Praise for Robert Wainwright

'undeniably compelling' *Sydney Morning Herald* on *Enid*

'. . . a skilful portrait of a woman who cut a London dash but remained a quintessentially Australian country girl.'
Australian Women's Weekly on *Sheila*

'The charm of Wainwright's biography is that he makes us see what an engaging, admirable and sometimes heroic quality it is to be a life-enhancer like Sheila.' *Daily Mail* on *Sheila*

'As social history Sheila Chisholm's life is fascinating . . . it's undeniably enjoyable to read of all that glitter and gold.'
The Spectator on *Sheila*

'Nothing short of impressive . . . Wainwright has revived a legend.' *The Lady* on *Sheila*

'While it is nigh impossible to capture what she was really like, her beauty and her boldness shine through this fascinating tale.'
Sydney Morning Herald on *Sheila*

'Well-written, well-paced, invariably light and interesting'
Canberra Times on *Nellie*

'Muriel Matters's name is apt: she certainly does matter . . . [a] highly readable biography.' *Daily Mail* on *Miss Muriel Matters*

'Wainwright's extensive research reveals an extraordinary story that is far more bitter than sweet.'
Herald Sun on *Rocky Road*

Robert Wainwright has been a journalist for more than thirty-five years, rising from the grassroots of country journalism in Western Australia to a senior writer with the *Sydney Morning Herald*, where he was a three-time finalist in the prestigious Walkley Awards. His career has ranged from politics to crime, always focusing on the people behind the major news of the day. He is the author of, among others, *Rose: The unauthorised biography of Rose Hancock Porteous, The Lost Boy, The killing of Caroline Byrne, Born or Bred?* (the story of killer Martin Bryant), *Sheila*, the award-winning *Maverick Mountaineer, Miss Muriel Matters, Rocky Road, Enid* and *Nellie: The life and loves of Dame Nellie Melba. Nell, the Duchess of Manchester* is his sixteenth book.

Nell

the Duchess *of* Manchester

ROBERT WAINWRIGHT

ALLEN&UNWIN

SYDNEY • MELBOURNE • AUCKLAND • LONDON

First published in 2025

Allen & Unwin
Cammeraygal Country
83 Alexander Street
Crows Nest NSW 2065
Australia
Phone: (61 2) 8425 0100
Email: info@allenandunwin.com
Web: www.allenandunwin.com

Allen & Unwin acknowledges the Traditional Owners of the Country on which we live and work. We pay our respects to all Aboriginal and Torres Strait Islander Elders, past and present.

NATIONAL LIBRARY OF AUSTRALIA

A catalogue record for this book is available from the National Library of Australia

ISBN 978 1 76106 898 0

Internal design by Lisa White
Set in 2.5/18 pt Minion Pro by Post Pre-press Group, Australia
Printed and bound in Australia by the Opus Group

10 9 8 7 6 5 4 3 2

MIX
Paper | Supporting responsible forestry
FSC www.fsc.org
FSC® C001695

The paper in this book is FSC certified. FSC promotes environmentally responsible, socially beneficial and economically viable management of the world's forests.

To Mariella

A woman who knows a thing or two about keeping alive a family dynasty. Thank you for your love and support

CONTENTS

PROLOGUE

18 July 1949

The vast lawns had been mown and carefully crosshatched into diamond shapes, and weeds—hairy bittercress, sticky willy and ivy-leaved toadflax—had been pulled from the white stone driveway and plucked from various cracks and crevices around the front staircase. Twin lines of red sequoias stood tall like ceremonial guardsmen along the route from the road to the forecourt of the great building with its Palladian pillars.

Kimbolton Castle in Cambridgeshire, the grand home of the earls and dukes of Manchester for more than three centuries, gleamed under bright summer sunshine. The future of the Montagu family, troubled but defiant, depended on their bastion being seen at its finest.

By mid-morning the front courtyard had become a parking lot, with family saloons, two-door shooting brakes, sleek touring cars and throaty roadsters massing in front of the entrance as people began arriving for a rare offering. The castle, once home to the tragic Catherine of Aragon, former Queen of England, was being opened to the public for the first time.

Inside, the remnants of the war years spent as a hospital depot had finally been cleared away, the damaged panelling patched, rugs vacuumed and furniture brushed. Heavy drapes had been drawn back to once again reveal the full splendour of the ground-floor drawing rooms.

The painted gaze of the previous dukes and earls and their children looked down from giant canvases as the townsfolk of Kimbolton wandered through the great rooms to see for themselves how their feudal masters lived, confirming the stories of opulence.

They were joined by dozens of Londoners—the curious and the opportunists—who, drawn by newspaper advertisements, had travelled by train from the city and ferried in on special bus services laid on from the station at the nearby town of Bedford.

They expected grandeur and were not disappointed. The works of art represented almost every great British artist or European master who had spent time in London in the seventeenth and eighteenth centuries, including the Venetian painter Giovanni Pellegrini, whose murals *Minerva* and *Triumph of a Roman Emperor* decorated the entrance stairwell. They were considered among the finest wall paintings in Britain, the colours as bright as when they had been daubed over a five-year period between 1708 and 1713, commissioned by Charles Montagu, the 1st Duke of Manchester and ambassador to France.

The crowds gawked at the giant works of famous kings and queens, politicians and courtiers, including a portrait of Elizabeth, 4th Duchess of Manchester and her son, George, who would become the 5th Duke. The pair were captured as Diana and Cupid by the great English portraitist Joshua Reynolds and dominated one wall of the great Green Drawing Room. On the opposite wall hung portraits of Oliver Cromwell, said to be the work of Victorian painter Charles Lucy, Charles I by John Russell and Catherine of Aragon by Hans Holbein.

A portrait of Queen Anne, by Sir Godfrey Kneller, hung in the White Hall, alongside William III by the seventeenth-century Dutch master Willem Wissing, while the Red Room next door held a painting of Henry VI, by Holbein, and Queen Charlotte by the German neoclassicist Johan Zoffany.

Most prominent above the fireplace in the great dining hall was a giant canvas, *Prometheus Bound*, painted in 1612 by the Flemish Baroque artist Peter Paul Rubens. It depicted the story of the Greek god paying the price for stealing fire from Mount Olympus for humankind, his liver being ripped from his body by an eagle sent by Zeus.

And on it went, through the Ivy and Archway rooms, the saloon and vestibule, Popham's Gallery, Queen Catherine's and King William's rooms and beyond to various bedrooms and even the night nursery. It seemed that each successive duke had commissioned grand and heroic portraits of his family, friends and, importantly, political sponsors. The dukes also collected art as they travelled through Europe, the names on the walls an astounding collection of masters—artists like Van Dyck, Mytens, Veronese, Claude, Bassano, Titian, Correggio, Tintoretto and Canaletto.

The furniture matched the artworks in scope and craftsmanship—Chippendale chairs by the dozen, Georgian serpentine chests and lattice bookcases, a Queen Anne bureau, a William and Mary gilt suite, the canopy of King William III's state bed, and the studded leather dowry chest of Catherine of Aragon, which took pride of place beneath the main staircase.

Among the crowd was the 10th and current duke, Alexander 'Mandy' Montagu, who had inherited the title two years before when his father, another William, had passed away. His Grace stood to one side in the White Hall, preferring to be in the background as strangers inspected and chatted about his family's history. Normally a convivial man with a reputation as being fair and competent in his duties to the town, he was wary to engage because of the circumstances of the event.

His long line of predecessors had been an important part of British history—earls first, then promoted in aristocratic importance to dukes. They had been advisors and confidants to kings and queens, including Henry VIII and Charles I and II, and to military leaders; they had filled important civic and diplomatic positions; and they had been frequently significant players in historic political tussles.

But times had changed. Alexander, aged forty-seven, was a naval officer and war hero but other recent dukes, his father and grandfather in particular, would be remembered not for contributions but weaknesses, their legacies more about moral decay and financial mismanagement. For Alexander, this day was not about pride, but shame.

More noticeable in the castle this day was the Duke's wife, a small, neat and efficient figure with engaging eyes and a sharp wit, dressed smartly in tweed and heels. Unlike her husband, Nell Manchester greeted many of the visitors with a smile, encouraging them to wander the rooms, and explaining the paintings and the artists.

Her ties to the family were marital rather than blood so the event was perhaps easier to accept—a temporary intrusion that would hopefully provide a permanent solution to their money worries.

Unlike her husband, Nell was not born in England, let alone into the aristocracy. Her 'common' background was more akin to that of the visitors, as she recalled her own awe and wonder when she had first explored the rooms and their treasures in the days after she had married Alexander, then Viscount Mandeville, more than twenty years before.

Rows of chairs for two hundred people had been set up in the dining room. The seats were filled by eleven o'clock when a tall, well-dressed man rang a bell and called the room to order.

The fire sale at Kimbolton Castle was about to begin.

1

A SEXY MAN DRESSED IN HIS UNDIES

6 August 1926

Misses Nell and Erin Stead . . . have gone for a holiday to Colombo.

By the time their sojourn was mentioned in the social pages of the *Prahran Telegraph*, the young Stead sisters, aged twenty-four and twenty-one respectively, had left Melbourne and were on their way to Ceylon, the tear-shaped island nation off the southern tip of India. It was a popular destination for adventurous, well-heeled Australians in the early years of the twentieth century, established as a tourist hub because its capital was one of the main ports of call along the shipping route to London via the Suez Canal.

The sisters were aboard the RMS *Cathay*, a 'luxurious modern oil burning steamship' launched by P&O barely a year earlier. Two nights before its 14 July departure, they were among the guests at an event hosted by a group of passengers in honour of the ship's officers. It was a bubbly affair, the dining tables decorated with bright red poppies and sprigs from olive-green gum trees. The officers returned the favour the next night by hosting a dinner at the Ambassadors Cafe for selected passengers who danced the Charleston, the latest craze from America.

Life for the sisters seemed promising although there was personal tragedy behind the holiday. It was a journey arranged by their father, Sidney, in the hope they could set aside for a while their grief for the loss of their mother, Lilian, who had recently succumbed to cancer after a two-year battle. She was just fifty-one.

Nell had always been noticeable, once turning a social writer's head by wearing 'an uncommon frock of tete-de-negre tulle, bronze metal lace with a design in Oriental colourings'. But it was her attitude that made her stand out in a crowd of eager young things—petite, almost pixie-like, with bobbed hair, large eyes and a challenge-me twinkle. Laughter came as easily as her unquestioned sense of self.

Ceylon, as modern-day Sri Lanka was then known, was their father's choice—a safe but exotic holiday where white folk could peer into the steamy culture of Asia without having to sully their hands, viewing the colour of street life from the shade of a rickshaw in the midday sun and taking English tea served by exotically dressed native staff. Besides, Sidney Stead had friends there who could keep an eye on his girls.

The three-week journey from Melbourne was comfortable, the cabins boasting the latest luxuries of electric lights, hot and cold saltwater bathrooms, a 'charming' music room and a library. But shipboard life had been largely uneventful between mealtimes, with no landfall between Fremantle and Colombo. The Stead sisters were now looking for some excitement and a little male attention.

Their father had perhaps foreseen his daughters' eagerness and arranged for a chaperone when they arrived. Gill Whitby, a half-dozen years older than Nell, had grown up in Melbourne and was now married to an Englishman, George, who managed a large tea plantation and would later serve as an MP in the Sri Lankan parliament.

After arriving in Colombo, the sisters joined the well-trodden tourist trail for a tour of the northern plains, through rubber estates, coconut and tea plantations, and thick jungle—where leopards and elephants were still hunted—before reaching the ruins of the ancient city of Anuradhapura. It was once the size of London until a marauding Tamil army had forced its largely Sinhalese citizens to flee and leave the buildings to the advancing jungle.

The trip then headed south, past the ruined city of Polonnaruwa with its artificial lakes, built to negate droughts but now filled with lazy crocodiles who kept frightened tourists awake at night with the swish of their tails. Next was the capital Kandy, where the relic of the tooth of Buddha lay in the royal temple, the approach past a dingy pool filled with sacred turtles and up steps lined with beggars—the blind, the lame and the emaciated—hoping for a miracle. Inside, amid the deafening noise of tom-toms and blowpipes, crowds bore offerings of flowers and scented bowls of jasmine and frangipani mixed with coconut oil.

The monsoon season was easing, although still with a threat of afternoon thunderstorms, when Nell and Erin arrived back in Colombo and checked in to the city's grand edifice, the Galle Face Hotel. The days were filled with humid sunshine and the temperature dipped only a handful of degrees after sunset, which ensured that evening coats were not required.

Built as a meeting place for 'colonial gentlemen' in the mid-nineteenth century, the Galle Face was remodelled as a hotel and expanded to become the epitome of colonial splendour and the epicentre of the city's social and business life. The four-storey hotel sat at the southern end of a stretch of green parkland behind a grove of stately coconut palms, the Indian Ocean lapping at its front gate. Guests were fanned each evening by cooling breezes that dulled the day's sticky heat, the air tinged with the hint of exotic spices and the whiff of incense. The forecourt jostled with rickshaws and snake charmers, and stilt fishermen sat above the waves on their *pettas* (crossbars attached to vertical poles) and cast their lines into the churning waters.

When he arrived here in 1896, the US writer Samuel Clemens—Mark Twain—was enthralled by the local people he saw along the red road that led from the port to the hotel, an experience he would call the most enchanting day of his life and that he described in aching detail in his book *Following the*

Equator: A Journey Around the World: 'The drive through the town and out to the Galle Face by the seashore, what a dream it was of tropical splendors of bloom and blossom, and Oriental conflagrations of costume! The walking groups of men, women, boys, girls, babies—each individual was a flame, each group a house afire for colour.'

It was here, among the wealthy white expatriates, tourists and visiting businessmen, that Nell and Erin were most at risk, at least by reputation. Mrs Whitby even checked in to the hotel herself to ensure the social safety of the pair. It was all about respectability.

The hotel attracted innumerable political leaders and luminaries over the years, including many Edwardian writers such as Somerset Maugham and Sir Arthur Conan Doyle; the latter extolled its position: 'Never . . . have I seen "the league-long roller thundering on the shore" as here, where the Indian Ocean with its thousand leagues of momentum hits the western coast of Ceylon.'

Inside, the doors to the best rooms were opened with oversized and brightly polished brass keys, and furnished with cane and mahogany divans and colonial wardrobes known as almirahs. The bathrooms were the size of parade grounds, according to one astonished military guest writing home to his wife, with antique pot-bellied tubs and dark teak floors waxed to perfection.

If the seas outside were calm, you could hear the sounds of the orchestra playing below in the lounge tended by Sinhalese staff in white skirts and bare feet, where the menu featured turtle soup, striped mullet and local curry dishes. A tortoiseshell hair comb worn by the head waiter signified his superior caste.

The temptation was to leave the windows open and allow the breeze to billow through the light curtains but there was a danger in doing so. Hundreds of crows gathered on lawns outside and an open window offered opportunity, as a notice in each room warned.

Beyond visiting the city's fragrant market stalls or myriad Hindu and Buddhist temples, the alternative daytime activity was a 10-kilometre journey along the seaside and inland to Mount Lavinia. Swimming in the ocean was regarded as a hazardous exercise, and bathers were warned of sharp rocks just below the surface and the potential for sharks. Instead, guests were advised to take a dip in the hotel's saltwater swimming pool, set in an open courtyard outside the Travellers' Bar and alongside a giant painted chequerboard. It was as much a place for social interaction and chance meetings as it was for energetic activity.

And so it would prove for Nell Stead.

The idea of not swimming in the sea seemed anomalous to Australian girls, but the saltwater pool was the next best thing. By the afternoon of their second day in Colombo, Nell and Erin were poolside in swimsuits, immediately attracting the attention of the men, among them officers from the British navy ship the HMS *Cairo*, which had docked in Colombo the previous day.

One of the men stood out for Nell, and from the moment each laid eyes on the other, the attraction was mutual. Lieutenant Alexander 'Mandy' Mandeville was athletic, stocky rather than tall, with a square jaw, blue eyes and a wide smile to match. Although he said only that he was a naval lieutenant, he had the presence and casual confidence that usually came with social position.

There would be three versions of how Nell and Mandy met.

Nell's account favoured a romantic version: they were both swimming in the hotel pool and collided in the water. 'I went to the swimming baths,' she would tell an American reporter some years later. 'There I actually bumped into the man who is now my husband. I had never met him before. He told me he was a lieutenant onboard the HMS *Cairo*.'

'That's quite true, and we had a jolly time afterwards,' confirmed Mandy without elaboration.

Two other versions that appeared later—they had met casually on the pool deck, or they had been formally introduced at a private party in a room off the pool area—were offered perhaps to avoid the idea of scandal in an age of social prudery.

Nell's entry in her diary a few hours after meeting Mandy was more forthright and appears to confirm that he was wearing swimming trunks: 'There was a sexy man standing near to me dressed in his undies.'

Barely a week after the poolside encounter, Nell boarded a ship with her sister back to Australia, besotted and betrothed—informally at least—to a man she barely knew and with a family history that was scarcely believable. Lieutenant 'Mandy'

Mandeville was in fact Viscount Alexander Mandeville, eldest son of the 9th Duke of Manchester, whose family owned three castles.

But what would she tell her father?

2

ROOTS

Nell Stead's family story began not in the fashionable cafes and society ballrooms of colonial Melbourne but in the anguished beauty of the Australian interior.

Widgiewa Station spreads itself across the Riverina district of New South Wales. The homestead is a couple of hours on horseback to the town of Jerilderie where, in 1879, the bushranger Ned Kelly locked up the town's police in their own cells and attempted to publish his manifesto about being forced to become an outlaw. The station's name was derived, so it was said, from a white man's version of an Aboriginal phrase supposedly meaning 'What do you want?', although it seems more likely that it was simply a word—pronounced *Widge-ee-wa*—that rolled easily off the tongue of the settlers.

In the last years of the nineteenth century, Widgiewa was a prosperous enterprise. Its twenty-five thousand merino sheep and several thousand Hereford cattle roamed across almost 200 square kilometres of open plains, feeding from a mix of hardy native plants—spear, saltbush and wallaby grasses, among others. During this time, the manager was a young man named David Sidney Vere Stead, known as Sidney, who had recently arrived from Ireland. His father, David, had made the journey across the world half a century before, staying several years around Geelong in Victoria until the harsh land and sun-beaten life sent him scurrying back to the gentle green of his homeland.

Sidney had grown up in Ireland hearing the stories of his father's adventures. David had built a homestead on a hill between the Moorabool River and Port Phillip Bay, where he had hung a bell from a tree to warn of impending trouble with local Aboriginal people. The confrontation never occurred but Bell Post Hill would remain part of the folklore and a landmark, even in the modern-day city; it is now a suburb in the north of Geelong.

Although David Stead had accepted defeat and returned to Ireland to raise his family, his son was sufficiently inspired by the romance of these adventures to make the journey halfway around the world himself. And, once settled, Sidney Stead would thrive.

From Melbourne, Widgiewa was reached via a weekly overnight mail train that left Flinders Street Station in the evening, steaming first through the heavily timbered towns of Benalla and Wangaratta, then crossing the mighty Murray River into New South Wales at the twin towns of Wodonga and Albury.

From there the line continued north to Wagga Wagga, where it swung west through rolling green pastoral land patched with sheep herds and clumps of eucalyptus. Flocks of grey and rose-breasted galahs rose in a scream of colour and noise from their branches as the carriages rolled past. The train would arrive in the town of Narrandera, on the Murrumbidgee River, by mid-morning before heading further inland through fields flaked with the bright gold of yellow daisies to arrive at Widgiewa, a railway siding with a raised platform and a tin shed, in the early afternoon.

Sidney would make the journey many times during the years immediately before and after the turn of the century, splitting his time between the city environs of Melbourne and the isolation of the Australian interior. There were also trips to its sister station, Yarrabee, 50 kilometres to the north. He managed both properties at various times, and another to the south called Goolgumbla.

He was a man of the land—not the kind who had red earth ground into his fingernails from tilling the soil but one who dressed in suits, trod the boards of cattle and sheep auctions, and understood the financial business of land and agriculture. He built a career managing these vast sheep and cattle stations on behalf of wealthy colonial landholders who expected healthy profits from their ventures. After all, land was an asset only if it produced something of value. Without a purpose it was a financial burden.

Sidney was not wealthy as such; rather, he helped create and manage wealth for others. He was, as his surname suggested, a man who conveyed a sense of competence and inspired trust, not only from his employers but from the colonial government, which appointed him to various posts as an adjudicator of disagreements and upholder of laws in the rough and tumble towns of rural Victoria and New South Wales. He served as a Justice of the Peace, overseer of liquor licensing and manager of district sheep-disease treatment and control, among other roles.

If anything, he was too steadfast. Friends would say that he never took a holiday—which, sadly, was ultimately to his personal detriment, as he would never see Ireland again. His only outlet was the occasional race meeting while maintaining a membership of the Victoria Racing Club and the Australian Club, and occasionally writing articles for *The Pastoralists' Review* about the future of land and agriculture.

For a time he lived in towns near the stations he managed, but all that changed in 1901 when he married Jessie Lilian Dickinson, known as Lilian, from the suburb of Croydon in Sydney. Their first child, Nell, arrived on 18 April the following year. There would be three more children—daughter Erin in 1904 and son, David, a year later, before a six-year gap to youngest daughter, Penelope. Sidney stopped managing stations soon after Nell's birth and began working for the Australian Mortgage, Land and Finance Company (AMLF), and the family settled in the affluent inner-Melbourne suburb of Armadale.

The AMLF would have a profound impact on Australia's rural landscape. Not only did it lend money for the purchase and development of properties, but it owned land, traded in produce, and built infrastructure such as the giant wool stores that would become a feature of Australian ports. And Sidney Stead was an integral cog in that wheel of rural finance, the man the company turned to in valuing land for acquisition and loan agreements across New South Wales and Victoria.

It was claimed that Sidney became a millionaire but the reality was much less glamorous. Although well off compared to the vast majority of citizens, he would leave a will worth a little over £20,000 when he died in 1929. His legacy was not in money but in his children.

If Nell—formally, Lilian Nell Vere Stead—had been looking for inspiration in life, then she would have needed to look no further than the incredible rags-to-riches saga of George and Esther Johnston, her great-great-grandparents on her mother's side. Lieutenant George Johnston was said to have been the first officer ashore at Sydney Cove when the First Fleet arrived in January 1788, and would become a notorious colonial figure, leading the only armed takeover of a government in Australian history and appointing himself lieutenant-governor. What is even more incredible in many ways is that his 'First Lady' was his mistress, Esther Abrahams, a former convict.

George had aristocratic links. He was born in Annandale, Dumfries, Scotland, in 1764 to an army officer of the same name who was aide-de-camp to Lord Percy, the 2nd Duke of Northumberland. The Duke obtained a commission for twelve-year-old George, and took father and son to fight the American War of Independence, during which George Sr was killed.

Lord Percy, regarded as a brilliant soldier, became the boy's guardian and watched over his military career until he volunteered to join the New South Wales Marine Corps, created to guard the prisoners aboard the six convict ships in the First Fleet. It was during the voyage aboard the *Lady Penrhyn* that George met Esther, a Sephardi (Spanish) Jewish teenager who had been convicted of stealing cards of black silk lace from a haberdashery in Piccadilly. Esther barely escaped the hangman's noose, pleading that she was pregnant, and she gave birth to a daughter while waiting for their departure in the notorious Newgate Prison.

With her exotic Spanish looks and middle-class upbringing (her father was a lawyer), Esther would have been out of place among the mainly poor young women aboard ship convicted of petty crimes. She caught the attention of the tall, blond, twenty-three-year-old officer; the jailer fell in love with his prisoner. Their shipboard romance would change not only their own lives but contribute significantly to Australian colonial history.

When the ship arrived at Sydney Cove, Johnston offered to be Esther's protector, perhaps worried about the baby and recalling the importance to his existence of his own benefactor. They would be together for the next thirty-five years, although it would be two decades before the relationship was formalised. In the meantime they would have seven children and become one of the most prominent families in the colony.

It was a life of highs and lows for the couple as Johnston led a conspicuous and controversial military career. He first served as adjutant to Governor Arthur Phillip before being made captain of what would later become known, because of its involvement in the illicit trade of alcohol, as the Rum Corps. Johnston was up to his neck in the trade and in 1800, now a major, he was charged by the lieutenant-governor William Paterson, the colony's administration officer, with selling rum to soldiers.

George demanded to be sent back to England for trial, where he was cleared of the charges, mainly because it was impossible to convince witnesses to travel from Australia and give evidence in London. Esther, who had just given birth to her fourth child, was left behind to manage for herself.

When he returned, triumphant, to Sydney two years later, Johnston brought with him a Spanish merino ram from the flock of the king, George III, as well as a commission to take command of the Rum Corps. Now a powerful political figure, he took a leading role in suppressing an uprising by Irish settlers in a confrontation at Castle Hill that left more than a dozen men dead. 'We took thirty prisoners and ten of them were hanged,' Johnston wrote to superiors back in London. He was rewarded with a land grant of 2000 acres (810 hectares) at Cabramatta from a 'grateful' Governor Philip Gidley King, who had replaced Paterson.

As his prominence rose, so did George and Esther's personal stocks. Not only did he receive the Cabramatta land but also property at Nepean and plots across what is now inner Sydney.

These included several homesteads at Bankstown and Georges Hall, as well as 300 acres (120 hectares) he would name Annandale after his home town. It was here that the couple lived with their children and ran merino sheep, horses and pigs; grew barley, oats and wheat; and established one of the colony's first vineyards.

The flourishing business even boasted a butchery, a bakery, a blacksmith and a brickfield where convicts made the bricks to build the expanding empire. George Johnston may not have had an aristocratic title but, more importantly, he had productive land and economic power.

Life changed again in 1806 with the arrival in the colony of yet another new governor, the unpopular William Bligh, who attempted to blunt the power of Johnston and close friend John Macarthur and their grip on the liquor trade. On the evening of 26 January 1808, in what became known as the Rum Rebellion, Johnston took four hundred troops to Government House and arrested Bligh, who was allegedly hiding beneath his bed. Johnston installed himself as lieutenant-governor, and Esther was suddenly the colony's First Lady.

With Bligh under house arrest, Johnston's military coup would last for six months until the arrival from England of a new lieutenant-governor, Joseph Foveaux. But rather than win praise for his actions, Johnston was court-martialled and forced to return to England to defend himself. If found guilty, he could be hanged.

Esther, now aged thirty-seven and having recently given birth to her eighth child, was left in charge of the complex series of estates and businesses. To make matters worse, and in retribution for her husband's actions, Lieutenant-Governor Foveaux rescinded a land grant made in her name at Bankstown where she kept cattle. She was also penalised because she and George had never married and her appeals, made under the name Esther Julian, that 'I have a large family' were rejected as inadmissible by the next governor, Lachlan Macquarie.

Suddenly, all the land that had been given to her husband was under threat but Esther clung on defiantly. Effectively squatting on her own land at Annandale, she hoped that George would be cleared and come back to reclaim their social position.

It would be a four-year wait and when George did finally return it was with mixed news. He had been convicted but spared the hangman's noose, instead cashiered—decommissioned—and allowed to return to New South Wales as 'any ordinary settler' complete with 'fine horses and ewes from the Duke of Northumberland'. It seemed that the Duke had waved his wand of protection over Johnston's charmed life. Governor Macquarie decided that George was 'a fine fellow after all' and returned all his land, insisting only that he and Esther marry to legitimise their union, and agreed to reinstate her 570 acres (230 hectares) at Bankstown.

Esther had managed the estates with aplomb while her husband was away, enduring derision and complaints from competitors who scornfully described her as 'Johnston's woman, a Jewess'. Now the formality of marriage gave her the social credibility she had craved. Touchingly, her eldest daughter Rosanna, and Rosanna's husband—a former convict named

Isaac Nichols who had become Australia's first postmaster—were the witnesses to the marriage.

Two of the Johnstons' three sons—George Jr and David—became prominent landowners in their own right. Robert, the second-eldest, followed his father into the military, becoming the first Australian to join the British Royal Navy, where he fought on the fringes of the Napoleonic Wars and the War of 1812. In 1816, aged only twenty-four and a lieutenant, he decided to head back to Sydney where he joined exploration parties, locating and naming the Clyde River near Batemans Bay.

Robert was about to return to England and resume naval duties when his older brother, George, died falling from a horse. Then, in 1823, his father died suddenly after a short illness, aged fifty-eight. At the time of his death, records showed that George owned more than 7000 acres (2830 hectares), which he left to his children. Annandale was bequeathed to Esther 'for the term of her natural life'.

It was here that the family fell apart. Robert, having now decided to stay in Sydney and eager to establish himself as a grazier, became frustrated at having to deal with his mother rather than take over Annandale. Relations between the pair quickly deteriorated and came to a head in 1829 when Esther attempted to raise a mortgage on the property and use the funds to return to England and be reunited with her own family after almost half a century apart.

Robert protested and took the drastic step of appealing to the courts to declare Esther insane, insisting that she drank too much and couldn't be trusted to manage her affairs. The case would shock Sydney; newspaper accounts of the case called it 'tragic'. Esther's lawyer conceded that she had 'the occasional practice of drinking too freely' but added—to amusement from the public gallery—that 'if all persons in the habit of drinking and committing extravagances in consequence were to be supposed mad', then 'it would be difficult to find jurymen enough to decide upon their cases'.

There was criticism of her 'driving most furiously' through the streets in her horse and buggy and telling neighbours that she was a victim of domestic violence from family members as they tried to curb her ways. The commissioners wondered if the periods of insanity were caused by drinking or if the drinking had been induced by insanity. Neighbours and friends gave evidence, describing her as a 'stirring industrious woman' who had changed in recent years. A reporter from *The Australian* noted sadly: 'Mrs J. sat at the table during the whole progress of this inquiry, sometimes interrupting the witnesses with a little impatience, but in a very quaint and pertinent manner.'

The jury pondered for an hour before returning a unanimous verdict: 'Esther Johnston is not of sound mind nor capable of managing her affairs.' She was declared to be a lunatic.

A trustee was put in place, and Esther went to live with David and his family at Georges Hall, the family's first homestead, where she would live another two decades. When she died in 1846, Esther was still one of the biggest female landowners in the colony.

Robert took control of Annandale and would become a successful grazier in his own right, marrying quite late and having nine children. His eldest daughter, Penelope, in 1863 married a businessman named Samuel Dickinson and they had seven children, among them a daughter named Jessie Lilian—Nell Stead's mother.

3

'I WANT TO BE UNIQUE'

There were two practical skills Sidney Stead figured that his oldest daughter would need in life—to ride a horse bareback and be a dead shot with a rifle. Pretty dresses and fancy shoes and hats were fine for the city, but out in the country—where he expected that Nell would find a husband and a future—there were far more practical talents that a young woman needed to shine and survive.

He was right but for very different reasons and circumstances to those he envisaged when, as a teenager, an eager Nell began to accompany him on some of his visits to outback properties. She was proud of her abilities, as she would tell a newspaper reporter many years later: 'I could cling to anything. I scorned a saddle.' In fact, Nell's diary would detail how she was taught to ride not only bareback but without a bridle, 'in case of emergency'. Earlier pages recorded in childhood scrawl a playdate with a friend to go hunting with guns. They were both aged six.

Among her keepsakes was a book titled *The Zoo Story*, written by an unnamed family friend. Filled with animal stories and decorated with magazine clippings, it included tales about monkeys and elephants, mules, ostriches and chamois. There was a strange, Dr Seuss–like bird called 'the Walla Walla' that feasted on peppercorns, and blue sharks whose deep dives caused 'South Seas bubbles'.

And dogs, from poodles and schnauzers to terriers and dachshunds. Her favourite, apparently, was a lengthy ditty about a 'country dog' named Runt, and his adventures and mishaps when he became lost in the big city. It echoed some of her own later experiences as she left Melbourne to explore the world.

These were pointers to the independently minded and forthright woman that Nell would become. Encouraged by her parents, she was sent to study first at Lauriston Girls' School in the Melbourne suburb of Armadale, which offered matriculation as part of a liberal education so that young women could lead 'fulfilling' lives.

Perhaps more important, however, were the final four years of her education at the Clyde Girls' Grammar School. The headmistress, Miss Isabel Henderson, was a prominent educationist of her time and championed the need for women to be schooled in languages like Latin and Greek, as well as mathematics and literature. She also believed the more traditional female subjects like cooking, sewing and deportment—the so-called domestic sciences—should be treated seriously and included in intermediate and leaving examinations.

Henderson had initially set up the school in the city but in 1919, in her quest for excellence, she bought Braemar House, a Victorian mansion in the former goldmining town of Woodend in the Macedon Ranges and turned it into a boarding school for eighty pupils—a rural haven. Their arrival in Woodend was controversial, and Henderson's methods were considered by some purists to be radical and morally loose, in a society that expected little of women beyond domesticity, and demanded conformity. Vicious rumours began to swirl and fester about her practices, which Henderson addressed angrily at a prize-giving for students at the end of the first year.

'It has been said, amongst other things, that the girls here have motors or ponies and that they think of nothing but dresses and money,' she told parents in the hall.

> This is absolutely untrue. There are neither motors nor ponies at Clyde; the girls dress just as simply—perhaps even more simply—as the ordinary schoolgirl one sees about Melbourne. It is said that the girls do no work at all, but are allowed to do just as they like, and that they smoke and play cards. Now these and all such stories are obviously not only lies but ridiculous lies yet they are still being circulated and, unfortunately, there are people to be found credulous enough to believe them.

Nell Stead was sitting in the audience that night, and earlier that afternoon she had been at the centre of the school photograph taken outside in front of the gabled and turreted edifice. While her schoolmates mostly smiled shyly at the camera, Nell was serious-faced, her head tilted slightly as if questioning the photographer hidden behind the canvas, her collar and tie deliberately askew, and sporting a stylish headband that was clearly not part of the school uniform.

School records would show that she wasn't among the prize winners that night and that her academic record in the final year was 'poor', but the education experience, according to the Isabel Henderson doctrine, was as much about character as it was academic achievement.

Another former student, the philanthropist Dame Elisabeth Murdoch (née Greene), would later refer to this aspect when she wrote the foreword to a book about the school's history in which she recalled the arduous journey just to reach the school:

> The trip up the mountain in old Mr South's wagonette was a thrilling experience. The track was appalling and quite perilous and the challenge to the driver, horses and girls was the forerunner of many endurance tests ahead of us at Clyde. Life was rugged during the long cold winter, but I believe we were the healthier for those Spartan conditions, which today would be considered unbearable, as indeed would be the isolation. Parents visited rarely, if ever. We became self-reliant and had to take the hard knocks, disappointments and the discipline, without which I consider we would have been less secure. We soon learned, living together for long periods, that concern and

> consideration for others were the best ingredients for happiness and satisfaction. Of all my treasured memories of my school days, the most precious would be that of the beauty and enchantment of our glorious bush and country surroundings.

If any further intrigue was required, the school and its students provided some inspiration for the characters and settings for the novel *Picnic at Hanging Rock*, written many years later by another former Clyde pupil, Joan Lindsay, about the disappearance of three schoolgirls during an outing at the famous Hanging Rock, which lies just 6 kilometres from Woodend. In a brief foreword to the psychological thriller, Lindsay noted tantalisingly that 'whether *Picnic at Hanging Rock* is fact or fiction, my readers must decide for themselves'.

By the norms of early-twentieth-century society, Nell Stead should have been married with a child or two by the time she reached her mid-twenties. But opportunities seemed to have passed her by, hindered, as it turned out, by events beyond her control.

Nell finished high school at the end of 1919, a few months after the Treaty of Versailles was signed, ending Australia's involvement in the Great War. Although the economic impacts of the faraway war would be felt for many years, the nation had emerged with a heightened sense of confidence and national identity—the Anzac spirit.

Like many young women, Nell was encouraged to ignore

higher education and a career in favour of becoming a wife and a mother. After all, the Stead family was respected and financially comfortable, thanks to Sidney Stead's flourishing career, and Nell was attractive and impish with a keen sense of humour and a lean figure that suited the fashions of the day, as hemlines rose and hair was crimped and shingled.

She quickly became a popular figure on Melbourne's social circuit. By April 1920 she had begun to appear regularly in newspaper society columns as having attended some of the many soirees intended to showcase young women in society, as *The Australasian* announced: 'Miss Nell Stead . . . who has just left school, is to make her debut during the festivities in honour of the visit of the Prince of Wales.'

Nell was among two dozen debutantes introduced to Edward, future King Edward VIII of England, at a ball held in the town hall and hosted by the lord mayor to welcome him to the city. The prince had arrived in Melbourne to begin a three-month tour of Australia. It was a critical visit to cement Britain's relationship with the colonies in the wake of the sacrifices of the Great War, and tens of thousands lined the shoreline between St Kilda and Port Melbourne to greet his ship, HMS *Renown*.

Despite the social importance and grandeur, Nell's entry in her diary was unadorned: 'I was presented at court. Proud.' There was no breathless description of the occasion, nor any sense of the nervous excitement she must have felt. It was not as if she was incapable of writing, rather that she was succinct and practical like her father. Not overawed, even when meeting a prince. It would hold her in good stead, so to speak.

It was difficult to imagine a better beginning in any search for a husband and a secure future, although, privately, she was far less comfortable with the process than her social success would suggest. Contrary to her appearance, Nell disliked being paraded and would have been far happier being on the back of a horse and riding with her father than conducting small talk at a society party. Despite her reticence, Nell knew there was little option unless she was satisfied with being a farmer's wife. There was a future for her out there somewhere beyond society's expectations.

'I am not ashamed of the way I look,' she wrote. 'I want to be unique.' It is difficult to know what she meant by this typically unadorned comment. Was it a response to some comment about her appearance or, more likely, her dress sense in a society that expected compliance? Whatever the reason, it reveals that Nell Stead saw herself as an individual, with her own mind and desires.

However 'unique' Nell may have been, she was embraced by Melbourne society. Over the next three years her appearances and newspaper mentions grew, from a name listed simply as 'among the others seen' at luncheon gatherings, to invitations to attend vice-regal balls at Government House and favourable observations by society columnists about her outfits. 'The beautiful effect gained by the blending of various tones of yellow was seen in Miss Nell Stead's georgette frock,' wrote the Melbourne *Herald* correspondent at a ball hosted by the Countess of Stradbroke a couple of months after Nell had turned twenty. 'From a foundation of deep orange, it merged into primrose yellow, cut in handkerchief points with a girdle of autumn leaves to complete it.'

She stood out as an unusual beauty, particularly the way in which she engaged with the camera—not with a beaming smile like those around her on the social pages but an inquiring stare that challenged the photographer to capture her thoughts. Photographs followed in magazines like *The Home*, which noted: 'Miss Stead's piquant beauty and graceful dancing make her a charming asset to the younger set of Melbourne.' The same magazine featured her again a few months later, showing off the latest hairstyle—the shingle—'one of the prettiest members of Melbourne's younger set' in thoughtful profile with the barest hint of a smile touching her features.

Nell's wardrobe was increasingly admired. At a winter charity dance in 1923 she 'favoured navy blue with brown furs and a . . . hatter's plush trimmed with a ribbon', and at the spring racing carnival a few months later, the *Table Talk* magazine columnist was enchanted by her 'biscuit satin baronet frock and scoop-shaped hat of terracotta fancy straw trimmed with quills in vivid colourings'.

The plaudits kept coming into the summer of 1924. She was 'charming' in azalea pink, 'decidedly attractive' in gold lace over tissue and 'outstanding and beautiful' in white tulle encrusted with pearls.

She was now a prominent member of the so-called 'Younger Set'—the Australian version of Britain's 'Bright Young Things'. It was the generation whose carefree celebration of postwar life pushed boundaries, their high jinks derided by the establishment and admired by their peers because they challenged churlish Victorian-era attitudes.

The war had ravaged the numbers of young men, not just as dance partners but, more seriously, as potential husbands. Some social events reported twice as many women as men in attendance, and wealthy families were now sending their daughters to America because there were more eligible men there.

Newspaper columnists rarely publicly linked single young women with men by name, but some of the connections were clear simply because the same people were repeatedly reported as being at the same events. For Nell, the name Keith Murdoch seemed to crop up frequently at events she attended during this period. Murdoch was in his mid-thirties and had recently returned from Europe to be appointed chief editor of the Melbourne *Herald*. He and Nell were not linked romantically although it is clear they were friends; they were often on the same guest lists and invited to each other's parties. Nell was one of his 'bagged bevy of pretty maids' in a *Herald* newspaper promotion for a charity 'poster and shawl' ball, and she sat next to Murdoch at a dinner he hosted afterwards at the Menzies Hotel.

By early 1924 the newspapers were noting that Nell wasn't just attending social events but was now playing hostess herself, including suppers at Carlyon's Hotel in the city, one of the haunts of the Younger Set. She was also frequently travelling interstate to Sydney, particularly for society polo tournaments, where she watched from the sidelines.

Now aged twenty-two, she had marriage in her sights. Her friends were choosing husbands and she at times found herself a member of a bridal party—a bridesmaid but not the bride—including the society wedding for close pal Mardie Syme, granddaughter of newspaper baron David Syme. Was there a man for 'one of the smartest girls in Melbourne', as she was described by one columnist enamoured with her beauty and style?

The autumn and winter of 1924 saw a flurry of engagements. She was among the select guests at an event hosted by the great opera diva Dame Nellie Melba at her home, Coombe Cottage. *Table Talk* magazine referred to her 'generational prominence', and when she attended the governor-general's grand ball that year, a reporter gushed: 'One of the most notable of the many notable frocks was a silver lace dress of Renaissance design, which was embroidered with red and worn by one of our smartest girls, Miss Nell Stead.'

But right then, just as her star shone at its brightest, life changed.

Nell's mother, Lilian, herself a frequent feature at gala social events, became ill with cancer and the diagnosis was serious enough for a mention in the columns she had once graced. As Christmas approached, *Table Talk* revealed: 'Mrs S.V. Stead's many friends regret to hear that she is invalided and her medical adviser insists on a complete rest.' Over the next two years there would be the occasional mention of her friends and family visiting her at their home in Armadale, or of her remaining ill at home and unable to socialise. It was a painful and slow descent.

If Lilian travelled, then Nell was at her side, the ever-vigilant daughter who was taking responsibility for her mother's care. As a result, Nell's appearances at social events around Melbourne became fewer and fewer. By late 1925, as her mother's cancer took its final hold, Nell had almost completely withdrawn; one of the few mentions was of her being on the committee for a fete in aid of the Girl Guides movement.

'Mother died today,' Nell wrote in her diary on 23 May 1926, the matter-of-fact simplicity of the entry indicating that she had been expecting this day for some time, and had already contemplated and come to grips with its sadness.

By this time Nell seemed to have given up on the idea of finding a husband, instead resigning herself to a life of taking her mother's place, tending to her father and managing the family home. She would even describe herself as a *spinster*—a woman beyond her prime and unlikely to find a husband—in a later, reflective diary entry. It was then that Sidney Stead decided to send Nell and her shy, bookworm sister Erin to Ceylon.

Life was about to change.

4

THE BOY WITH BRAINS

Castle church bells pealed in celebration in England and Ireland when Alexander George Francis Drogo Montagu was born on 2 October 1902.

Dukes hold the most senior title in Britain's creaking feudal system of nobility, ahead of marquesses, earls, viscounts and barons in that order. The birth of a son and heir to a duke was an occasion to be hailed.

There were only thirty dukedoms in the United Kingdom, six of them held by members of the royal family. Of the rest, the Duke of Manchester, created in 1719 for Charles Montagu, Ambassador to Venice and France under the reign of George I, was considered the eighteenth most senior title by the two bibles of aristocracy, *Burke's Peerage* and *Debrett's*. Mandy—nicknamed because of the traditional courtesy title, 'Viscount Mandeville', that he would carry as a youth—was destined to become the 10th Duke of Manchester and take a seat in the House of Lords, where his ancestors had played prominent roles in the nation's governance for at least five centuries.

The sense of occasion was confirmed a few days after his birth when *The Guardian* carried an announcement. 'The Queen has consented to be the godmother to the Duke of Manchester's child,' it read, adding: 'Her consent was conveyed in the following telegram to the Duke: *I am delighted to be godmother to your little son. Alexandra R.*'

The baptism was a lavish ceremony at the Chapel Royal in St James's Palace in front of a 'fashionable congregation'. Queen Alexandra, wife of Edward VII, held the boy during the ceremony, during which his head was anointed with holy water from the River Jordan while choristers in blue and gold heralded his arrival.

The family's seat was Kimbolton in Cambridgeshire, an imposing medieval castle that was, in 1920, three hours north of London by car. It had been the last home of Catherine of Aragon, the banished first wife of Henry VIII. The earls and dukes of Manchester had owned the estate for three hundred years, and the family also owned Tandragee Castle in Ireland, 50 kilometres south of Belfast, which had come to the family estates via a marriage dowry in the nineteenth century. A third castle would soon be added when Mandy's maternal grandfather, an American railroad baron named Eugene Zimmerman, bought Kylemore Castle in Connemara, County Galway, Ireland, in celebration of Mandy's arrival.

It seemed that money and privilege flowed in abundance for the Montagu family. Its noble house could be traced back to Norman warrior Drogo de Montagud, a descendant of the Viking king Rollo; he had accompanied William the Conqueror across the English Channel to fight the Battle of Hastings in 1066 and was rewarded with lands in Somerset.

But modern aristocratic life was much more complicated. Behind the pomp and adulation, the Montagu family had struggled in recent generations to keep alive their great estates, weighed down by heavy taxes and rising costs. It was one thing to own vast acreages of land and cavernous castles, and another to have the money to maintain them.

The impact of inheritance tax on real-estate assets, made more punitive in 1894 to help pay off government debt, was increasingly devastating for wealthier families as great houses, their contents and parcels of land were sold off in bits and pieces to pay the death duties. Auction companies like Sotheby's and Christie's handled most of the bonanza of sales of valuable household items—boxes of jewellery, fine furniture and paintings. In 1950 alone there would be three dukes, two Marquesses, nine earls, five viscounts and fourteen barons who would sell off family valuables to pay taxes.

Lady Irene Lawley had to move out of the family home at Escrick Park, one of the largest estates in northern England, because of heavy death duties owed when her father, Lord Wenlock, died in 1912. The earls of Strathmore had their estate taxed twice in six years during the 1940s, meaning they effectively handed over more than three-quarters of the family's wealth to the government. Death duties hit the earldom of Chichester three times in sixteen years.

For those who survived, it was merely a matter of time; three, perhaps four generations would be enough to hand the wealth to the state, or to force a sale and breakup of the estate itself. In the meantime the costs of managing such properties took their toll, much of it caused by a land tax on the estimated capital value each year, irrespective of an estate's income—which was often less than the tax.

The Montagu family was lucky in many ways because Mandy's father, the 9th Duke, had inherited in 1892, just two years before the new tax came into effect, but it was only a matter of time before they, too, would face the reality of a death tax demand.

In the meantime, the family's financial affairs had come under a different pressure: profligacy.

Many of the great aristocratic families were rescued by America—specifically by the eligible daughters of American industry barons, who were happy to provide huge dowries in exchange for an aristocratic title and entry into British society. What might have appeared to be in poor taste was actually a rare moment of noble pragmatism, famously initiated when, in 1874, Lord Randolph Churchill married a Brooklyn girl named Jennie Jerome, the first of the so-called 'dollar princesses' and the mother of Winston Churchill. Few of these marriages would last, most ending in divorce, or estrangement and adultery by consent, but then love was never a likely ingredient in these transactions.

Mandy's mother, Helena, was an American from the Midwest city of Cincinnati, and his father's mother, the dowager duchess Consuelo Yznaga, had been a Cuban-American heiress from New York, a childhood acquaintance of Jennie Jerome. Consuelo had married George Victor Montagu, the 8th Duke of Manchester, in 1876, bringing with her a dowry worth US$6 million that would become the financial backbone of the family.

George and Consuelo would have three children—a son and twin daughters, Alice and Jacqueline, who both died young, from tuberculosis and malaria respectively. The marriage would be a disaster, and George was just thirty-nine years old when he died in 1892, leaving their fifteen-year-old son William to inherit the title as the 9th Duke of Manchester.

'Little Kim', as William was known—in deference to his father's nickname, 'Kim'—was still a schoolboy, and it would be a decade before he took his seat on the Liberal benches in the House of Lords to re-establish his family's presence in the parliament. When Sir Henry Campbell-Bannerman was elected prime minister in December 1905, William was appointed Captain of the Yeomen of the Guard, a ceremonial post dating back to the fifteenth century. Two years later he was appointed a member of the Privy Council, one of a select group of politicians who gave advice to the sovereign of the day.

He and Helena, whom he married in 1900—much to the annoyance of his own mother—would have four children. Mary, known as Alice, arrived in 1901, the year after their marriage, followed by Mandy in 1902, Edward in 1906, and Ellen, known as Louise, in 1908.

But the marriage would follow the norm and fall apart, and the children grew up mostly in an estranged household. William moved to his London townhouse, where he launched various questionable business schemes, and he sent his sons to boarding schools. Helena, who had been living mostly at Tandragee, took her daughters with her and lived between Paris and New York. The breakup and scattered childhood would have a profound effect on all the children.

Mandy's upbringing was short on love and attention and long on neglect dressed up as caring parental strategy, as his father would recall in his 1931 memoir *My Candid Recollections*:

> If my eldest son Mandy fell down, instead of sympathising with him for hurting himself I made him take a second tumble, on the principle that if one knocks a funny bone one immediately knocks the opposite funny bone in order to ease the pain of the first. I was anxious to prevent him from suffering from physical fear and to make him manly. It is fatally easy for a parent to sympathise with a small child who tumbles, but the consequences is [sic] that the tumble immediately becomes magnified in the child's mind into something of a great importance, and frequently it will fall again through sheer fear of being hurt. Now, Mandy could take a toss with anyone.

Mandy's recollection of childhood lessons from his father included learning to shoot from either shoulder and with either hand: 'When I was quite young, my father would say "Mandy, we shall require snipe and salmon for breakfast." I knew that if I didn't deliver them he would beat me. Later on, when I began to be invited to shoot pheasant or grouse, my father made me wait until I had spent a year learning to shoot left-handed.'

Mandy was indeed a resilient young man, and his father would have been pleased with his manly parenting skills as he watched his son performing on a rugby pitch. Mandy shone as a sportsman during his school days at Eton, particularly in rugby where he was lauded for his 'pluck' and regarded as a player of great promise.

'The boy has brains as well,' the Duke told a newspaper reporter proudly after watching one match in which Mandy starred while playing rugby for Blackheath. This London club was synonymous with sporting icons, such as the cricketers Andrew Stoddart and C.B. Fry, and boasted it had more capped England players than any other club.

But a sporting career would take a back seat when, soon after his eighteenth birthday, Mandy dropped out of Cambridge University to pursue a career as a naval officer. He enrolled at the Royal Naval College, Osborne, where Prince George, the fourth son of King George V, was among his cohort.

Mandy was commissioned the following year as a midshipman aboard HMS *Lowestoft*, a light cruiser. Life aboard ship was a mix of strict routine and, as pages from his training manual revealed, a concoction of demands placed on the behaviour of gentlemen officers, ranging from saluting properly to dress standards. There was a particular disdain of overdressing 'in sou'westers and seaboots like men on sardine cans' when on watch. Dinner-table behaviour was of the utmost importance, particularly arriving on time and dressing properly. Bad language was not tolerated, nor were proposing toasts or making bets, whistling or singing or ever mentioning a lady's name. 'Don't curse domestics during meals because the food does not meet with your approval,' he and his fellow officers were warned.

He settled well and impressed his commanding officers sufficiently for them to promote him the following year to sub lieutenant, an appointment the mention of which found its way into the social pages alongside news about Prince George. Although they served on different ships, the pair would remain close friends.

But then a change of plan. In 1923, just a few months before his twenty-first birthday and with another promotion in sight, Mandy sought extended leave, apparently to go searching for gold. Whatever his superiors thought of this rather bizarre move, they agreed to let the young man head off to Canada, where his father was trying to establish a gold mine in the wilds of Ontario. Some saw it as his attempt to re-bond with his errant father.

The Duke had taken the lease of 6000 acres (2430 hectares) of virgin forest a dozen or so kilometres from an established mine that had struck it rich some years before. He had told British newspapers that he was taking his valet, Chilton—'a remarkable fellow'—and a team of local prospectors and woodsmen first to clear virgin forest and then to begin to dig for 'great veins of gold'.

Mandy spent several months with his father as the Duke struggled to make headway at the mine. Eventually the older man headed back to Europe while insisting to newspaper reporters who found him at the local airport that the decision was forced upon him by bad weather and that he could not continue working the claim in the winter. He promised to return the next summer but never did, leaving a line of angry creditors behind him.

Mandy did not head back to Britain immediately but crossed the border into the United States. He was still there on 2 October when he turned twenty-one and crossed the threshold into adulthood—a tradition that originated as the age at which a young man could become a knight, but now tied to voting rights, marrying without consent and signing legal contracts. Back home in England the church bells, in spite of his absence, rang out across Kimbolton once again to celebrate this momentous birthday. Flags were hoisted and villagers celebrated. The same celebrations occurred at Tandragee Castle, where town councillors sent telegrams in the hope they would reach the young man, who newspapers declared was now one of Britain's most eligible bachelors.

Social writers concluded that Mandy's time in America meant he was on the hunt for a rich American heiress—or they observed that he should be. After all, his father and grandfather had both made the same trip and come back with brides.

But even if Mandy had been searching for a wife in America, he came home a few months later empty-handed. Now there were to be formal celebrations at Kimbolton of his coming of age, with his mother in attendance and his father absent. Watching his parents' marriage founder had entrenched in Mandy the need to take life seriously. Try as he might, he was no playboy. Marriage, for him, would be an affair of the heart and not of the wallet.

When he finally reported back to Admiralty House in early 1924, the young man was sent to HMS *Dryad*, a 'stone frigate' at Portsmouth, which was home to the Royal Navy's warfare school for torpedo and gunnery courses. These would qualify him for the next rung on the ladder.

The indulgence in allowing Mandy a little freedom was not just because of his title, as his record would demonstrate. Not long after being promoted to lieutenant, an assessment was made by a Captain Edward Cochrane, who described Mandy's future as an officer as very promising, noting: 'Forceful personality, physically fit and very strong. Good gun rifle shot and speaks fluent French. Shows promising leadership with tactful management with ratings'—junior sailors—'although he tends to be rather abrupt.'

In 1925 Mandy was commissioned to join the HMS *Cairo* under the command of Captain Cochrane. This was the ship that would determine not only his navy future but the course of his life—and his attempts to save the family fortune.

5

BANDAGES, BOUQUETS AND BELLS

27 March 1927

> Miss Nell Stead, with her sister, Miss Erin Stead, and Miss Marjorie Sutherland, left for England by the Cathay today.

The note, in the society columns of the Melbourne *Herald*, hid the real story. It was six months after Nell had met the young naval lieutenant, and she had told her friends that she was going to London to visit an aunt, a Mrs Shields, who lived in Kensington Gardens. Nell and Erin, accompanied by their friend Marjorie Sutherland, would be in London for the spring and then take a car trip on the Continent—France, Switzerland and Italy. The trio would then head back to London for the Season—the cultural heartbeat of upper-class British society—during which Mrs Shields might provide social introductions for the sisters and their friend.

There was no mention of Lieutenant Mandeville and a rekindling of their Ceylon dalliance. In fact, Nell had not told anyone but her father of their chance meeting in Colombo, and Sidney wondered why their chaperones, George and Gill Whitby, had allowed the sisters to go swimming. Still, it would have been impossible to disapprove of his daughter mingling with a naval officer who also happened to be a member of the aristocracy.

But why would Nell keep such a wonderful secret from her friends? Perhaps it seemed too far-fetched for others to believe, or maybe she still didn't quite believe it herself.

And yet the romance was real enough. In fact, just a few days after meeting Nell in Colombo, Mandy proposed marriage. After arriving back in Melbourne, Nell had accepted by letter, realising that she was in love, and the letters between them had continued to flow for the six months they had been apart. Mandy knew that she was making the journey halfway around the world to see him.

The sisters stopped once again in Colombo, but this time only for a few days before reboarding the ship and travelling via the Suez Canal to the port of Marseilles. Here they were met on the dock by Mandy with news that he had been assigned a new ship, the HMS *Hood*. He was on two weeks' leave while the battle cruiser was in port getting repairs, so he could escort Nell, Erin and Marjorie to London.

London was a city of contrasts when they arrived a few days later. It was a time of transition on city streets, when double-decker 'motor buses' jostled for space with horse-drawn carts and the occasional flock of sheep being herded down the

Strand by a farmer on the way to market. Likewise on the footpaths, where rich, poor, young and old mingled in disharmony: raucous flower-sellers pushed their wares onto gentlemen in frockcoats and silk top hats; anxious hotel bellboys in oversized braided jackets ferried suitcases for haughty ladies; and weary sandwich-board men trudged past restaurants filled with the leisure classes out for afternoon tea.

Nightlife sparkled. Theatre programs were crammed with musical revues and there was a proliferation of late-night clubs dominated by jazz at the peak of its popularity. Crowds flocked to cinemas, which now showed talking pictures, and King George V and Queen Mary ceremonially opened the iconic Mayfair Hotel in Piccadilly. Women, empowered by the vote, were exploring risqué fashion, with shorter hair and shorter dresses, and were smoking and driving motor cars. The Flapper Girl had arrived—girl power, 1920s style—bringing with her the right to be reckless and wild.

But there were also long shadows. In Britain, the flowers on the war memorials in Whitehall were still fresh and replaced every week, and carefree celebrations of the immediate postwar years had become fading memories for the working and middle classes. The hard economic realities of rebuilding a battered society began to bite, and by the middle of the decade there were an estimated two million people out of work. In 1926, the year before Nell arrived, some northern towns were reporting 70 per cent unemployment, creating the ill feeling that had ultimately led to the biggest general strike in the nation's history.

As promised, Nell and Erin lodged in Chelsea with their aunt, near the banks of the Thames and within walking distance of the city's dazzle. It was Nell's first visit, as she would later tell reporters, and the city was overwhelming for a young woman whose experience of city life was Melbourne—which was still, in essence, a colonial town.

Mandy was her guide, and the real reason she was there—far from home and family, and eager to start a new life as a wife and lover. If they were to marry, the ceremony had to be now, before Mandy was due back aboard his ship, which would be gone for months.

But Nell and Erin only had one suitcase when they arrived, the rest of their luggage held up in customs down at Southampton. Somehow, Nell found that she had agreed to a wedding within a week, with no clothes to speak of, and little time to prepare.

In hindsight it would have been better to have taken the train, but the romance of driving to London to pick up his bride-to-be and taking her back to Kimbolton the night before the wedding was too powerful an urge for Mandy.

He and Nell had an early supper at her aunt's Chelsea townhouse and headed off to be at Kimbolton by sunset. Mandy drove through the backstreets of one of the city's plushest neighbourhoods and into Stanhope Gardens, pausing briefly before swinging left into Cromwell Road across from the Natural History Museum.

Perhaps consumed by conversation about the next day's ceremony, Mandy misjudged the speed of another car approaching on the same side of the road. The other driver could not brake in time and slammed what the young naval officer would describe as 'broadside' into his car, spinning it in a vicious circle before it flipped on its side. Nell, caught by surprise, was flung around inside the car, smashing her right knee into the door frame. She felt the pain immediately and when the car stopped she looked down, expecting to see blood or even bone. She saw neither, but knew she had been injured. Her elbow hurt and she felt dazed, although she couldn't recall hitting her head.

Mandy, who had somehow escaped with a few bruises, was fraught and, despite Nell's protestations, insisted on an examination in a nearby hospital for his 'plucky' bride-to-be, as he would later describe her. Her knee had swollen like a purple balloon by the time she was examined but, miraculously given the accident, there was no broken bone. Although walking up the aisle in a few hours' time seemed a ludicrous proposition, Nell demanded that her knee be bandaged for stability, to give her the option of walking the next day.

In the meantime, a hire car was arranged and a now demure Mandy set off again, with his best man, fellow junior officer Lieutenant Douglas, now in the back seat alongside Nell. It was well after dark and their intended evening drinks were reduced to a swig from the neck of a whiskey bottle as they drove north to Kimbolton.

Should the wedding be called off?

Nell was insistent when she woke the next morning, sore but determined that the ceremony would go ahead as planned. She had travelled halfway across the world and a limp was not going to stop her getting married.

'Feeling sore and whiplashed,' she acknowledged in her diary. It was a simple entry, considering how the crash had impacted on her special day, and it indicated her propensity to understate situations and emotions—and her determination to press on regardless.

The next morning—5 May—the sun shone kindly, although the springtime chill remained. The ceremony would be held at the fourteenth-century St Andrew's Church, at the top of the Kimbolton high street a few hundred metres from Kimbolton Castle, before guests retired to the castle for modest celebrations.

The couple had wanted a quiet affair but it would have been impossible for the Viscount, heir to the title, to marry without the townsfolk of Kimbolton expressing their congratulations.

Word had spread swiftly the previous evening and by the time the couple alighted from their car outside the church, the street was decorated with colourful streamers and lined with dozens of wellwishers waving flags. Nell, dressed not in bridal white but a primrose coat trimmed with fur over a biscuit-coloured frock, black satin cloche hat and carrying a sheaf of lilac, was clearly limping as she disappeared into the church on the arm of her beau. Mandy was dressed 'mufti'—in a civilian suit rather than his naval uniform.

Inside, amid the hastily arranged flowers and choral singers, only the front pews were needed to seat the knot of family who would witness a ceremony that in another day and age would have been a grand society wedding. Her coat now discarded, Nell's bandaged knees were clearly visible as she and Mandy made their vows.

The service was over in half an hour; when the couple emerged, there was a group of newspaper reporters gathered by the car. News had spread fast of the exotic love story and the injured bride. Nell stopped to talk to them, Mandy by her side. 'My knees were badly cut and bruised and they are giving me considerable pain,' she said. 'It was only with the greatest difficulty that I managed to reach the altar. I am compelled to wear bandages and in a few minutes I have to see a doctor.'

And what of the romance in Ceylon? Nell laughed and recounted the chance meeting at the swimming pool: 'It was a real romance. Rather like a novel actually.' There was an extra challenge in terms of the wedding, she admitted. Despite being in London for a week, her luggage had not yet been delivered from the boat: 'My sister and I came here each with a single suitcase, and out of this I had to take clothes in which I was married today. Fancy a bride with only a suitcase!'

Mandy smiled at the attention—no doubt arranged by his publicity-seeking father—and batted away questions about the rush and perceived secrecy. He and Nell had fallen in love on sight, he insisted, and wanted to be together. Who could want for a better reason to marry as soon as possible? Their attraction was only intensified by their separation after leaving Ceylon so it was just a matter of getting Sidney Stead's approval and making arrangements for Nell to travel to England.

As for a honeymoon, there was little time because he had to be back aboard HMS *Hood* in a couple of days. He was a member of the Royal Navy and took his duties seriously.

Back at the castle, as champagne corks were popped in a tent set up on the unused tennis court, Nell had time to consider what was to come. The new Lady Mandeville had become effectively the female head of the Manchester family, given the long absence of her mother-in-law, Duchess Helena.

Although the castle was mostly shut, there was an estate to run day-to-day and social expectations to fulfil, all while her new father-in-law played fast and loose in the gambling clubs of London and her new husband was away at sea. It seemed that she had swapped managing the Stead household in Melbourne for managing the Manchester ducal lands in England.

Despite the wedding's lack of grandeur, or perhaps because of it, a handful of formal photographs taken at Kimbolton that afternoon would remain as poignant reminders. There was a simple joy and confidence in Nell's expression as she posed, hand on hip, with a slight cock of the head as if challenging any inquisitor, and sporting a modest diamond ring on her wedding finger. Was she really aware of the enormity of the decision she'd just made? Not only had she known this young man in person for just a few weeks in total but she was on the other side of the world to her family, and in a society and a culture of which she had only fleeting experience.

A little more than eight months before this day, she had been a single woman in her mid-twenties with few prospects, trying to evaluate the world and her place in it. Yet now her name carried a title of import—Viscountess—and she had married a man who would one day carry the title of duke, and own three castles and as many baronies—Montagu, Mandeville and Manchester—as well as being the nephew of the Duchess of Hamilton and the countesses of Derby and Gosford.

The bride and groom sat for photos with their guests beneath the soaring stone pillars of the castle's grand portico. It was a happy moment and yet there was sadness in the faces of some of the older men who sat at the back, perched on the grand staircase staring out across the estate grounds, as if remembering what had been and what lay ahead for the family and its heritage. At the front, Nell and her sister Erin grinned at the camera, happy but oblivious, while Mandy's siblings—Lord Edward, and sisters Lady Alice and Lady Louise—looked studious, trapped by the past and at a loss about the future.

Most telling of all were the photographs of Nell and Mandy in unguarded moments, so engaged in each other's company that they seemed unaware of the camera. It seemed such a short time to have grown so attached and yet Mandy's protective arm about his new wife's shoulders expressed care and love.

At sunset there was a gathering of some import. The vast majority of servants who had tended the needs and desires of this once grand home were gone, no longer needed by a duke who preferred to live in his city flat at Grosvenor Square.

But some staff and estate hands remained and, as the sunset spread its rays across the vast lawns, they gathered in a circle around the newlyweds to wish them well. An elderly retainer named Hewitt raised a toast with a glass of ale brewed in the town:

I wish you all health,
I wish you all wealth,
I wish you all the gold in store,
And when you die to Heaven you go,
What could I wish you more?

Later that night there was a knock on the great castle door just as sixteen guests sat down to dinner in the Great Hall. The housekeeper answered the door to two women who stood outside with a touching gift for the newlyweds—a posy of Australian navel-orange blossoms.

As the newlyweds retired to bed, the papers back in Melbourne and Sydney were being alerted to the union. It was not the first time that an Australian woman had married into the British aristocracy—there were at least a dozen countesses, marchionesses and baronesses as well as wives of royal families scattered throughout Europe—but this was at another, rarified level, with a duke holding the most senior English title after the royal family. Little Nell Stead stood in line to become Australia's first duchess, no less.

Social columnists rushed to recall her, searching their clipping files to find plaudits for a young woman who had faded from view in recent years through the circumstances of her mother's illness.

'Her last social appearance in Melbourne was at the Sargood wedding, where she was frocked as usual to perfection,' noted the 'Melbourne Chatter' columnist for *The Bulletin*. 'She is dark-eyed with a complexion like a blush-rose, rather shy and reserved for this generation.'

'Nell Stead's photographs do not adequately convey her looks,' concluded the correspondent for *Smith's Weekly*. 'She has a good taste in dress, a nice appreciation of colour and form. The firm chin also indicates a character of her own.' *The Argus* agreed: Nell had been prominent but relatively quiet and reserved among her peers. Dark-eyed and attractive, rather than beautiful, she always dressed well with a graceful figure: 'She has the gift of being always what the French people describe as "bien soignée".'

Although they all commented on her appearance, it was Nell's character that was held to be most admirable—not only a devoted daughter to a dying mother, but discreet enough to keep her engagement a closely guarded secret for more than six months after returning to Melbourne, although it wasn't made clear why public discretion was so important. 'Until her mother's illness, Nell was considered one of the smartest girls in Melbourne,' crowed *The Age*. 'It is part of the thoroughness of her character that she relinquished most of her pleasures and devoted herself to her mother until she died. She presents that unusual combination—fair to reddish hair and melting brown eyes—that all men find irresistible. She is not actually a beauty but dresses well with quite a French touch. Miss Stead, being a skilled needlewoman, made herself a small but exquisite trousseau.'

The English newspapers described the event as being to the 'great astonishment to London', given that society weddings were usually large and ostentatious affairs, announced publicly well in advance to generate publicity about the union of two great families. This was deliciously clandestine and had the drama of the traffic accident to boot.

They praised the 'charming and plucky' bride and wrote of her ability to hunt, dance, and play tennis and golf—important skills for a noblewoman, it seemed. The groom was a 'motoring enthusiast', they noted, in clear reference to the accident, and known as a promising rugby player and cricketer. His connection to Prince George at the Royal Naval College was also acknowledged.

But some UK papers were cynical about the reason for the union: it was all about money, they insisted. After all, Nell was an heiress and the daughter of a 'very large landowner' and multimillionaire. Such was the infatuation with creating a moneyed purpose that the *Daily Telegraph* in London even claimed, falsely, that she was related to a well-known vicar whose grandfather had emigrated to Australia many years before and 'owned the whole of the ground on which Melbourne is built'. It was front-page news in the *Evening Standard*, which labelled her a 'millionairess' who had been rushed to the altar two days after the wedding licence had been granted.

The Duke, who'd recently delayed his divorce from Helena Zimmerman and given the bride away in the absence of Sidney Stead, did nothing to dissuade the coverage, smoking a cigar and beaming as he spoke to reporters: 'They met, and—there, you have it,' he chuckled, inviting the scribes to draw their own conclusions. 'I knew only two days before that they intended to get married although, of course, I had heard of the engagement. I am sure my son will be extremely happy. He has married one of the most charming girls I have met. I am sure she will make an ideal wife, and they both have my blessing.'

But for all the compliments, some journalists wondered whether the marriage would last and if Nell was up to the job. After all, three other Australian peeresses—Lady Cheylesmore (formerly Nora Parker, a Tasmanian chorus girl), Marchioness Conyngham (formerly Bessie Tobin of Melbourne) and Lady Headley (formerly Barbara Baynton, a writer from Scone in New South Wales) had recently been through the divorce courts.

'Australians don't seem to be able to pull it off as peeresses,' declared *Truth*, which described the response to the wedding as merry twitter: 'It is to expect something in the nature of a miracle for a girl who has spent the greater part of her life in a suburb of an Australian city to take her part in the Great World, as she must, as an honest-to-goodness duchess, with any real hope of making a "go" of it.'

And yet, in spite of the legitimate observations about her closeted upbringing, there was acknowledgement that 'Australian girls' were rather an unknown quantity: 'It must be admitted that no one knows the half of what an Australian girl is capable.'

6

A LEGACY OF TITLES

The River Kym has flowed through the middle of Kimbolton for thousands of years. It is more of a stream really, especially in the summer when reduced to a series of pools with stepping stones for townsfolk to cross. But in the winter it can swell with melted snow and floods from heavy rains to become more menacing as it carves its way through the Cambridgeshire countryside before emptying into the Great Ouse and eventually draining into the North Sea.

It was flowing when a small Roman settlement was established on its banks around AD 50, and mentioned a thousand years later when the *Domesday Book* was published, noting that the town, then known as Kenebaltone, had one hundred and twenty-one residents, two men-at-arms, a water mill, a church and a priest. The town was a quiet village surrounded by fertile land measuring twenty 'ploughlands'—a unit of measurement based on how much a team of oxen could till in a season—which made it a prominent settlement in England.

The river was the cornerstone of life in Kimbolton, even as the town grew and then stagnated, its buildings clustered around the St Andrew's Church spire, built in the thirteenth century. Inside, the church was filled with the remains of earls and dukes, with the monuments and regimental colours of wealthy donors, long dead, whose gifts—bread and coins mostly—were emblazoned with gilt letters on black boards under the organ gallery.

It was said that King Harold Godwinson, the last Anglo-Saxon king, whose reign ended with his death at the Battle of Hastings in 1066, had owned a hunting lodge nearby and worshipped at the local church. The invading Normans reached Kimbolton a few years after Hastings and built a wooden motte-and-bailey castle on raised ground. Its remains are still visible centuries later as a low grass mound surrounded by a ditch.

By the thirteenth century there was a new building on the site, a fortified manor house built by Sir Geoffrey FitzPiers, the Earl of Essex, a confidant to the Lionheart, King Richard, and his successor, younger brother King John. The manor and lands would change hands frequently over the next two centuries as wealthy families fell in and out of favour with the passing parade of monarchs.

The building would also grow and evolve into Kimbolton Castle, becoming not only a visible part of British architectural history but intrinsically connected to the fragile politics of court society, with links to almost every king and queen over the next five hundred years. Most critically, in the early sixteenth century it was given to the diplomat and courtier Sir Richard Wingfield, a Knight of the Garter appointed by King Henry VIII.

The Wingfield family remodelled and expanded the building to create a castle of note. In 1534 it became the home of Catherine of Aragon, Henry's first wife, who was banished to the castle after refusing to accept Henry's ruling that they were no longer husband and wife. He had turned to Anne Boleyn, Catherine's lady-in-waiting, to provide him with a male heir. It marked his break with the Catholic Church and the bloody beginning of the Church of England.

The castle would be Catherine's prison where she spent the last years of her life in almost total isolation. Banished and forbidden to see her daughter, Mary, she spent more than eighteen months holed up in a few rooms at the south-western corner of the building with a handful of loyal servants. Her failing health was blamed on the climate but, based on descriptions at the time, it was more likely to have been a form of cancer. By January 1536 she was confined to bed and hardly able to eat. In one last, defiant act, she dictated a letter to Henry from her Kimbolton prison, 'pardoning' him for his actions against her and the Catholic Church:

> The hour of my death now drawing on . . . I pardon you everything, and I wish to devoutly pray God that He will

> pardon you also. For the rest, I commend unto you our daughter Mary, beseeching you to be a good father unto her, as I have heretofore desired. Lastly, I make this vow, that mine eyes desire you above all things.

Catherine died a few days later, her body embalmed with spices, wrapped in waxed linen and encased in lead before being left in the castle chapel for three weeks. Afterwards her body was driven 40 kilometres north to be entombed at Peterborough Abbey. In one final act of cruelty, Henry refused to allow their daughter, Mary, to attend the funeral.

There was a last reminder of Catherine's time at Kimbolton—a studded leather coffer that contained her most personal belongings. Almost four centuries later, the empty coffer was still in the castle, placed in the central hallway beneath the grand staircase.

Catherine's ghost was said to walk the halls, appearing as legs and lower body projecting from the ceiling, while on the floor above, her head and shoulders would be seen gliding along a hallway. It was as if her apparition was haunting the building as it had stood in her time, long before its transformation.

The Montagu family arrived at Kimbolton in 1615 when the castle was bought by Henry Montagu, a lawyer and politician, and a member of the so-called Star Chamber court that sat in the royal Palace of Westminster. He became Lord Chief Justice of England, confidant to King Charles I, and best known for sending the explorer Sir Walter Raleigh to the executioner for his alleged role in the plot to dethrone the monarch.

Henry's royal rewards first came with junior peerages as Viscount Mandeville and Baron Montagu of Kimbolton. Then in 1626 he was appointed Earl of Manchester, a newly created title. Manchester was then a modest Lancashire town; two centuries later, driven by the industrial revolution, it would become one of the great manufacturing cities of the world.

Henry Montagu's son Edward, the 2nd Earl of Manchester, was a politician and commander for the Parliamentary forces during the First English Civil War. His second in command, for a time, was Oliver Cromwell, with whom he later fell out. Despite fighting against the Royalists, Edward felt the same as many MPs and opposed the trial of Charles I, who was eventually beheaded for treason. Edward later became a key figure in the Restoration and subsequent return from exile of Charles II.

The Montagu family's proximity to power continued into the next generation when Robert, the 3rd Earl of Manchester, served as Gentleman of the Bedchamber to Charles II. Despite the family's social prominence and apparent wealth, Kimbolton Castle was falling into disrepair and was in need of refurbishment by the time the title was handed down to the 4th Earl, Charles Edward Montagu, in 1683.

Charles served as England's ambassador to France and later ambassador to Venice during the reign of William, Prince of Orange. After the partial collapse of the castle's south-east corner in the late seventeenth century, Charles commissioned the radical architect and dramatist John Vanbrugh, and his collaborator Nicholas Hawksmoor, to redesign and rebuild the front of the castle.

Vanbrugh was in demand; he had just completed construction of Castle Howard in Yorkshire, and was also building Blenheim Palace in Oxfordshire, both of which would be hailed as 'English Baroque' masterpieces. Kimbolton was a different challenge as he persuaded the Earl to allow him to reface all sides in a classical style and keep a sense of its history as a fortified building with battlements—'a castle air'.

A classical portico was added and the courtyard rebuilt while, inside, the great halls were divided into a series of state rooms and saloons, the family chapel restored and a grand staircase added. The work took three years, after which the Earl brought the Venetian painter Giovanni Antonio Pellegrini to England to paint murals for the new rooms—including the wall and ceilings of the main staircase, the musicians' gallery and the chapel. A portrait of the Earl's children would adorn the main wall of the largest of the halls.

Pellegrini's airy, illusionistic compositions, with their bright flickering colour, set a new standard of rococo elegance for English decoration. To complete the effect, French upholsterers were commissioned to design and make gilded Louis XIV–inspired furniture.

Not long after the work was completed, Charles Montagu received an appointment to the household of King George I. In 1719 the King then created a new, upgraded title for his trusted aide—the Earldom of Manchester had become the Dukedom. With the title came a coat of arms with the crest of a mythical griffin above a shield of eagles and diamonds representing mountaintops. The 'supporters' were a heraldic antelope, representing harmony and purity, and a griffin, representing strength and leadership.

But it was the motto—*Disponendo me, non mutando me*—that would attract the most attention and discussion over the years. Translated from the Latin, it means 'By disposing of me, not by changing me', but the interpretation, revealed in an 1837 guide to the British peerage system, provides the most interesting aspect. The Montagu family believed it meant 'Pay me well and I am yours,' and referred to the role of Edward, the 2nd Earl of Manchester, in the restoration of the crown to Charles II.

It also said much about the questionable character of some of the dukes who were to come.

The Montagu men may initially have been the dominating voice in the family but, as Nell would discover as she roamed the saloons and drawing rooms of the castle over the few days of her honeymoon, there was plenty of character and intrigue among their wives. It was the duchesses who would hold sway over the family and its finances for much of the first three centuries of the dukedom.

Lady Isabella was the wife of William Montagu, the 2nd Duke of Manchester. The couple was childless, which led to her decision to help establish the Foundling Hospital, a charity that worked to save children abandoned by their parents due to poverty. In 1730 she was one of twenty-one 'prominent lady petitioners', as they were dubbed, whose signatures persuaded King George II to give the charity his royal seal.

The hospital would become the world's first incorporated charity and play an important role in managing London's overwhelming child poverty crisis. Its supporters included the painter William Hogarth, who established Britain's first public art gallery as a fundraising initiative, and the composer George Frideric Handel, who held an annual benefit concert where he would present a performance of his masterpiece *Messiah*.

Lady Isabella was also admired as a talented amateur artist, receiving acclaim from the writer and art historian Horace Walpole, who noted that she painted 'remarkably well in crayons'.

Elizabeth Dashwood, wife of George, the 4th Duke, was also an artist of some note, and her pocketbook was acquired by the Royal Academy of Arts. It was George and Elizabeth who would save the castle and rebuild its crumbling walls; many of the treasures and acclaimed artworks that came to hang inside it were attributed to her eye. She commissioned paintings by such artists as Joshua Reynolds, whose portrait of the Duchess and her son, titled *Diana Disarming Cupid*, would later hang in the Victoria and Albert Museum.

Lady Susan Gordon, wife of William, the 5th Duke, was famous not for charitable works or artistic endeavours but for shocking polite society. After bearing eight children in twelve years, the Duchess stayed behind in England when her husband, a notorious philanderer, was made governor of

Jamaica in 1808. When he had not returned four years later, she eloped with one of her footmen, forcing her wayward husband to negotiate an unusual financial settlement that banished her from the castle and left it abandoned for almost a decade until his own return.

The 6th Duke of Manchester, George, married Millicent Sparrow, who brought with her the keys to Tandragee Castle and its estates in County Armagh, Ireland, as well as Brampton Park House, a magnificent eighteenth-century mansion near the village of Brampton, a dozen kilometres east of Kimbolton. It was in Brampton that the diarist Samuel Pepys was said to have buried his fortune of gold coins in a panic after the Dutch navy invaded the River Medway in 1667.

Tandragee, once the home of the powerful O'Hanlon clan, had been largely abandoned but with Millicent's money, it was redesigned in Scottish baronial style, including a turret where the Duchess had light to do her needlework. She was loved in the town, where the Manchesters were considered good landlords and where Millicent established schools, clothing funds and an orphanage for Protestant girls. Mandy, who was born at Tandragee in 1902, would later follow the lead of his great-great-grandmother as a landowner who provided for his tenants.

Louisa von Alten was a German countess who would become known as the Double Duchess after first marrying William, the 7th Duke of Manchester in 1853 and then, when he died forty years later, wedding Spencer Cavendish, the 8th Duke of Devonshire. In truth, the relationship with Cavendish had been going on for years as she and William became estranged.

She was typical of a woman who lived what was regarded as a fast life and was once called 'a social climber with a nose for power'. She became a great friend of the Prince of Wales, later King Edward VII, and managed to wrangle herself into the position of Mistress of the Robes to Queen Victoria. In 1897, at Devonshire House in London, she hosted a costume ball to mark Victoria's Diamond Jubilee. The event would become known as one of the city's most successful social events, attended by at least one member of every European royal family.

Her marriage to the 7th Duke had set a pattern, and henceforth the dukes of Manchester would look past Europe and other noble houses for their wives, starting with George, the 8th Duke of Manchester, and Consuelo Yznaga, a renowned Cuban-American beauty. Consuelo's story was one of the inspirations for her friend Edith Wharton's unfinished novel *The Buccaneers*, which followed the stories of five wealthy and ambitious American women and their unhappy cross-Atlantic marriages.

Consuelo and George were doomed to failure for one reason: George was a drunken wastrel who took Consuelo's money and burned it on gambling and a music-hall actress named Bessie Bellwood. As George and his wife drifted apart and he was ostracised by his peers for being an inebriate (he would die of cirrhosis of the liver, aged thirty-nine), Consuelo was becoming a prominent society figure in London and among the intimate circle of Edward VII.

For all her wealth, it seemed that Consuelo had a social conscience. She championed causes in poverty, education and health during her lifetime, although media attention at the time of her death in 1909 focused on her money and chattels, particularly the ruby-and-diamond bracelet she bequeathed to Queen Alexandra. Also the Manchester tiara, created for her by Cartier, for which she had supplied more than one thousand brilliant-cut and four hundred rose-cut diamonds; this would end up in the Victoria and Albert Museum.

Helena Zimmerman was the daughter of Ohio businessman Eugene who made his fortune investing in oil as a business associate of John D. Rockefeller, and then parlaying his profits into railways as the American interior was opened up in the late nineteenth century. His big mistake was to let William Montagu, 'Little Kim', the young 9th Duke of Manchester, walk through his front door and charm his daughter.

Two years later, after seeing off a Polish prince as rival suitor and promising to give his bride Tandragee Castle, William married Helena in secret. The move enraged his mother Consuelo, the dowager duchess who, clearly influenced by her own matrimonial experiences, refused to believe that her son had repeated his father's dishonesty until she went to the church and demanded to see the register for herself.

Eugene Zimmerman's response was more charitable when the newlywed couple travelled to America after the wedding. 'He has the potential to be a good husband, even if he is in debt,' Zimmerman was reported to have said, while quietly establishing a US$1 million trust fund for his daughter that the Duke could not touch.

The newspapers greeted the marriage with a level of cynicism. One columnist remarked of the Duke: 'Besides being affable, fond of horseback riding and auto-mobiling, he knows every chorus girl in London.'

Nell Stead must have pondered how she could fit into this legacy of titles, politics, prominence, wealth and waste. She was none of these things: a woman of modest means, at least in comparison to the women who had come before her, and certainly without the social position that they all occupied.

But there was one important thing that she had to offer the Montagu family: a marriage born of love rather than opportunity, and a relationship sincere enough to survive life's challenges, of which there would undoubtedly be many.

7

A GIRL MADE GOOD

The grandeur of Kimbolton Castle, and Mandy's stories of the family's past wealth and power, had been an all-too-brief experience. The honeymoon was over in a few days and Mandy was off to rejoin his ship.

Suddenly the castle became overwhelming, its cavernous interior and myriad rooms a physical reminder for Nell of the enormity of the change in her life. One night she woke, alone in bed, and needing a drink of water. Unsure of where to go, she descended the grand staircase in search of the kitchens below and became lost in the rabbit warren. She was found the next morning, curled up asleep on the stone floor of a downstairs passageway.

The castle would not be their marital home, at least initially. A few weeks later she settled into Park Lodge, a grand estate house that sat within 12 hectares of land and gardens on a gentle hill not far from the village, facing the castle across the valley and next to the estate's farm. Originally a Tudor hunting lodge, it had become a secret retreat for the friends of various dukes to entertain their lovers, among them Edward Prince of Wales, later King Edward VII, who used the lodge as a safe house where he could entertain the socialite and actress Lillie Langtry.

Nell was unlikely to have known this story, of course. It was not one to be told by her new husband, or by her father-in-law, who had scarpered off back to London while her mother-in-law flitted between Paris, New York and occasionally Cannes.

The eyes of Kimbolton were now upon a twenty-five-year-old from colonial Melbourne, who was suddenly the day-to-day face of the town's ancient traditions and modern expectations. The Duke of Manchester was not only the principal landowner and employer but was also expected to be seen, like a town mayor or the local vicar, and Kimbolton had long missed the Duke and his family in their community celebrations and events.

Nell Stead was a willing although slightly overawed participant. The splendour of the castle was like a fairytale and yet she somehow felt at home at Kimbolton. Perhaps it was the humble, almost shambolic castle interiors or the relaxed relationship with the staff, most of whom she spoke to on a first-name basis. Or maybe it was the fact that Kimbolton was, after all, a country town and she was a country girl.

A few weeks after becoming the new Lady Mandeville, Nell was called on to unfurl the Union Jack at Kimbolton's Empire Day ceremony. The next month she gave out trophies at the secondary school athletics carnival and was a keen observer at the Midland Counties sheepdog trials. In the summer there was a speech to give at the ceremony to open the cricket season, and a VIP box to sit in when she attended the circus. She judged flowers, vegetables and cakes at the annual Peterborough Show and sat in the family pew each Sunday at St Andrew's Church.

Despite her insecurities, Nell decided to remain very much herself. She shocked and thrilled the townspeople by daring to wear trousers while she shopped in the high street. She rebuffed the vicar, Canon Frank Powys Maurice, when he offered to have his daughter make her a 'proper countrywoman', and attempts by others to interest her in breeding and showing Pekingese dogs. She insisted she preferred the pack of retrievers and 'nondescript' dogs that were kennelled on the farm for hunting.

She made attempts to fit in with the coterie of wives of local dignitaries, who smiled and invited her for tea but privately made fun of Nell's background, Australian manner and attitude. It would take time for her to be embraced by a society in which one usually required either distinction or money, and preferably both, to be accepted.

Her life was no hardship of course, surrounded as she was by servants and living in a grand house, even if it wasn't a castle. That move would hopefully come later, after Mandy inherited the title. Perhaps there would be money from his mother's fortune that could be used to restore the castle to its former glory. They could only dream.

For the moment there was an endowment from Mandy's grandmother Consuelo, set up in a trust fund that was administered by executors in faraway America; they tried to ensure that the Duke steered well clear of the money beyond his cut, which was quickly swallowed up by his outrageous lifestyle. Mandy, as the oldest son of the Duke, received a more generous allowance than his siblings but he was regularly called upon to bail out his father as well as his younger brother, Edward, who was in Canada somewhere and seemed to have inherited their father's attitude to life. Mandy's older sister Alice lived in America when she wasn't with her mother and, according to Mandy, struggled with depression.

The youngest, Lady Louise, was a female version of her eldest brother, in looks and attitude as she raced cars and learned to fly a plane. She and Nell had already struck up a bond at the wedding, drawn together by their socially unconventional views and tomboyish behaviour, both as comfortable in jodhpurs and hunting boots as they were in heels and ball gowns.

Beyond the Montagu money, Nell also had her own source of income, more modest but a contribution nonetheless. It included a stash of shares in a relatively young Australian mining operation, the Broken Hill Company, which had begun as a silver venture but had recently begun investing in steelworks at Newcastle back in New South Wales. Her father had the foresight to invest in rural businesses and his instincts would prove right when the company later became one of the world's largest mining companies, BHP. (By a strange quirk of fate, the company's first silver-mining venture had been opened by William, the 7th Duke of Manchester, during a visit to Australia in 1881.)

London, the jewel of high-society life, remained something of a mystery to Nell until Mandy was home on shore leave several months after the wedding. Nell, the outsider and future duchess, caused immediate interest as she mingled easily with a cabaret cast who were dancing on tables in a Green Park restaurant. At a 'dance and splash party' at Grosvenor House in Park Lane, Nell cast modesty aside, changing from her ball gown into a bathing suit and easily winning the swimming races.

They were suddenly considered among the fringe members of the city's so-called 'Bright Young Things', the group of bohemian aristocrats and socialites who ran amok through London in the late 1920s, fond of flamboyant parties and crazy stunts, all eagerly reported by the tabloid press. Their more prominent members included Cecil Beaton; Nancy and Diana Mitford; Evelyn Waugh; the Sitwell siblings Edith, Osbert and Sacheverell; and another Australian, socialite Sheila Chisholm.

Nell drank it all in, luxuriating in the frivolity, but there were weightier things on her mind, Australia among them. She missed home and would never come to terms with the English weather, which she found miserably wet and cold, even in the summers. Letters from her sister Erin, which she would keep among her personal papers, were filled with updates about family events involving her other siblings, Penelope and David, as well as Erin's own betrothal to a businessman named John Grimwade.

The letters also made clear that there was unfinished business in terms of her journey across the world and the surprise marriage. Their father had given the union his blessing, but only from afar. Although he had known of the real reason for his daughter's visit to England—to rekindle the romance with the young viscount—and may have suspected there was a likelihood of marriage, the first he had heard of a wedding was a cable from Mandy the day before the event asking for his permission for this 'sudden decision'.

This meant that Sidney had no chance to attend the ceremony and bask in the fortunes of his oldest child. It was time for the prodigal daughter, albeit one who had boosted rather than squandered her future, to return to Melbourne and introduce her new husband.

In terms of homecomings, Nell's arrival in Melbourne in late February 1928, nine months after her marriage, was lowkey. When the SS *Ormonde* docked in Melbourne, there were reporters to photograph the 'girl made good' and her handsome beau, but the couple made it clear that this was essentially a private visit rather than a media parade.

When Nell continued to resist interviews, the frustrated reporters, unused to being refused, resorted to commenting disdainfully on her appearance to fill their society gossip columns. 'Lady Mandeville has not altered her appearance since she left Melbourne just eleven months ago,' noted 'Cecilia' for the Melbourne *Herald*. 'She still wears her curly brown hair shingled, although rather longer in cut than has been customary here for the last few months.'

Her mother-in-law, Duchess Helena, was said to be anxious to present Nell to court but would have to wait until next Season while her daughter-in-law enjoyed 'the country life of dogs and shooting far more than the prospect of London social gaieties'. It was all supposition as the reporters clutched at straws.

The media would have to wait until the couple made a brief visit to Sydney before they got an opportunity for photographs. But when Nell finally stepped out socially, she paid the price for ignoring their overtures. At a horseracing meeting she was said to be dressed 'plainly' in black-and-white satin, and at a dance to celebrate the end of the polo season she wore a necklace of large sapphires set in diamonds from the Manchester collection, which prompted this catty observation: 'It was so magnificent a piece of jewellery that it seemed as if it needed age and dignity to show it off.'

Nell and Mandy would leave a few weeks later with even less fanfare as they travelled through the Pacific to Honolulu and on to Los Angeles; there, by contrast, they happily posed for photographs at the Biltmore Hotel. This was Mandy's stamping ground, given his American mother and Cuban-American grandmother. 'With a whole flock of maids, valets and baggage, the Viscount and Viscountess Mandeville are here for a few days on a honeymoon visit,' crowed the *Oakland Tribune*. They queried Mandy—'bronzed, blue-eyed and handsome'—about his hunting whims as the couple announced they were off to Yosemite National Park. Joking that there were no lions, 'I must content myself with shooting a round of golf,' he quipped.

Nell—'stylish, girlish and democratic'—joined in the mirth and grinned when her husband revealed her skills on a horse and with a rifle. The reporter decided to test the claim: 'Why does the Prince of Wales fall so often from his horse?' he asked, in reference to several recent riding accidents by the future Edward VIII.

Nell threw back her head and laughed: 'I'll tell you. He hasn't any seat or any hands.' The reporter looked quizzical. 'Now, if he had learned to ride bareback in the beginning he could cling to anything. Down in Australia I scorned a saddle but, of course, I'll use one in England.'

Nell and Mandy's marriage was the real interest. Could a marriage that began around a swimming pool be real or was it more of a 'companionate' arrangement? The question implied that Nell was merely a companion or lover, rather than a partner in life. Mandy seemed offended as he looked across at his wife: 'Companionate marriage? It sounds rather silly.'

Nell chipped in: 'Ours is a real love marriage. We did it ourselves. You Americans are always creating new fads and I think this companionate marriage business is only a passing fancy on the part of a group of people who always must have something new to talk about.'

They toured for several weeks, visiting the Grand Canyon, Arizona, Chicago and finally New York where Mandy's mother, Duchess Helena, was waiting in a hotel opposite Central Park to meet her daughter-in-law.

Like Sidney Stead, she had not been told of the marriage until it was too late to make the journey to England, and it was said that she had been upset. Any doubts about the marriage were quickly erased as the three of them boarded the same liner to cross the Atlantic back to Europe, where the Duchess returned to Paris, and the Mandevilles to London and onwards to Kimbolton.

First, there was another trip to make before Mandy returned for a new stint at sea, this time to Tandragee in Northern Ireland, where Mandy had been born, and where the townsfolk had been waiting since the marriage to congratulate the couple despite being largely ignored by the family over the past decade.

Tandragee Castle sat on a hillside overlooking the Cusher River. The area's brisk winds probably led to the naming of the town, from the Gaelic *Toin re Gaoith* or 'backside to the wind'. But he had not been to the town for almost a decade and neither had anyone else in the family, as the chairman of the local council pointed out sourly in his welcoming speech: 'We regret that of late years these visits have been all too infrequent and we hope with deep sincerity that it may be possible for your Lordship and Viscountess Mandeville to come amongst us very often in the near future. We are proud of the fact that you are a Tandragee man and we follow your career with personal interest.'

Mandy responded by insisting that Tandragee was his heart place. The crowd cheered, even though many thought privately that he was simply being polite. They cheered again when Nell was persuaded to speak and said her husband had underplayed how beautiful the countryside was and how much she'd like to visit regularly. A bonfire was lit in the market square to celebrate.

The good feelings continued the next day when they were feted by the nearby Portadown Council, a 'brother town' which had also benefited from what the town clerk described as 'the munificence of scions of the House of Montagu in bygone days'. This included the People's Park, the cholera hospital, the town quay and the fair green.

Like Tandragee's elders, the Portadown aldermen hoped the couple would take up permanent residence in a castle that was now empty, and play a role in public life. Mandy assured them in return that he and Nell would visit more often: 'As a representative of my father I thank you for the loving and loyal way in which you have all looked up to the House of Montagu in spite of all the troubles we have had.' The goodwill trip had been a success.

There would be two additional private visits before the couple returned to Kimbolton. One was to Kylemore Abbey at Connemara in the west of Ireland, which, despite having been sold off years ago to pay his father's gambling debts, held powerful memories for Mandy, who spent an afternoon trout fishing with some of his local boyhood friends.

The other visit was for Nell. Just 40 kilometres south of Tandragee was Rostrevor, a picturesque village of myth and legend on the shores of a lough that spills into the Irish Sea, and set against the backdrop of the Mourne Mountains. This was the home of the Stead family, where her father, Sidney, was born in 1861.

A few days after returning to Kimbolton there was reason to celebrate the future, a trip to the doctor confirming that Nell was pregnant.

8

THE SPENDTHRIFT'S TRUST

'Spendthrift' is a curious word—the joining of two opposites to describe wasteful extravagance. Yet the etymology of 'thrift', an Old Norse word for prosperity, would suggest that spendthrift actually means *spend to thrive.*

Certainly that seemed to be the view of William Montagu, the 9th Duke of Manchester, who literally spent his life away with an abandon that few could match, even if they were stupid enough to try. He regarded every effort to curb his spending as a challenge for him to simply squander more.

Perhaps it was rebellion against his impoverished childhood, if the account in his memoir, *My Candid Recollections*, is to be believed. As a boy, he had only been given a small amount of pocket money—'one penny a day'—for which he had to work under the directions of one of the foremen on the Kimbolton estate. 'I had my choice between the mason, the carpenter or the stud groom, and the foremen had instructions from my father to give me a docket to exchange for a penny when my task was finished to his satisfaction. By working every day, including Saturday, it was possible to make my earnings amount to sixpence by the end of the week.'

His mother, Consuelo, had endured the consequences of indulgence during her own marriage to William's father, George, and recognised the same character flaw in her beloved son when he assumed the mantle as duke. She never spoke about her concerns but they were revealed after she died in 1909. In a carefully constructed will, which would take decades for British and American courts to interpret and settle, Consuelo attempted to protect her son from himself. She stipulated that no matter what he had spent, the American trustees of her multimillion-dollar estate were obliged to top up his personal coffers by £8000 each year.

But what was supposed to protect her son and perhaps teach him how to be responsible with his money accomplished the exact opposite. Eight thousand pounds was an enormous sum, given that the average working man's annual wage was roughly £100. Even as his debts mounted, 'Little Kim' simply spent more, knowing that his magical bucket of money would simply refill as the year ended and another began.

His bankruptcy cases regularly came to court as infuriated creditors struggled to be paid at least a few pence on the pound or cents on the dollar, depending on which side of the Atlantic the jurisdiction fell. There was some poetry in the fact that he had been declared bankrupt on the day he first sat in parliament (because of a £400 debt) as well as the day he was married. By 1928 he had been personally involved in more than sixty such bankruptcy hearings in London alone.

The lurid tales of his spending titillated the newspapers but did little to satisfy those silly enough to lend him money simply because of his title. Creditors were outraged during one hearing in London to learn that he had paid a doctor £250 to treat him for indigestion, an extraordinary sum for the time, and then clocked up £1000 playing tennis, justifying the cost because the same doctor had prescribed tennis as a cure and 'whenever he plays tennis he likes a new racquet and a fresh box or two of balls'.

The creditors accepted that the Duke might have to maintain appearances in society by spending several thousand dollars on suits each year but questioned why he had spent £260 on socks: 'Does he have to throw them away after wearing them once?' they asked. 'Can't he send them to the laundry?'

The £4000 he spent on dresses and jewellery looked awkward given that his wife bought her own clothes, as did the £1000 bill for staying at a hotel in Mayfair when he already owned a luxurious flat near Hyde Park. There was another £2000 on theatre tickets and £4000 on dinner parties.

Then there was the gambling, and an unthinkable amount lost on the gaming tables of Europe. The Duke was unrepentant, as he made clear in his autobiography:

> Gambling, if it be a vice, is one to which I am still, and expect in the future to continue to be, unrepentantly addicted. Some

> of the biggest thrills of my life have been at the tables, and though I have lost a great deal of money at various times I have also won a great deal, and as it is my golden rule in life to never to keep accounts I have not cast the balance. I can safely certify, however, that I have had my money's worth.

The more the Duke spent, the more people were prepared to lend him, and he continued to be offered seats on company boards. During a 1928 hearing, at which he hoped to be relieved from bankruptcy, it was noted that he was a director of two aeroplane companies and a lorry company. His lawyers even argued that the pressure of being 'assumed rich' was a good enough excuse to keep running up debt.

The Duke sank £7000 of borrowed money into a bizarre search to find a cure for tuberculosis, arguing in court that the venture was a virtuous and charitable escapade. He raised another £3500 from unsuspecting American admirers to pour into his Canadian mining exploration—for no return. He did the same with a company called the International Education League, whose aim was to put films into schools and churches, even hiring a team of actors to go to the Middle East to enact Bible stories and produce 'clean' movies. The project never got off the ground but the money was gone.

At one point it was calculated that the Duke owed creditors £129,000. He offered to settle for £90 of jewellery from the family collection that was not his to sell. When asked by creditors gloomily if that was all he could manage, he explained that he had been 'as careful and economical as a duke could be'.

Even authorities seemed to shy away from overt criticism of his behaviour. When the Duke was applying to be discharged, yet again, from bankruptcy, the registrar of the London Bankruptcy Court only observed that, 'Although it might be difficult for a man to be economical when he is a duke, I think, at any rate, he might behave like a gentleman.'

The suggestion that he wasn't a gentleman stung more than his financial reputation. 'Merely spite, these stories,' he told reporters sourly as he relaxed at the Hotel Devon after one hearing. 'Really, one despairs. Jealousy, that is all.'

It all came under threat when one of the American creditors, a businessman named Clarence Hamilton who had helped fund the failed film venture, sued and won a court order for the trustees to hand over income that was due to the Duke from the trust fund so he could clear the debt. But the trustees, led by Henry Taft, famed New York lawyer and brother of US president William Taft, ignored the order and forced Hamilton to take his claim to the Supreme Court, which then reversed the decision.

The key was the wording of a single paragraph that gave Mr Taft and his trustees the absolute right to determine how much and when to pay. More critically, they could decide *who* to pay. The Duke, it seemed, had an obligation to use the money 'in a proper manner for the maintenance of himself and children'. If there was even a hint that he was borrowing on the basis of money he had not yet been granted, then they could decide to give him nothing and instead give the income to another member of his immediate family.

The Duke was clearly not behaving in a responsible manner, so the trustees had decided some years before the court case to pay someone else in the family. The man chosen to receive the income was the Duke's uncle, Lord Charles Montagu, who was then able to slip his nephew a 'gift'. The creditors were furious at this legal trickery, particularly when the New York Court of Appeals then upheld the decision, creating a legal precedent that would become known in wider circles as the 'Spendthrift's Trust'.

But in victory there would also be defeat: the decision ensured that the Duke would never again benefit directly from his mother's will. Not that he showed any concern. On the day that the *Hamilton v. Drogo* judgment was published in New York, in January 1926, he was in London, outside a jeweller's shop in Jermyn Street.

As he stood there, perhaps contemplating another gift he couldn't afford for a woman he shouldn't be wooing, a pair of would-be thieves, both young men, ran up next to him. One flung a brick through the window and the other reached in through the shattered pane to take a tray of rings. As he did so the Duke grabbed the man by the arm, holding on with surprising strength while police were called.

The first man ran off as a crowd began to gather, cheering the Duke as he held on to the struggling thief. When the law finally arrived and took the man into custody, a relieved and beaming Duke stood accepting the applause of the crowd before hailing a cab and driving away waving, as a monarch might to his adoring subjects. It was then that he reached for his pocketbook to find it was gone—stolen by a pickpocket as he had bowed to his admirers.

Only one man had ever seemed to take a stand against the Duke's attitude to money—his father-in-law Eugene Zimmerman. Initially Zimmerman had helped his son-in-law out of bankruptcy within a few years of his marriage by buying up the mortgages that hung over the Manchester estate, including Kimbolton, Tandragee and Brampton Park House, and placing the properties into a trust that the Duke could not touch.

The longer the marriage to his daughter lasted, the more angry Zimmerman became about the financial drain on the family fortune. He had offered the Duke a job, only to be turned down—even though the Duke's forays into journalism, filmmaking and gold prospecting had failed. Eventually, Zimmerman told his daughter to stop bailing her husband out of financial binds.

The final straw for Zimmerman came in 1914 when he got wind that the Duke had hired a special train to take a group of New York showgirls to Newport for a party. Asked publicly about the revelation, the businessman remarked: 'I have advised the Duke of Manchester to go to the Front and get out in front.' His reference was, of course, to the Great War that had just begun in France.

A few months later, while eating at the Queen City Club in Cincinnati, Zimmerman had a heart attack and died. He had written his will in such a way that the Duke could not get his hands on a cent; it banned his daughter from using any of the money—estimated to be between US$6 and $15 million—to pay her husband's debts.

If Helena died before the Duke, the remaining funds went into a trust for twenty-one years before being distributed to her children. If they too died, then the money would go to St Paul's Episcopal Church in Seattle where Helena's late mother, Etta, used to pray.

9

A BIRTH AND A DEATH

5 February 1929

> Lady Mandeville gave birth to a son this morning at Kimbolton Castle, Huntingdonshire. Both mother and son are doing well.

The news of the birth of Nell and Mandy's first child in 1929 was carried by the London *Daily Telegraph*'s private wire service and spread quickly. The birth of a noble son, particularly a future duke, was considered important news to the townsfolk and villagers of middle England and the myriad of regional newspapers that kept them informed.

He was named Sidney Arthur Robin George Drogo Montagu and carried the courtesy title Baron Kimbolton. Instead of taking the name of one of his illustrious paternal ancestors—William, George or Charles perhaps—the little baron was named after his maternal grandfather: a commoner from Australia, the son of an Irish migrant, who was not born to power and money but made his own fortune. It appeared to be as much a statement of the respect the couple had for Sidney Stead as a slap in the face to the Duke.

The celebrations would reflect the perceived importance of the occasion. They began with the laying of a ceremonial stone outside Kimbolton House, a seventeenth-century inn on the high street; it bore the inscription *Spes durat avorum*—'The hope of the ancestors lasts'—echoing the family's desire for a turnaround in fortune.

But it was the choice of godparents and the baptism setting a month later that told a more accurate story of the Montagu family's fall from political and social grace over the past two decades. The question was whether this had been caused by the poor behaviour of the Duke, who had recently been dubbed by the press as 'the uncrowned king of Soho' or, as another newspaper suggested, by Mandy's decision to marry 'a socially unknown young woman'.

Either way, the baptism of Sidney was a very different occasion to that of his father. Instead of the Queen of England as his godmother, Sidney's godmothers were his great-aunts, the ageing sisters of the late Consuelo; the godfathers were two of Mandy's naval colleagues.

And rather than being christened at the royal chapel in front of socially 'fashionable' people, heralded by choirboys and anointed with holy water, Sidney was baptised in a ceremony held at Kimbolton, inside St Andrew's Church, and officiated by the local vicar in front of a small group of family members.

But what the ceremony lacked in pomp was made up by the warmth of the community in response to the birth, as one hundred and thirty townsfolk joined the celebrations at Mandeville Hall, in the town, with a supper and entertainment by the Magpie Concert Band from Cambridge, as reported by the main local paper, *The Peterborough and Hunts Standard*:

> During the evening Mr William Brawn, of Wornaditch Farm, made a presentation on behalf of the estate tenants and employees. He handed the Viscountess Mandeville a very pretty plate and spoon which constituted a nice and appropriate gift to the infant, Baron Kimbolton. The plate was inscribed with a coronet and the words *From the Kimbolton Estate Tenants and Employees*. In making the presentation Mr Brawn made a very able speech. After supper Viscount Mandeville proposed the loyal toast. The company broke up at 10 o'clock after a very happy evening.

In Ireland, the burghers of Tandragee and Portadown also celebrated loudly with a bonfire and speeches imploring the couple to make their future home in the old castle. It was all to no avail, of course, although Mandy and Nell would keep their promise and make regular visits to the castle over the next decade.

The arrival of the baby—Lord Kim, as he would quickly become known—had indeed prompted a move for the young family, not to Ireland but into Brampton Park House. The house, its imposing turreted exterior reminiscent of Nell's old school, Clyde Girls' Grammar School, had been partly destroyed by fire twenty years before, then used to house German prisoners during the Great War before being abandoned. Nell and Mandy were now rebuilding. 'Already the gardens are receiving attention, as it is understood that Lady Mandeville is a great lover of flowers,' the local paper trumpeted.

But there were more money issues to complicate their lives. Across the Atlantic in New York, Consuelo's will was being challenged again, this time by three of her grandchildren. Mandy's siblings—Edward, Alice and Louise—were objecting to the way part of the estate was being interpreted and managed by the United States Trust Company of New York.

Their grandmother had set up the trust fund of £50,000 for the benefit of the 'younger children' in recognition that, unlike Mandy who stood to inherit the title and estate, they would need financial help—not only as children but as young adults finding their way in the world. The trustees were expected to make an annual payment based on the income earned from the trust fund, which had been salted away in carefully selected shares and bonds. The question was to whom the payments should be made.

The answer was obvious during the first years after Consuelo's death, when the children were minors: the money would be paid directly to the Duke, in the hope that he would use it wisely to help take care of the children. He didn't, of course, instead throwing the money onto the roulette tables of Monaco where, in one night—according to his own account—he won £19,000 and on another night lost £27,000.

But by July 1929 the three siblings had all become adults. Alice was almost twenty-eight, Edward about to turn twenty-three and Louise had just turned twenty-one. The will had stipulated that the money went to their father, the Duke, until Edward came of age and his sisters either came of age or had been married 'with the consent of the trustees'.

But there was another clause—a contradictory one that complicated matters further. Consuelo had stated also that the arrangement should be in place 'during the life of my son' and, given that the Duke was still alive when all his children became adults, the trustees interpreted this stipulation as a green light to continue paying *him* rather than *them*.

Justice Frankenthaler sided with the siblings, concluding that the discretion only applied to what happened in the event of the Duke dying before his children had turned twenty-one. In that situation, the money and responsibility would fall to Mandy, but that had not occurred. The judgment was clear: 'Each of the younger children of the Duke is entitled to receive from the American trustee the full income from his or her allotted share of the £50,000 trust under the will.'

The Duke had lost another ready source of income.

Sidney Stead died on the morning of 4 September 1929. A heart attack felled him at the age of sixty-eight—'sudden' was the description used by the newspapers, which would laud his contribution to Australian rural life, first as a station manager and later as an important liaison between the farmer and his financial resource. He had always believed it was better to support a struggling business in the hope it would come good rather than cut it loose and lose a man on the land.

He understood firsthand the complexities of the Australian landscape and how to ride the bucking-bronco pattern of weather conditions, which could turn from flood to fire within a season. If he had ever visited his eldest daughter at Kimbolton he might have been a useful mentor to resurrect its ailing agricultural business. But he never made the journey.

Nell was in England when her father died, nursing his first grandchild, who was now seven months old. Her trip to Australia the previous year had turned out to be a blessing, and had allowed Sidney to see for himself that his daughter's rash dash into marriage had been genuine and a success.

Erin, now aged twenty-four and about to be engaged, was at Kimbolton at this time as well. She had booked a passage to Europe as soon as Lord Kim was born, to give Nell some familial support; Erin would now cut short her trip and head back to Australia, even though she knew that the six-week journey meant she could not get back in time for the funeral. But there was another sister who would need help in the aftermath of their father's death: Penelope, who had just turned seventeen. She had been the only sibling at Amesbury, the family home in Melbourne, when their father collapsed.

Their brother, David, was in the far north-west of New South Wales, where he was following in his father's footsteps and managing a sheep station called Dumble, just south of the Queensland border. It was, as they say, the back of beyond—more than 700 kilometres north-west of Sydney—but he and two colleagues set out to drive for fourteen hours to meet an overnight Sydney–Melbourne train and make it to his father's funeral.

Such was the challenge on the rough dirt roads that their dash was covered in the local paper, *The Narromine News and Trangie Advocate*, which noted inevitable tyre trouble and marvelled at the achievement of them travelling the 120-kilometre stretch between Nyngan and Narromine in just under two hours. The funeral at Brighton Cemetery the next day would be delayed by several hours until David had completed the rest of the journey to mourn with Penelope at the graveside.

The experience would help spark a change in David Stead's view of life. Rather than continuing to endure the hardships and isolation of rural Australia, David would soon decide to follow his older sister's lead and begin to explore the world. Europe beckoned.

10

'I'D RATHER DRIVE WITH AN ECHIDNA'

If Alexander Montagu had one weakness, it was his love of motor cars.

While he eschewed most of the social vices of his father and grandfather, Mandy could not resist the throaty roar of an engine or the thrill of driving as fast as possible along the bumpy highways and narrow country lanes of England.

In particular, he seemed to settle on cars produced by the American manufacturer Stutz, a niche manufacturer of high-end luxury cars. In the late 1920s, Mandy bought two of its Vertical Eight saloon touring cars. The model was marketed as motoring's first 'safe' vehicle, with a low centre of gravity for better road handling, and safety glass. One was for use by his father, and the other was for Nell, much to the annoyance of British manufacturers who wanted the nobility to support local car-makers.

What really interested Mandy was not safety but speed, and it was not uncommon to see him flying along the narrow roads between Brampton Park House and Kimbolton in a two-seater Stutz Blackhawk Roadster capable of speeds of more than 160 kilometres per hour.

In media parlance, he was a 'motoring enthusiast', which meant one thing: racing. He often took his cars down to the Brooklands racetrack in Surrey to pit himself against the stop-watch, once hitting more than 190 kilometres per hour on the famous banked track. Nell eventually convinced her husband to throttle back on racing because, she insisted, he was a father and it was too dangerous.

In 1931 his enthusiasm bubbled over into hosting a 'speedway' event called Students of Speed, with a course through the heart of the Kimbolton Estate forests. The cinematic news agency British Pathé filmed the event, with motorbikes and three-wheeled sports cars racing along a path carved through the trees in an event called a speed hill climb.

But there was another, problematic side to his love affair with motoring. Mandy was prone to accidents and by the time he married Nell, the young naval officer was already known for his motoring misadventures. The first of these to make the news had been in February 1923; the then twenty-one-year-old was driving through the village of Cranford, west of Huntingdon, when he collided with a horse and cart ridden by a market gardener named Henry Trussler. Both vehicles were damaged but there were no injuries to the men or the horse.

The combination of Mandy's youthful exuberance on the tight, haphazardly laid roads, and the relatively poor handling of the early vehicles was a recipe for frequent bingles and it was no surprise when he was involved in a crash on the eve of his own wedding. There were several minor incidents and accidents over the years, including being caught speeding while racing his car around Regent's Park in London one evening in 1929.

He wasn't always at fault but problems seemed to follow him. Nell, a new mother, was with him one evening in May 1930 when his custom-built Bentley six-speed saloon burst into flames as they were driving back to Kimbolton. Both managed to get out of the car uninjured but the flames were so fierce that they were unable to douse them, and one side of the car's chassis was destroyed despite the efforts of the local fire brigade.

There is a postscript to this misadventure: it turned out that the car would be saved. Its chassis, separated from its burnt-out carriage, was rebuilt, used and adored by a British family for almost four decades on roads across Europe and America. Incredibly, its damaged carriage was kept and stored, forgotten, in a shed, then later discovered, repaired and reunited with its chassis to make it one of the rarest of Bentleys.

Mandy's accidents seemed to be getting progressively more serious and in April 1932 he suffered internal injuries when the car in which he was a front-seat passenger was involved in a collision on the Barnet Bypass at Hendon. He was being driven back from London by a friend when the accident happened. Nell was in Paris, having taken Lord Kim to visit his grandmother, and rushed back to be at Mandy's bedside while he spent several weeks in a nursing home.

The reason that Mandy was a passenger in the car, not its driver, was that he had had an accident just a week before, this time near the town of Deal. His new Bentley had been involved in what was described as a 'smash-up' from which he and two passengers had a miraculous escape. Newspaper accounts implied that the Viscount was driving too fast in wet conditions; his car had left the road and mounted a grass bank. He tried to brake, leaving a 50-metre-long skid, but hit a small tree and ended up in a ditch just outside the gate to the local golf club. Mandy's only injury was a cut finger and his passengers were unhurt, but the car was so heavy that it broke the crane of the breakdown lorry used to try to haul the wreckage from the ditch.

He had yet another collision near Hendon in 1933 and this time the matter ended up in court. Mandy told the magistrate that he had been driving at 40 miles per hour (65 kilometres per hour) along the bypass. As he drew abreast of the other vehicle its driver, without warning, moved to the middle of the road, as if she was about to turn right at the approaching traffic lights. Thankfully, there were no cars coming the other way. The judge fined the woman £1 for not using her indicators.

In February 1934 he was back in court, this time because he had been driving a car that had struck a motorbike head-on in Ospringe, Kent. The Viscount was sued for causing the accident by a local labourer, who had been riding pillion on the back of the bike ridden by his friend. They were behind a truck and moved to overtake when Mandy, coming the other way, moved to the centre of the road and sideswiped the bike as they crossed paths. The passenger was knocked unconscious and ended up under the stricken bike with injuries to both legs; he claimed that Mandy had been negligent because he lost control of his car while trying to light a cigarette and had swerved into the middle of the road.

Mandy denied the accusation and said he had only seen the oncoming motorbike just 50 yards (45 metres) away, going very fast to overtake the truck. He swerved twice to try to miss it, but had always stayed on his side of the road. He called an expert witness, described as an Automobile Association scout, who testified that he had examined the tyre marks on the dirt road. These showed, he said, that the Viscount's car had never left its side of the road.

Judge Clements told the jury that they must ask themselves whether Lord Mandeville had come to court to tell a wilful lie. 'If so, he has committed gross and wicked perjury,' he said fiercely. The jury believed Mandy and blamed the bike's driver, ordering him to pay his friend £33 in damages.

Despite his exoneration, it just seemed a matter of time before there would be tragic repercussions of Viscount Mandeville's seemingly daredevil driving. As Nell would comment in her diary after a third accident in twelve months: 'Mandy is erratic. I'd rather drive with an echidna.'

It had been a pleasant few days in January 1934 with a group of friends, old and new. It had ended with a lazy Sunday lunch in the warmth of Brampton Park House. By late afternoon, grey skies set in overhead, unlikely to budge. Snow had been expected but had not arrived, although the temperature outside had dropped below zero.

Among the overnight guests was an American banker named Martin Hofer, who had designs on Mandy's sister Lady Louise. Hofer had brought with him a colleague named Albert Suprenant who had recently arrived from New York. There were also two Frenchmen: Count Chauzel, who was an attaché at the French embassy in London, and businessman Baron de Vaufreland, who had been making himself known on London's social circuit.

There were also two young Cambridge University students who had hired a car to make the 35-kilometre trip to Brampton. Frederick Ponsonby was the twenty-year-old son of the Earl of Bessborough; he had recently returned to England from Canada, where his father was serving as governor-general. Just as Mandy was a viscount, in line for his father's title, so too was Ponsonby, who was known as Lord Duncannon. He brought with him a fellow student named Henry Hyde.

The lunch had dragged on pleasantly until three o'clock, the visitors intrigued by the Montagu story and the legend of Kimbolton Castle. There were a couple of hours of sunlight left in the day when Mandy bowed to pressure and agreed to give his guests a tour.

It would be twenty minutes by car, a winding drive alongside the vast Grafham Water reservoir and then cutting across through the hamlet of Stonely, with its ancient priory. They aimed to see Kimbolton Castle and its grounds before the low winter sun finally set in the west. But they would need to take two cars.

Mandy led the way, with Hofer beside him and Baron de Vaufreland in the back seat. The car behind was being driven by Lord Duncannon. Count Chauzel was beside him in the front passenger seat, with Hyde and Suprenant in the back. The road was unsurfaced and narrow. Hedgerows lined the route, tall and lush in the summer months but barren and leafless now, in the dead of winter, and allowing a broad view of the rolling countryside.

Mandy raced ahead, slowing through the village of Buckden and then speeding up so that Duncannon's car slipped from view behind him. The road followed the line of gentle hills towards the village of Perry, famous for its historic mansion Gaynes Hall, once home to Oliver Cromwell.

A kilometre before Perry, there was a dip in the road leading to a stone bridge spanning a stream. The road twisted left then right, the subtle change caused by the terrain and difficult to see with the sun behind in the fading light. Perhaps sensing the dangerous combination, Mandy stopped his car at the top of the next hill and looked back to see if Duncannon was still behind.

He might have told his young friend beforehand that the road curved without warning and that the camber of the road was suited more to carts and horses than motor cars, but he hadn't done so and now regretted this oversight, watching as the Austin 12 coupé appeared over the hill and descended towards the stream. The young man was clearly trying to catch up to Mandy and misjudged the hill, changing gears to slow down as he approached the bridge. Instead he lost control and the car skidded sideways, one way then the other, before flipping and landing back on its wheels.

Mandy leaped from his car, the others behind him, and ran back down the hill towards the stricken vehicle. Henry Hyde had been thrown out of the car as it flipped and had landed in a roadside hedge. The windscreen had been torn off and the car's radiator was found in a nearby field. Mandy pulled Hyde clear of the hedge; the young man was cut on both arms from the branches but otherwise uninjured.

The driver, Duncannon, was lying half in and half out of the car, dazed and bleeding from cuts. Hofer helped him to his feet while Mandy went to help the other two men, who had somehow ended up on top of one another in the middle of the road.

Chauzel was on top and screamed in pain as Mandy and Baron de Vaufreland lifted him clear of the American lying beneath. Chauzel, who was babbling in French, had several broken ribs and would recuperate in hospital, but Suprenant was clearly much more seriously injured, unconscious and bleeding from a gaping head wound.

Realising the urgency, Mandy asked his two friends to stay with the injured men while he went for help. He stopped first at Frank Robinson's garage at Buckden and asked them to send a breakdown gang and call the police; then he went to the house of the local GP, who was out on house calls, so he returned to the accident scene.

The garage proprietor arrived soon afterwards; Robinson loaded Suprenant into his car and took him to the county's hospital. He was followed by Mandy, who had placed the Count into his own car.

Albert Suprenant died three hours later, having never regained consciousness.

The combination of the involvement of two young noblemen and the death of a foreign visitor caused nationwide interest when an inquest was held two weeks later. The courthouse at nearby Huntingdon was packed as Duncannon and Mandy faced accusations of negligence, particularly when another witness stepped forward.

Ernest Mann, who owned a farm next to the bridge, had been standing outside his barn when the cars came down the hill; he stopped to watch. They were both going too fast, he told the inquest. 'Do you think the car travelled much faster than others you have seen?' asked the coroner.

'Yes,' replied Mann without further elaboration.

Local police said the road was deceptive, but there were no warning signs. They had examined three skid marks left by Duncannon's car, one of them more than 20 metres long, and concluded that the car had drifted onto the grass verge when Duncannon lost control, causing it to flip. There was no sign that he had tried to use the brakes. The county surveyor said the curves in the road were potentially dangerous and agreed there should have been warning signs.

Count Chauzel was still in hospital, but Henry Hyde gave evidence. The car was going too fast, he said, but his friend had tried to regain control using the gears. Like Duncannon, he remembered nothing after the car began to slide.

Duncannon, who was sporting facial cuts and bruises, confirmed that he had tried to use the gears to slow the car when he was going down the hill and realised he had miscalculated the first bend in the road. Instead of turning the wheel in the direction of the spin, he tried to right the car and it skidded left and flipped. The next thing he recalled was sitting in the road and seeing Mandy placing a cushion beneath the head of the stricken Suprenant.

Asked why he hadn't turned with the spin, Duncannon showed his driving inexperience: 'I didn't know; my instinct was to keep it on the road.'

'Were you trying to catch Viscount Mandeville?' probed the coroner.

Duncannon shook his head: 'No sir. I was trying to keep a convenient distance between us.'

Mandy was also defensive about the issue of speed. 'I knew that he wasn't familiar with the road, which was why I stopped,' he said. 'The car was coming toward me, so I couldn't estimate how fast he was driving.'

The jury took less than an hour to clear Duncannon and return a verdict of accidental death. The coroner added: 'Mr Suprenant was not an inhabitant of this country, but everyone would regret that a visitor should have met with such a dreadful death during his stay here. I think we must also say that his three companions in the car had a most merciful escape. Looking at the scene and reconstruction of what happened it is amazing that they were not all killed.'

It wasn't the end of the matter, and the following month Duncannon was charged by police and fined £10 for 'driving a car without due care and attention'.

It seemed a small penalty for a man's life.

11

ERRANT BROTHERS

'Susan' made her way across the marble foyer of the Australia Hotel in Castlereagh Street, Sydney, and headed for the cocktail bar. It was a Friday evening in early April 1933 and the crowd of mostly city office workers was growing, particularly in the far corner where a group of women had gathered to toast an important arrival.

Susan drew closer, standing just outside the circle as she searched for the woman she'd been sent to interview for a social column in the *Daily Telegraph*. Lady Mandeville was easy enough to spot if only because she was the centre of attention, a glass of gin in hand as she smiled and chatted with wellwishers, some friends and other strangers who wanted to be her new friend.

Susan took a moment to study the Viscountess and in particular her outfit. There was an expectation that visiting aristocrats would set a standard, perhaps introduce something new or different fashion-wise from London or the Continent when they arrived. Lady Mandeville would not disappoint, as Susan would later write:

> When everybody else in Sydney is wearing a little chapeau turned up at the back and down over the eye, along comes the smart little Viscountess Mandeville in just the reverse. Yesterday evening . . . her frocking exemplified the latest in overseas styles. She wore a little hat of white stitched satin, caught up in front with a bow, and partly covering at the back her attractive Titian hair. Her high-necked frock of black crinkly crepe was of superb cut, its only adornment being a diamond brooch. The finishing touch to the black and white ensemble was the black flared nose veil.

But Susan thought there was something else about the Viscountess that was different from the women around her. She looked closely and realised that it was her hands. Well, her nails actually—lacquered vivid red, almost scarlet, which stood out against the glass in her hand. By comparison, the other women had painted their nails muted shades of pink and brown.

Susan waited for a break in the conversation before taking a step forward to introduce herself, asking if they could have a few quiet words. The Viscountess Mandeville obliged, excusing herself from the throng and stepping to one side where the pair might chat and her photograph could be taken.

Susan began by asking about her red nails. The colour was striking and unmissable, she told the Viscountess, who laughed and pointed at her feet: It wasn't just fingernails. Women in Europe were discarding stockings for evening wear: 'We dance in sandals with our toenails painted vivid colours. The last London season was the gayest for some years. I think people have reconciled themselves to the change of times.'

Bare legs, sandals and red nails in a time of change. The combination was daring, a suggestion that British people believed their nation had turned the corner economically and had begun emerging from the gloom of the Great Depression. Certainly, Nell's husband, Mandy, was convinced that England was on the cusp of an industrial revival. Fashion was following society's relief; it was embracing change and modernisation.

Susan turned to more personal matters. The lady had left Australia on a whim six years before and travelled halfway around the world to marry a man she hardly knew. Now she had returned as a prominent member of the aristocracy, a future duchess and a mother. Had the transition been difficult?

Lady Mandeville nodded. 'Initially I missed my old friends,' she told the reporter. 'Everything in England was strange. It all happened so quickly and I wasn't really prepared for not only a new place but a completely new life. But now I love it. I have met a host of charming people who have been wonderfully kind to me. We also spend a great deal of time in Europe and America. I was in Paris just before we left to come to Australia.'

And what was it like living in a castle? Nell shook her head: 'Kimbolton is a charming old place but it has no electric lights or modern conveniences.' Instead they lived at Brampton Park House and hosted house parties and hunting weekends.

'Everyone is very keen on hunting, although I don't do a great deal myself. Life is really full of fun.'

Interview over, Lady Mandeville returned to the party while Susan slipped away to go back to the office and write her story of young Nell Stead's return for the next day's paper, summarising the Viscountess as 'Scarlet tipped, slim and dark and fascinating.'

Nell and Mandy had been in Australia since late February, arriving first in Fremantle, where Lord Kim had been the centre of attention after celebrating his fourth birthday during the six-week voyage. On their honeymoon visit in 1928, Nell had been reluctant to be interviewed; now she was happy to talk about her life in British society. Five years had passed and she felt more comfortable and accepted as a legitimate viscountess and future duchess.

But first she needed to mend a few fences. It was a pleasure to be back in her native home, she told the assembled reporters: 'It's so exciting to see Australian sunshine again,' she exclaimed, adding that it was doubly exciting to be introducing her son to his Australian relatives.

The photo calls and interviews would become routine over the next three months as the three of them travelled between Australia's major cities and attended a seemingly endless array of dinners, dances and formal functions that challenged her wardrobe. Being in the spotlight meant she would be scrutinised wherever she went: She dined at Romano's 'frocked in violet lace and a striking white arctic fox collar'; she attended a Government House event sporting 'a spray of orchids on her mink coat' and 'her toque was of black tucked taffeta'. She was vibrant at the Randwick races during the autumn carnival, on one occasion in 'a coat of powder blue marocain' and on another, 'most attractive … in a suit of burnt amber boucle cloth'.

She may have been an exotic addition to London society but here, back in her homeland, 'the former Miss Nell Stead', as she was invariably described in social columns, was a glamorous exception—the closest thing Australia had to a queen of society, the first to wed the son of a duke, and therefore a woman of substance.

There was a fourth member of the party on the trip. Lady Louise Montagu had travelled to Australia with Mandy, Nell and Lord Kim. Bright and adventurous, she made an immediate impact when they arrived in Adelaide. Although she was fond of dancing, the twenty-five-year-old told reporters that she preferred the thrill of the hunting season to the hunt for a husband during London's social season. 'I am just crazy about going on a kangaroo hunt,' she declared, explaining away her American twang as a product of a cross-continental childhood. 'My mother is American and I can't help but copy voices,' she laughed. 'I won't be in Australia three weeks before I am talking Australian. I will be mistaken for a real Aussie.'

When Nell showed enthusiasm to join her, the idea of a kangaroo hunt was lapped up by the local press, which pictured two daring and glamorous aristocratic women on horseback galloping through the Australian outback. The two women even had a property in mind: the sheep station Widgiewa in northern New South Wales that Sidney Stead used to manage and was now owned by family friends. Nell was returning to her roots.

Lady Louise was a handsome, swashbuckling figure rather than a pretty socialite. She was inspired by literature like John Masefield's *Salt-Water Poems and Ballads*, a book of poems about life at sea that she was currently reading: 'Anything about the sea fascinates me. My life's ambition is to sail before the mast. Windjammer days must have been thrilling,' she declared, echoing Masefield whose most famous poem, *Sea-Fever*, included the line: 'All I ask is a tall ship and a star to steer her by.'

But it would be something far more domestic that captured the headlines a few weeks later when Lady Louise and Nell's brother, David, met and fell for one another within days of her arriving in Melbourne. On the surface it seemed to be a repeat of their older siblings' love affair as news leaked out that they planned to marry. 'Melbourne is all a twitter about their engagement,' the *Herald* announced, noting that when they arrived in the southern capital, they all stayed at Amesbury House, the Stead family home that had been turned into a palatial set of flats by Nell's sister Erin and her husband John Grimwade. 'For David Stead, it was only a matter of popping upstairs to pop the question,' the paper joked.

There were no details about the romance, only that they were spending all of their time together, lunching almost every day at the Quality Inn at the top of Collins Street and dancing at the Rex, a cabaret club in Swanston Street which had hosted members of the English cricket team during the recent second Test of the infamous 'Bodyline' series.

The engagement had not been announced formally and Louise would only tell her mother after she returned to England, via America. But their plans were interrupted by more drama when Mandy, eager to display his prowess on the rugby field, injured his knee during a game and was hospitalised. Nell moved out of the hotel and into a flat while her husband recuperated.

On 30 May, after a three-month visit, they finally boarded the ocean liner *Monterey* with a nanny for Kim and a valet for Mandy, who was still on crutches. There was also an extra passenger joining the group: David Stead was not going to let Lady Louise out of his sight. The group headed to London via the South Sea Islands, Honolulu and America, where more family drama awaited.

Edward Montagu took after his mother in looks—tall and slight, rather than muscular and thickset like his father, the Duke, and his elder brother, Mandy—with his dark, curved eyebrows, and jet-black hair swept back off his forehead à la Errol Flynn. He even carried his mother's cultural heritage in his middle names, Eugene Fernando.

Named after his godfather, King Edward VII, he seemed to have the world at his feet, born to luxury and ease. At Harrow he had been hailed as a brilliant student and fine athlete, with the promise of a diplomatic career. But somehow these green pastures were sowed with weeds and by his early twenties he had begun to talk about his title being a 'menace' to his existence.

He sought a future across the Atlantic, working as a farm labourer in Canada before quitting and drifting from job to job, first as a cook and then a taxi driver. He tried selling cars and working as secretary at an oil company, where he met and married a young woman named Norah Potter. The couple had a son and settled in Edmonton, where Edward took up an interest in the local dramatic society.

It seemed he had found his feet professionally and privately when he scored a job as a reporter with a newspaper, but his domestic peace was short-lived and his wanderlust returned. By the time his son turned three, he had gone; he moved to San Francisco where he served coffee and sandwiches from his own stall while searching for adventure.

Life changed dramatically and mysteriously in late 1932, when he joined the vagabond crew of a schooner named *Carma*. It was about to embark on an 'adventure cruise' to the South Pacific organised by its charismatic and mysterious owner, the colourfully named Captain Walter Wanderwell, who was a quixotic soldier-of-fortune character at one time suspected of being a spy.

Those aboard the *Carma*, a former rum-running vessel, included an actress, a waitress, a Hollywood cameraman, a writer and several students, all of whom paid US$190 for their passage. It was never determined if Edward had taken a job as a seaman or was one of the paying customers, but the adventure never began. A few nights before the planned departure,

Captain Wanderwell was murdered, shot in the back on board his own boat by a visitor shrouded in mist.

Edward was in his cabin at the time of the shooting and gave brief evidence at the trial of William 'Curley' Guy, a former crewman who had left after an argument with Captain Wanderwell on a previous voyage. He lived nearby and was immediately suspected by police to have been the killer.

Edward told police he heard the shot but knew nothing more. He had joined the boat seeking adventure and when questioned about his marriage, he replied: 'We are not separated, so far as I know.'

The case received widespread publicity largely because of the characters involved, including Edward, the son of a duke. William Guy, whose family insisted he was at home at the time of the shooting, was acquitted and the killing remained an unsolved crime.

Edward hightailed it out of California after the court case, across the border back to Canada. But instead of returning to Edmonton, to be reunited with his wife and son, in March 1933 he headed for Victoria, a city on Vancouver Island in the west of the country. Ever the opportunist, he launched a scheme to make money from his involvement in the case by doing public lectures, accompanied by slides and photographs of Captain Wanderwell's burial at sea. But that was just the beginning of another odyssey that, if it had not been detailed in yet another bizarre court case, might have been dismissed as pure fantasy.

Edward's lectures were a flop, but he was still in Victoria a month later. Although he had very little money, he'd somehow managed to acquire what he described as a 'gas boat' called the *Merman.* He told the media he intended to explore the coast of British Columbia before 'going to meet my brother, Viscount Mandeville, who is returning from Australia'. It seemed that Edward was much better informed about Mandy's movements than the other way around.

But, as usual, Edward's plans changed. On 8 June he left port on the *Merman* with five men he claimed to have just met. He was bound for Vancouver across the straits, even though there was only sleeping quarters for two people.

Trouble struck the next day when they ran aground off one of the tiny islands in the gulf between the two cities. Using the dinghy the men managed to get ashore, onto Jones Island, where they waited for the tide to rise and inspect the damage. The *Merman* had been holed below the waterline but it was a small hole so, if they were careful, they might be able to make it back across the strait to get help.

The proviso was that two of the men had to remain behind, to reduce the weight on the already overladen and stressed vessel. Ronald Kindersley and Max Newman agreed to stay behind while the others—Edward, John Forbes, Cecil Brooks and Humphrey Ramage—headed for the nearest town to arrange repairs. It was only after the men had left that Kindersley and Newman discovered there was no fresh water on the island. They had to survive two days before being rescued by local fishermen, who saw their distress signals.

In the meantime, the four men had reached the small town of Sidney and found a boatyard where the *Merman* could be repaired. While they waited, the men camped outside the town and one night got drunk and began fighting among themselves. The situation was calmed but trouble flared again the next night after they returned to the *Merman*. In the melee that followed, Forbes ended up in hospital with head injuries, including a broken jaw.

Police were called and arrested Edward and Brooks; both were charged with assault. When neither man could produce the CA$50 bail money they were jailed, causing a media sensation across Canada because a British aristocrat was behind bars.

The tiny courtroom was packed two days later when the court case began and Edward was put on the stand. He seemed to enjoy the attention, calmly dismissing the incident as a minor scuffle between English public schoolboys (he'd gone to Harrow and two of the other men had gone to its rival, Eton).

Instead, Edward blamed Forbes for the kerfuffle, insisting that he had got wildly drunk on whiskey, was threatening the others and had to be dealt with. 'There was nothing to it—Harrow versus Eton,' he smiled. Edward was also quizzed about his life, and he conceded that he had no permanent home in Victoria other than the *Merman*.

'What is your occupation?' the prosecuting officer asked.

'I am a gentleman.'

'Yes, but can you be more specific.'

Edward smiled. 'I haven't an occupation now.'

Brooks backed up Edwards' story and claimed that the incident had been overblown, admitting that he was the one who had punched Forbes once to stop him 'acting like a monkey'.

But his evidence was countered by a doctor who revealed that Forbes' injuries were more extensive than a single punch; then Kindersley, a former policemen, accused his fellow passengers of dragging Forbes behind the boat on a rope. He also accused them of planning house break-ins as they traversed the waterways. Even slaughtering sheep.

The magistrate found the pair guilty of assault with intent to do grievous bodily harm. He fined Brooks CA$50 and Edward $20, calling their behaviour reprehensible. Edward, who found the money to pay the fine and avoid more jail time, was unrepentant. 'It had taught me a lesson. I won't be playing Good Samaritan to Etonians anymore,' he quipped as he boarded the *Merman*, which he now intended to raffle in yet another money-making scheme.

The publicity had died down by the time Mandy and Nell arrived in California a few weeks later, aware of the first drama in California but not the second court case in Canada. Mandy decided to track down his errant brother, who he assumed was still in San Francisco, but his inquiries caught the attention of the media and sparked fresh stories that Edward had somehow gone missing.

'We only hear about him when he gets his name in the papers,' Mandy told the New York *Daily Mirror*, which then raised the possibility that Edward, who they dubbed a 'modern-day Dick Whittington', might have been the victim of foul play.

Under the lurid headline 'Lord Edward Montagu missing? Kidnapped or murdered', the story quoted Ronald Kindersley, who described himself as a friend of Edward's and suggested that he might have run off to join the Foreign Legion in Morocco.

The story spread like wildfire, not only through the US but back to England, where the *Liverpool Echo* asked: 'The evasive Lord Edward Montagu. Is he missing?'

Edward's father, the Duke of Manchester, was angry and perplexed: 'I don't know who originated the story. Nobody in the family knows anything about it. My daughter-in-law [Edward's wife Norah] was terribly upset by reports that he had been murdered or kidnapped. He was probably playing golf so she did not telephone him, but tonight she is putting through a call and tomorrow she will cable me.'

Two days later Edward emerged. He was staying alone in a cottage near Elk Lake, north of Victoria. 'I have no intention of joining the Foreign Legion or embarking on any other adventure,' he declared. 'My main idea now is to keep out of the newspapers.'

He would fail.

12

A BRUSH WITH THE LAW

It was just after one o'clock in the morning on 29 August 1934. A dozen uniformed police followed their senior officer into a courtyard off Piccadilly, opposite the famed department store Fortnum & Mason. All was quiet at this time on a Wednesday, even in the centre of London. The weather was still warm but clearly on the turn, the long days of summer over and the longer autumn nights ahead.

The footsteps of the police echoed across the cobblestones of one of the city's most exclusive addresses. The main building at the end of the courtyard, The Albany, was a once-imposing eighteenth-century mansion that had been converted into apartments now coveted by the city's wealthy and famous. Lord Byron once lived there—'spacious', with 'room for my books and sabres', he said of his rooms. The novelist Aldous Huxley, bathing in the success of his dystopian masterpiece

Brave New World and fighting writer's block to pen a sequel, was trying to sleep inside an apartment he'd recently leased there.

Superintendent Angus Ralph, the officer leading the raid, ignored the main building. He was interested in a smaller, stately townhouse to its left, which had been divided into three separate residences. In the darkness of the courtyard, the lights at number 6 were still ablaze.

Ralph and his men were responding to a complaint that the house was being used as an illegal gambling venue. There had been regular parties for at least four months, often lasting through the night. The wealthy guests would leave after dawn, their ermine stoles and white silk cravats slightly askew as they headed off, mostly poorer, to find cabs or a breakfast of kippers and eggs.

Gambling was illegal but for the most part police turned a blind eye. Resources were scarce, crimes were difficult to prove and, besides, most of those inside number 6 on this night had money to lose. They were only hurting themselves.

Convictions were also difficult to secure unless those involved were caught in the act. Canny operators dressed up gambling nights as privately hosted parties with admission only possible by private introduction; the clientele, perhaps surprisingly, was mostly women. Police had received complaints that crooks were fleecing unsuspecting women from charity organisations who were using such premises to host fundraising roulette parties. The conmen would covertly increase the number of counters that had to be repaid to the house at the end of the evening, in some cases by thousands of pounds.

Such concerns had been part of the police application to the local magistrate to approve the raid on this night. The man who rented the house at number 6, an antiques dealer named John Pincott, had been arrested before for running illegal gambling premises, and had served prison time in New York for the same crime.

Superintendent Ralph knew the raid was not going to be quiet and would very likely wake everyone else inside the courtyard. *So be it*, he thought, as one of his men rang the doorbell at the front. A head appeared out of the upstairs window almost immediately, the man's face anxious as he peered down into the half-light, counting the uniforms below.

'Police!' he yelled back inside, before disappearing from view.

He was clearly the doorman, tasked to ensure that only invited guests were admitted inside. The inspector didn't hesitate. 'Break the door down,' he ordered.

Police charged up the staircase to be confronted by another locked door. When they got inside, there were a dozen or so well-heeled patrons in their finest evening wear and jewellery standing quietly around the edges of a room dominated by what was obviously a roulette table, even though its wheel was missing, taken by someone in a vain attempt to hide its purpose. But the green cloth covering the table was clearly marked for play and there were counters of different denominations on the table, as well as a pile of banknotes and two croupier rakes.

Smaller tables and chairs had been placed around the room, most covered with glasses filled with varying amounts of wine, whiskey and gin. The habit of gambling-den owners was to provide drinks free of charge so as to purport to be private hosts rather than commercial operators. It was also an inducement to gamble as patrons became less inhibited.

While the patrons—twelve men and six women—were ushered away, bundled into a Black Maria, as police vans were known, and driven to the Vine Street station to be charged, police searched the rest of the house. In a room off the main living area there was a card table set up for chemin de fer, a baccarat-style game. Cards, money and counters were strewn across the table, a hand clearly interrupted by the arrival of police.

Noises above alerted police to a roof access, where they found Pincott and his wife, Dorothy. It was Pincott, noted as a sinister-looking fellow with a 'scarred countenance', who had taken the roulette wheel and tried to hide it. As the inspector was reading the arrest warrant, Pincott admitted his involvement: 'All right, I take full responsibility for the games here. It is my establishment.'

Staff were rounded up as the search continued. The croupier's name was Charles Wolsley, a well-known West End pianist. The doorman, Ernest Ryan, was hiding in a downstairs room and the drinks waiter, John Ibbotson, tried to pose as a gambler, hoping he would be let off with a small fine.

Police also found a stash of IOUs, the house clearly winning against gamblers with no apparent concern for losing their money. A list of names and invitation cards also gave police a clue as to the gamblers' identities and their losses for the night. The patrons were all clearly prominent citizens of some type but one name stood out among the others—Viscountess Nell Mandeville. The police had caught themselves an aristocrat.

News leaked of Nell's arrest within a few hours. Raids were becoming more frequent events across London as authorities tried to crack down on gambling's prevalence. Invariably in this part of the city there were prominent people among those arrested, but it was rare that their identities were made public. More often than not the arrested provided aliases—Jones, Brown and Smith—to avoid embarrassment; their cases were funnelled through the Marlborough Street Police Court, whose magistrates viewed their situation favourably.

But not so Nell Mandeville. She had 'declined anonymity', according to court records, and even provided a real address in Portland Place, Marylebone, where she was staying while in the city. It showed either her refusal to be cowed by what she considered an inconsequential breach, or highlighted further the fact that she was a stranger to the culture of the English nobility. Perhaps a bit of both.

And now Viscountess Mandeville sat in the dock of the Marlborough Street Police Court with the other 'frequenters', as they were described, in front of a courtroom full of newspaper reporters eager to clap eyes on her. She was tired, from little sleep, and still dressed in her clothes from the outing the night before, which had begun at the Ritz, just up the street. There she'd had dinner with Vera Crawford-Kehrmann, widow of the Marquis de Bourbel, who had chosen to be identified by her maiden name in court to hide her title. There were other prominent citizens caught up in the raid, including several leading military officers, who were unrecognised by the media because they did not use their titles.

There was a single lawyer to represent everyone who'd been arrested at number 6 Albany Court Yard. Claude Hornby was a well-connected defence lawyer; he told his apprehensive clients that, if everything went well and the magistrate, a former crown prosecutor named Edward Boyd, was in a decent mood, then they would likely be let off with a caution and bound over for a period of probably twelve months, during which time, if they were arrested again on gambling premises, then they could face jail.

There was an argument for mitigating circumstances, given the differences between Britain, where gambling was illegal, and France, where casinos flourished in seaside towns like Le Touquet and along the Côte d'Azur, where many wealthy Brits spent their summers in hotels advertised in British papers for their gaming rooms. The whole thing seemed hypocritical.

'The persons summonsed as frequenters are all people of position and presumably if they choose to go to this place they are able to lose such money as they have lost,' Hornby told Magistrate Boyd:

> I am not here to quarrel with the law of the land. What is legal on one side of the Channel is illegal here and these places are not permitted by law. There is no suggestion that anybody was drunk or that any liquor was sold. These sorts of parties are given in people's houses and I suppose it is not unusual to provide some sort of refreshment for them. It is obvious after

this raid that these places will have to stop. And there will be an end of such profits as have been made. As a matter of fact, I am assured by my clients that the bank has had a very bad time lately.

Magistrate Boyd was unmoved. He'd heard it all before and his judgment was swift and succinct. Nell and the others would be bound over for twelve months and be immediately fined £20 if caught again inside a gambling house.

Hornby was also representing John Pincott, who had been foolish to try to hide the roulette wheel, submitted Hornby; but he had admitted his crime, as had his wife, who had been managing the chemin de fer table when police arrived. These were mitigating circumstances that should be taken into account when sentencing.

Magistrate Boyd, scowling from the bench, was not convinced of Pincott's sincerity. 'There has been extensive gambling going on here. How long has it been operating?' he asked Superintendent Ralph.

'Since April,' the policeman replied, adding that Pincott had a criminal record in New York for gaming offences but not in the UK. He also used an alias, 'Jack Gordon', which raised suspicions about his character. The magistrate fined him £250 with £25 in costs. Dorothy Pincott was fined £50 for her role.

The staff employed by Pincott should be treated leniently, Hornby argued, particularly Wolsley, who had once found fame as a member of a successful stage variety revue but had fallen on hard times: 'Since then he has found things rather hard. As a matter of fact, he has not had any regular work except for the occasional concert engagement for the last two years. He has a wife and two children to keep and gets a small salary of £7 a week from the proprietor.' Magistrate Boyd again was unmoved, fining Wolsley and the other employees £30 each.

Nell made no attempt to rush away after the case was over. While the other gamblers who'd chosen to attend court left quickly, ignoring the reporters who had regathered, Nell stood around expectantly.

Finally, one reporter approached and asked if she had any response: 'I was there at the club and I cannot escape that fact, nor would I hide my identity,' she said without emotion. 'There are many people who enjoy the entertainment of a little gambling. Many of us gamble in France in the summertime and, although we know it is technically illegal in London, the police have tended to ignore our little events, although not on this occasion. One wonders if the menfolk in their clubs might be concerned.'

The reporter pressed. Her father-in-law, the Duke of Manchester, was known as a habitual gambler whose financial misfortune in life was largely caused by gambling in one form or another. And now she had been labelled by the court as a 'frequenter' of gambling houses.

Nell shook her head: 'I don't accept that description. I don't make a habit of it and I know what I can afford to lose. I can't comment on my father-in-law but he has been very upfront about his lifestyle. The court has said that I cannot go to a club for the next year, so I suspect this was the last time.'

It would not be Pincott's last brush with the law. The following year he was a prime suspect in an FBI investigation into the swindling of an American businessman, but he avoided arrest by staying in London. Nell would probably have counted herself lucky if she had known the extent of his criminal activities.

Far from being humiliated by the incident, Nell found herself featured in a rush of largely positive newspaper stories, lauding the decision of the 'Australian beauty' not to remain anonymous. The *Liverpool Post* described her as 'impulsive but plucky', recounting the romance of her engagement and being married with bandages because of the car accident.

Across the Atlantic, the American papers that picked up the story were perplexed about the fuss over her gambling activities and hoped she and the Viscount would one day return to their shores. The *Oakland Tribune* in particular ran a front-page story and photograph of the couple, happy and smiling during their 1928 honeymoon spent in California and their subsequent visit with four-year-old Sidney.

In Sydney and Melbourne there was a range of responses. One front-page story about the court case was accompanied by photographs of Nell strolling down a city street, wrapped in a cape of lynx instead of the usual fox. 'Australia's Viscountess Mandeville has established a new fashion in London,' the caption proudly claimed.

But there was also criticism. Some insisted that she was somehow representing Australia and therefore should be more considered in her behaviour and dress sense. One syndicated social writer complained that, while she had been in Tasmania the previous year, Nell had 'wrangled' her way into a dinner party aboard the HMAS *Canberra*, rather than being invited, and then turned up 'stockingless, wearing sandals and pink lacquered toenails'. The outraged writer, with the nom de plume 'Florence', insisted that Nell 'made straight for the seat on the captain's right, and was gently but firmly told it was reserved for someone else, and to take the seat on the left'.

If that wasn't bad enough, wrote Florence, there had also been reports about Nell's visit to Fiji after their recent trip to Australia, when she had entered a Suva bank dressed only in shorts and a brassiere. 'Bank officials would not do business with her,' the columnist reported. 'If Fiji climate is anything like what we have been feeling—as if in a glass house with every door shut—one feels inclined to ask, "Why the brassiere?" Was it prudishness, or ostentation—or perhaps merely swank?'

But for all Florence's protestations—described by rival journalists as 'brisk and cattish'—Nell's brush with the law had made her something of a rebellious heroine rather than a shamed socialite. Back in London, Nell had begun receiving fan mail in the wake of the court case. One man invited her to the Belgian city of Ostend to try out a new gambling system. Another suggested going into partnership with him in a covert gambling establishment, lending her name and presence to invitations 'as bait to Mayfair'. There were also a number of younger men who wrote asking for a signed photograph.

'It's as if I am a film star and really quite bewildering,' she confided to the correspondent for *Table Talk* magazine as they crossed paths along Bond Street. Until this moment, Nell had felt slightly overawed by her new world, uncertain of whether she would fit in. But notoriety had changed everything. Now she belonged.

13

THE BROKE DUKE WITH THREE CASTLES

The elderly, hawkish man, his jeweller's loupe scrunched into his right eye, stared intently at the baubles spread out before him. He appraised them slowly—a heavy diamond ring and a cluster necklace—and admired the craftwork. It wasn't often that he dealt with such luxury, even in Westminster where he and his partner had run a pawnshop for decades.

It was January 1933 and the collection was being offered by a well-dressed man, squarish rather than portly, with snowy hair and apple cheeks. He waited apprehensively, as if the broker was going to find that the jewels were paste. 'An unusual man,' one of the pawnshop staff would comment later.

It was not the pawnbroker's place to ask why a man who looked as if he had all the money in the world wanted a loan and was prepared to put up family jewels as collateral. The only thing that mattered was that the jewellery and the owner were genuine. He was now in the process of deciding the former and, to satisfy the latter, he had insisted the man sign a contract stating that the jewels were his to sell. The handwritten note sat beside him on the appraisal table. It read, in part: 'It is my property and I have a perfect right to deal with same.'

The broker finally stood up, unscrewed the eyeglass and gave the necklace one last rub between his fingers: 'Righto! Is £650 satisfactory? Good, good. Here'ya sir.'

'Thank you too much,' murmured the man, taking the large notes and folding them away in his pocketbook before disappearing quickly through the door and into the street, where he scurried away before being recognised.

William 'Little Kim' Montagu wasn't normally a man to be shy of acknowledgement—his courting of publicity suggested the opposite was true—but on this occasion the Duke of Manchester preferred anonymity because he was pawning his dead mother's jewels.

After Consuelo died in 1909, the collection was secured in a city vault by a jewellery firm, and items released on request while he fumbled in and out of debt and marriage, the second in 1931 to a West End actress named Kathleen Dawes. Finally, though, he had been forced to reach for the family jewels. The financial well was about to run dry; his allowance from the family trust was not enough to cover his untethered spending habits, and he needed cash. Pawning a few items would be a loan, he figured, which he would one day pay off to reclaim the valuables. No one need know.

But he was wrong. According to the terms of Consuelo's will, the necklaces were not his to sell; rather, they were controlled by the trustees of her estate. Consuelo had feared that her son would otherwise sell it all and her grandchildren would get nothing.

When the pawnbroker, Thomas Sutton, found out he'd been duped, he decided to press charges against the Duke for obtaining money under false pretences. But Sutton died before police had finished their investigation and the matter seemed closed—until it was reopened two years later at the insistence of the trustees.

One mid-morning in March 1935, police knocked on the Duke's door and were shown to his bedroom, where he sat in bed propped up on pillows and drinking tea. They read out the charges. He must appear in Westminster Police Court in a fortnight, they said, before leaving.

The case was front-page news. The bad boy of the British establishment, a Privy Councillor, had finally crossed the line, or so it seemed. Despite his outrageous lifestyle, the Duke was a popular figure, gregarious and largely harmless to everyone except himself—and those creditors silly enough to lend him money, and the finances of one of Britain's most senior aristocratic houses. His misfortunes made great headlines but somehow he always managed to fall on his feet. Would this be the same?

First, a magistrate had to decide if the case should be dismissed out of hand or taken before a jury.

The matter had begun two days before Christmas in 1932, when a telephone message was received at the offices of Cambridge's, a prestigious jewellery firm. The Duke wanted access to the collection for his new wife Kathleen's personal use and this was allowed under the terms of the will. It required a written request, which arrived a few hours later, signed not by Helena but by the Duke.

Despite this anomaly, the manager handed over the requested items. After all, it was hard to say 'no' to a duke. In court more than two years later, the manager was asked by the barrister for the prosecution to account for his actions.

'Can you tell me how it came about that the jewellery was handed over contrary to the express instructions you received from the trustees?'

'I thought he was the Duchess's agent.'

'But he wasn't, was he?'

'No sir.'

In the first days of January 1933, the Duke visited the pawnbrokers, where he was served by Thomas Sutton and signed the false declaration. The necklace and ring were still missing from the collection a year later, when the trustees finally noticed and asked for their return. The jewels were safe, the Duke insisted before admitting that he had used them as collateral to take out a loan, which he was still paying off.

The pawnshop confirmed that the Duke had made regular repayments and the jewellery had not been sold. But they wanted the £650 back, plus interest, to release the jewels, which were in the office safe.

The Duke stood in the dock calmly as his lawyer, Mr Edward Mayer, argued that the Duke had believed he had the right to dispose of the jewels. Besides, he never planned to sell them and now, just as the charges were laid, he was expecting to come into some money that would clear the debt.

'I submit there is no evidence of an intent to defraud,' Mr Mayer concluded.

The magistrate pondered the complexities of the case. There seemed little doubt that the Duke had erred—the will was clear—but did he do so deliberately or, as his lawyer argued, because he was misguided? 'All right,' he said finally, ruling that he would give the Duke the chance to plead his case before a jury.

The trial was set for 10 May 1935. That morning reporters were waiting outside the Duke's Mayfair flat, hoping for a photograph of the quasi-celebrity. After years of financial blunders and a string of bad debts, he was facing the prospect of jail time. The Duke did not rush to his car, even though his chauffeur held the door open for him. Instead, he took his time, stepping from his front door and pausing on the pavement to smoke a cigarette while the photographers clattered about him.

'People think being a duke is great fun,' he told them wistfully. 'My one regret in life is that I was never allowed to go into business when I was a boy. I have four estates but I live in a flat because I can't afford to live in any of the castles. I've been so broke that I have only just been able to pay for my valet's meals.'

Sir Henry Curtis-Bennett KC loved publicity as much as the Duke. They had once been parliamentary colleagues, albeit on opposite sides of the political fence, until Sir Henry resigned to concentrate on his legal career, defending mostly high-profile clients and on one occasion cross-examining the wartime spy Mata Hari.

But Sir Henry was very much on the side of the Duke as he stood in court to defend his old sparring partner. 'The Duke has been very ill recently,' Sir Henry explained, no doubt hoping to evoke a little sympathy from jury members, as the Duke walked slowly to the dock to give evidence. He looked much older than his fifty-eight years.

'Would you like to sit?' the magistrate offered.

'I'm alright. It's quite all right,' the Duke countered, his stoicism now a badge of honour.

Sir Henry took him through the events, beginning with what he had requested from the trustee. As well as the ring and necklace, he had taken four brooches of emeralds and diamonds, a diamond-encrusted tiara, and an emerald-and-diamond necklace.

Why did he take the jewels, Sir Henry asked.

'I thought I would give her a surprise for Christmas,' the Duke replied, explaining that he expected his wife Kathleen to wear them. But she had refused, insisting that they did not suit her because of the light weight of the fabric of her dress compared to the heavy dresses worn by Consuelo.

Instead of returning them to Cambridge's, as he should have done, the Duke placed the jewels in the family safe, where they sat for several months until the day he decided to take them to the pawnshop.

'Why did you go to Sutton's that day?'

'I was involved in certain lawsuits and pressed for money,' the Duke offered. He said he had sought legal opinion, which confirmed his view: 'I felt sure I had the right to dispose of them.'

Sir Henry's strategy was clear from his line of questioning. 'Had you any intention of defrauding Mr Sutton of the money you were obtaining?'

'Absolutely not,' the Duke huffed. 'I asked at the time if they would be kind enough to write me a letter to remind me of the time the interest became due as I was certainly not going to let things go. They did so, and I paid the interest.'

'Are you ready and prepared at this moment to redeem the article by payment of the full amount and interest?'

'I am.'

Turning to the jury, Sir Henry made his pitch: 'It is not an offence to be hard up and in difficulties with creditors,' he began.

> The Duke, having taken advice from a reputable member of the Bar, was entitled to act upon it. Yet two years later someone starts a prosecution. No request, as I understand it, was made to the Duke to redeem those articles before the prosecution was started. The question the jury has to decide is whether the prosecution has proved that, at the time he went to the pawnbroker, did the Duke have the intention to defraud.

The magistrate was also intrigued by the Duke's mindset: 'Did you honestly believe when you went to Sutton's that the jewellery was your property?'

The Duke was adamant: 'I thought I had them for life.'

'And did you believe you could dispose of them?'

'I thought it was my right to pledge them temporarily.'

'Did you believe you were giving the pawnbroker the right to sell these goods in case of default?'

'In case of default—yes.'

Mr Edmunds for the prosecution weighed in, targeting the Duke's reputation for reneging on debt: 'You are not suggesting that your personal guarantee for these items was worth anything, are you?'

The Duke was offended: 'I think it was . . . I had pledged things before without having any questions asked at all.'

Mr Edmunds pressed further. It was absurd for him to believe that the Duke was a man to be trusted over money.

How many times had he been bankrupted? 'Twice.'

How many petitions was he facing for unpaid debts? 'Sixty-seven.'

How much money did he owe from previous judgments? 'It might run to three figures.'

Nell watched from the back of the court. She and Mandy were footing the legal bill, of course. The invoice had already been sent and would remain filed among the family papers, not for any purpose other than as a reminder of the complications her father-in-law presented.

Mandy adored his father in spite of his flaws. They were very different men, but Mandy admired the Duke's free spirit. Life was always exciting and full of possibilities, and failure was an accepted risk. His younger brother, Edward, was a similar character and had his own difficulties in life. Nell was fond of the Duke as well. From the moment they had met at Kimbolton, on the morning of the wedding, he had accepted her immediately, as part of a family and a history that she would otherwise have feared.

Some of her friends might have suggested that Nell should steer clear of the court on this day, particularly in light of her own run-in with the law the previous year. But loyalty was important, and the Duke needed his friends.

The jury filed out of the room and were back barely an hour later. The case was either easy to dismiss or easy to convict; their solemn faces and the way they avoided looking at the accused man indicated the latter. The Duke stood quietly, one hand in his jacket pocket, as the foreman read the verdict: 'Guilty.'

Sir Henry leaped to his feet. The Duke would appeal the result: 'I ask that you remand the prisoner while the appeal is organised.'

'Certainly not. I sentence him to nine months in prison,' the magistrate retorted. 'He must see a judge in Chambers to organise an appeal.'

The Duke looked shocked, as if the possibility of prison had not previously crossed his mind. He bowed to the magistrate, almost politely, then turned slowly and with dragging steps went down below.

As he disappeared from view, reporters rushed out to file their stories, ignoring Nell, who put her head in her hands.

An hour later the Duke of Manchester was sent off in a taxi between two uniformed warders to Wormwood Scrubs Prison, where he was examined medically, bathed, dressed in prison garb, and given a Bible, a prayer book, a mug and a metal plate before being led to a holding cell for the night. He was no longer 'Your Grace', but a prisoner with a number. A man with three castles was living in a three-metre-square concrete cell.

The Duke would be incarcerated for twenty-five days, mostly in the prison hospital, before an appeal was arranged to set him free. A trio of justices decided that the magistrate had not summed up sufficiently to give the jury the confidence that it could clear the Duke, basing an acquittal on the Duke's belief that the legal counsel he had initially received was accurate and that there was a likelihood that he did not intend to defraud the pawnshop owner.

The Duke walked free a few minutes later, but there was no attempt by reporters to interview him about his innocence. It seemed that the Duke of Manchester was only newsworthy when he was in trouble.

The Duke wasn't the only family member clogging up London courts and creating newspaper headlines. Less than a month after her father won his appeal, his youngest daughter, Lady Louise, was also in court and giving the tabloids some juicy aristocratic fodder.

Lady Louise's relationship with David Stead had petered

out a few months after they had arrived in England from their Australian trip, although Nell's brother did not hightail it back to Australia. Instead he had remained at Kimbolton where he enjoyed his brother-in-law's hospitality and began to carve out a social life of his own, seen as something of a charmer by local women.

Louise had no shortage of male admirers but was especially taken by Martin Hofer, the American banker who had been involved in the car crash near Perry a year earlier. The pair hit it off over their love of flying, and Lady Louise travelled back and forth across the English Channel with her boyfriend whenever he had to tend to business in Europe.

Now, in court, she was defending him against claims that he owed £367 in medical bills to a doctor for treating her for a nervous disorder.

A West End doctor named John Precope claimed that Hofer, who was living in a flat in Mount Row, Mayfair, had asked for his services. It was the first week of December 1934 and Hofer had returned from a business trip to Amsterdam with what he called 'an attack of dipsomania'.

The forty-five-year-old was normally teetotal, he insisted, but occasionally had a drink and 'went off the rails'. On this occasion he had been on a bender for a week, which he blamed on the pressure of finalising a valuable business deal, but the truth was that Hofer had a serious drinking problem.

A friend was so concerned about his health that, when he returned to London, he called in Dr Precope to attend him for a week. Hofer resisted the intervention but eventually complied and, according to Dr Precope's version of events, had then asked the doctor to 'look after' Lady Louise, who was living around the corner in Bourdon Street and apparently suffering from a nervous disorder.

There was another complication. 'Lady Louise doesn't have a shilling so to save her embarrassment, please charge her a nominal amount and send me the bill for the rest of your fee,' Hofer instructed the GP.

Things then got out of control. Instead of treating her for a few days, as requested, Dr Precope began visiting Lady Louise almost daily over several weeks, taking her to lunch and dinner and even writing her a poem. This ended in a violent confrontation on New Year's Eve, when Hofer turned up at her flat and found a group, including Lady Louise and Dr Precope, 'playing jolly card games'. He accused the doctor of using his visits as an excuse to insert himself into their social set and becoming 'too familiar' with his girlfriend.

The newspaper reporters in court lapped up the juicy detail of the skirmish; the two men had ended up in a punch-up when Dr Precope retaliated by calling Hofer a cad. 'He hit me and Lady Louise got between us. I hit him back and Lady Louise rushed for the police,' an indignant Dr Precope told the magistrate.

When Hofer took the stand, he admitted being drunk and emotional, which explained his confrontational behaviour. The police prosecutor asked him if it was true that he wanted to marry the twenty-seven-year-old Lady Louise, but that she was not keen to wed him. 'Yes, I suppose that is so,' he conceded.

Dr Precope, who admitted that his bill—for an astonishing

£50 a day—included the time he spent having dinner with Lady Louise, claimed that he was being a friend, trying what he called 'auto-suggestion' as part of her treatment. Lady Louise, he said, was drinking heavily and threatening suicide.

It was a claim that Lady Louise strenuously denied. 'There is not a word of truth to the statement,' she retorted, describing herself as an average drinker and insisting that she had had a cough and had taken a dose of sleeping draught: 'When that didn't work, I took a second dose and it made me feel ill.'

One house call by Dr Precope should have been sufficient and she had regarded his subsequent visits as purely social, his attempts at poetry as 'funny'.

The magistrate, Justice Mackinnon, decided that Dr Precope had indeed inflated his £367 bill and that the time he had spent with Louise in a professional capacity had been greatly exaggerated. 'I think £42 is a reasonable amount', he concluded.

Far from being a woman with a nervous disorder, Lady Louise Montagu was a thrillseeker who shared her brother's love for Stutz cars and even raced at Brooklands. In August 1934 she joined a rare group of women and got her pilot's licence flying an Avro Club Cadet biplane from Heston Airport in Hounslow.

Her daredevil nature knew no bounds. Mandy and his friends would tell of the morning that their shooting party at Kimbolton was disturbed when a plane appeared overhead. It was Louise, who then proceeded to dive-bomb her brother, as family friend James Wentworth Day would recall: 'She came down out of the sky like a thunderbolt and dispersed every pheasant in panic. She was lucky not to be shot.'

Despite their eighteen-year age gap and her reservations about him, Lady Louise married Martin Hofer in New York in 1936. It was a splashy affair, with the reception held at the Waldorf Astoria and covered by the press, who described her as 'a quiet member of a rather sensational family'.

14

A PRODIGAL SON RETURNS

Edward Montagu was back in London and back in trouble with the law. In late September 1935, having recently escaped a dangerous driving charge with a two-year driving ban and a £30 fine after hitting a woman with his sports car, he had been charged with forgery while working as a secretary for a rich Kensington widow and businesswoman.

The night before his appearance in court, an intrepid reporter from *The People* newspaper sat with some of Lord Edward's friends, who wanted to explain why life as a titled man was so difficult for him. They used phrases like 'handicapped' and 'misunderstood' to describe his lifestyle, which jarred with most people's perception of the titled class.

The difference, according to his earnest friends, was money; without wealth, a title became a negative. One did not go without the other, at least in the eyes of the general population. It was an argument that had been frequently proffered by his father, although there were significant differences in their challenges. Little Kim had inherited an estate and a senior aristocratic position in society; his second son had a courtesy title without an inheritance beyond a small stipend, paid from America, the value of which rose and fell with exchange rates and markets.

He was trapped between two worlds, unable to mix socially in his supposed 'class' because he had no money to spend, and resented among the working class because he was presumed snobbish or 'not one of them'. If he was friendly he was accused of being condescending; if he was quiet and reserved he was being stand-offish.

Edward was not afraid of working but struggled to find his place, such as the time he was driving taxis in Alberta, Canada, under the assumed name of Edward Markum. He had been in the job for three weeks when the boss called him into the office and demanded to know his real identity. When he admitted who he was, he was sacked. The offence was not using an alias but having a title. 'I don't want moneyed people working for me,' the proprietor had said.

Credit was the devil: easy to obtain because of the presumption of wealth, difficult to resist and impossible to clear.

And the trial he was about to face was a perfect example of being a marked man. Thousands of men and women appeared in courts each day charged with similar or worse crimes, but their cases went unreported because they were 'ordinary'.

The journalist reported the tale, almost as lurid as his father's rollicking adventures, and raised the obvious question: if Lord

Edward Montagu was so talented as a youth then why wasn't he able to pursue a decent, well-paid career in London? It went unanswered. Edward's friends were perplexed about this themselves.

There was another aspect that they might have considered in their plea for understanding, one far more acceptable than simply complaining about Edward's lack of money. Lord Edward Montagu may have been born to luxury but he was raised without something far more important—a family. His parents were estranged, his sisters had lived with their mother in America and his older brother was off exploring the world in the navy. His father was, at best, an absent figure whose life he learned about by reading the newspapers. Instead, Edward was sent off to boarding schools from the age of seven and emerged as a grown man without a rudder or a moral compass to guide him.

The court case, far from spotlighting the character of Edward Montagu, quickly became an examination of the memory and accusations of the complainant, Mrs Violet Van der Elst, who arrived at court in a white Rolls-Royce. Edward's barrister, Mr Maude, decided that the best way to defend his client was to attack the elderly woman's reputation, and the proceedings descended into chaos as she fought back against this tactic.

First Mr Maude suggested that Mrs Van der Elst was a student of black magic, all because she had used a medium to try to contact her dead husband, a Belgian painter, beyond the grave. 'I am a brave woman,' she declared to the magistrate. 'I'll not have mud thrown at me. I won't let it stick. Tell him to stop.'

The magistrate told her to calm down and answer the questions simply, 'and we will all get through this'. But the anger returned when Mr Maude tried to paint a picture of a woman trying to run too many houses and businesses to be able to remember accurately what cheques she signed or did not sign.

Edward and his lawyer had picked the wrong woman to attempt to defame. Violet was wealthy through her own talents rather than marriage; she was the daughter of a washerwoman and a coal porter, and had once worked as a scullery maid, but had become a successful businesswoman. Experimenting in her own kitchen, she invented Shavex, the first brushless shaving cream. She was also a writer, would-be politician and tireless campaigner against capital punishment.

Mrs Van der Elst had employed Edward Montagu for the very reasons about which he and his friends complained—that he was young, he was misunderstood and he deserved a chance to find a place in life. She was a self-made woman who had risen from adversity and recognised the challenges that he faced, if from an entirely different starting point. She gave him a job as a secretary, dealing with paperwork for her businesses, and hoped 'he would stick to it'.

The disputed cheque had been paid to Mrs Van der Elst by a betting company, David Cope Ltd. She enjoyed the occasional flutter on the horses and in the casinos of Le Touquet, and on this occasion had had a decent win on a race at Ascot. The cheque for £17 5d was placed in an office drawer where Edward was working on her accounts.

Some weeks later, and without explanation, he failed to show up for work and did not return. It was soon afterwards that Mrs Van der Elst discovered the cheque was missing. She put two and two together and called the police, even though it was against her better judgment: 'God knows, I didn't want to charge him but I was forced to.'

Police traced the cheque to a city bank, which had cashed it for Edward based on an endorsement signed by Mrs Van der Elst on its back. It was this endorsement that police insisted was a forgery. When they found him at the bar in the Strollers' Club, his explanation was that he had not shown up for work because he had fallen ill. The cheque had been given to him by Mrs Van der Elst in lieu of settling some accounts and owed wages.

A few days after he was charged, Edward accepted an invitation to visit Mrs Van der Elst. 'I wanted to know why he did it,' she told the court. 'He said he was poor and had a wife in Canada. I gave him a cup of tea and a couple of pounds.'

The jury believed Mrs Van der Elst, who cried out in despair when the foreman declared 'Guilty'. She then rushed to the bench and pleaded, 'I ask for leniency', before being taken back to her seat.

Somewhat sympathetic, the magistrate said that forgery was a serious crime, requiring premeditation and careful execution, and he had little choice: 'It is my painful duty to sentence you to nine months' imprisonment.'

As Edward was led away to Wormwood Scrubs, Mrs Van der Elst made one last effort: 'I didn't want to charge him.

It would have been much better if it had been left to me. I would have helped him . . . I wanted to help him . . . I did everything I could . . . but he wouldn't let me.'

Mrs Van der Elst left the court crying. Edward Montagu had lost the best sponsor he could have hoped for—a sympathetic if eccentric woman, whose belief in helping others was genuine. She would ultimately run a successful fifty-year campaign to end the death penalty in England; on the night in 1965 when the law was changed, it was said that she was given a standing ovation on the floor of the House of Commons.

Edward served his time and on release faced new court proceedings, this time finalising the divorce from his long-suffering Canadian wife, Norah Potter, with whom he had had a son. Two days after it was dissolved he was married again, this time to a West End actress and aspiring theatre producer named Dorothy Peters. The ceremony was a quiet affair in the Brighton Registry Office and the union proved to be a successful one, giving Edward a new line of work—acting.

Given his father's propensity for West End actresses, it seemed that the apple had not fallen far from the tree.

15

THE ENIGMA FROM DOWN UNDER

Nell was a complicated figure in small-town life. Here was a woman who had willingly taken on the role of a British noblewoman and yet was determined to remain resolutely, and rather bluntly, Australian. She divided opinion.

Many intriguing stories were unearthed years later, when her former neighbours recalled some wild tales about her behaviour behind closed doors. Most notable was a recollection of a dinner party hosted one night by Captain Hugh Duberley, the squire at nearby Staughton Manor, and his wife, Saffron.

Nell arrived in an exotic dress 'made of mink', but it wasn't the dress that got tongues wagging; it was her decision after dinner to dump the dress and step out naked. On the face of it, this act seems out of character. Nell was a bold and forthright woman with a habit of challenging social expectations about fashion, but there was no evidence of lewd conduct by either her or Mandy. Rather, they were seen as quite serious—certainly compared with the Duke—and as a couple devoted to each other.

The story of her naked dinner party act was told by the Duberleys' daughter, Grey, who said her father had regarded Nell as uniquely Australian and risqué; he decided after the dinner that he and his wife 'should stop trying to keep pace with the Mandevilles'. Grey, in her late teens at the time, was captivated by Nell's complete disregard for social norms. She was 'extraordinary, amazing'.

Hugh Duberley was a man of some importance, a local councillor and senior office holder of the powerful Country Gentlemen's Association. Whatever their feelings about Nell's outlandish behaviour, it did not initially dissuade the Duberleys from mixing socially with the Mandevilles.

Grey Duberley's theory was that country life was boring for a woman like Nell Mandeville and that she was merely trying to make life interesting. She was also under the misguided impression that Nell had turned the chapel at Kimbolton Castle into a bar and that the whiskey glasses all depicted pornographic images 'of the most interesting kind'. In fact, the chapel was always kept as it was, as a chapel, which casts some doubts on the veracity of Grey's other stories about Nell. There was no doubt, however, that Nell and Mandy enjoyed a drink, and alcohol was a central component of socialising and weekend hunting parties. Even outdoor lunches were served with beer.

They also built an impressive bar at Brampton Park House, the shelves lined with dozens of mixers and carefully placed glasses, although none of them bore pornographic images of the kind reported by Grey Duberley. However, there was a curious sign on the back wall that read 'Spanish Fly', presumably in reference to its supposed aphrodisiac qualities.

The writer Marcus Scriven interviewed several neighbours and their descendants around Kimbolton while he was researching *Splendour & Squalor*, his 2009 book that told the story of four black-sheep sons of aristocratic families, including the Montagus.

The picture that Scriven painted of Nell was of a woman who ultimately didn't fit into the conservative fabric of aristocratic society. Recounting a series of rumours, he claimed that she wasn't faithful to Mandy and slept with some of the men who visited Kimbolton, and even some of the estate workers who she found 'very attractive'. By contrast, Scriven wrote, Mandy was always smitten with Nell and never strayed.

If Nell's diaries are to be believed, then most of the stories were just that—stories and innuendo. There was just one instance in which Nell may have strayed, or at least thought about it. And it was her father-in-law, a man who had cheated on his wife without compunction, who saved the marriage.

Nell detailed in her diaries how she fell for a footman and even considered 'dumping Mandy', but Manch—as she called the Duke—stepped in and begged her to stay. The unnamed footman was quietly sacked and life moved on. The incident, several years into the marriage, was the only time that she had such thoughts, or at least put them to paper. If Mandy was unfaithful then she never found out about it.

It was the house parties and the line-up of famous and exotic visitors that generated the most gossip. Family photo albums, lovingly collated by Mandy, recorded dozens of events through the 1930s—images of happy, well-dressed guests, often sprawled casually across one another and fine old furniture, giving the impression of a carefree lifestyle even as the world ground its way through the Depression years.

One of the most frequent guests was the famed racing driver Joel Woolf 'Babe' Barnato, one of the so-called 'Bentley Boys', who had met Mandy at Brooklands Raceway during the 1920s. Barnato had inherited his father's diamond fortune and used his wealth to buy the Bentley Motor Company and then drive its cars to victory at the Le Mans 24 Hour race in three successive years.

Prince George was another guest. He and Mandy had remained friends since their days at the Royal Naval College, and the Duke of Kent, as he was now titled, had a reputation for being a 'party prince' who indulged in cocaine and morphine and, although married, had affairs with both men and women.

The Russian prince Emanuel Galitzine, a descendant of Catherine the Great, was another guest who attended winter hunts for fox and pheasant on the estate. Prince Emanuel, whose family had escaped post-revolutionary Russia, was known for throwing his own glamorous parties. His flamboyant behaviour included one occasion when he dived into the Thames wearing white tie and tails and swam to the other side.

One of Nell and Mandy's more intriguing guests was an exotic Austrian noblewoman named Baroness Violet von Gagern, who had moved to London after fleeing Vienna in 1919, in the midst of the communist uprising and declaration of martial law. A Greta Garbo lookalike, she was a successful model who wrote travel stories and book reviews for *Tatler* magazine, even adopting the nom de plume 'Iris Orklid' to hide her aristocratic connections when appearing in French and Belgian movies. She and Nell had met during the latter's jaunts to London, when she would visit the 400 Club at Leicester Square, dubbed 'the night-time headquarters of society'.

The baroness, described by her agents as 'a particularly good horsewoman and fine rifle shot', was at Kimbolton one weekend in December 1937 when the Mandevilles held a two-day shoot to rid the estate of a rabbit plague. She was among a dozen or so guests in a group photograph published by a sporting magazine at the end of the first day's hunting, when almost seventeen hundred rabbits had been shot.

The photograph makes an intriguing study of relationships and personalities. Nell, dressed in a tailored jacket, gloves and boots, has clearly not been hunting, but is clinging to the arm of 'Babe' Barnato while looking over to the baroness, who returns her gaze. Mandy stands between the two women, legs crossed casually, and looking down at his wife. Barnato stares intently, almost menacingly, at the photographer.

Some of her neighbours, like the Duberleys, might say the photo is evidence that Nell was having an affair, or at least flirting with Babe, and that it was tolerated by Mandy. But it is impossible to draw any firm conclusions other than Nell's comfort in front of the camera.

The family photo albums contain many more images of hunting days—for rabbits, pheasants, foxes and even ducks. One taken in October 1936 is especially illustrative of the hunting life, Nell posing with her gun amid a dozen or so well-dressed friends with a mountain of dead birds at their feet. 'The bag at lunch time—final bag 288 ducks,' the caption reads.

Typical of the whispers about Nell was that one of her 'favourites' was Albert Suprenant, the American banker killed in the car crash in 1935. But this couldn't have been true because Suprenant was a friend and colleague of Martin Hofer; before the fateful day, he had only just arrived in the UK, and had not been to Brampton or Kimbolton before.

It appeared that being Australian made Nell either a victim of small-town whispers and innuendo, or of wider anti-colonial and class sentiments. Not that she seemed that bothered by it all in the least.

12th May 1937

I woke up at 530 to a gun salute outside. I rang for my maid and she brought in a silk dress and my coronation robes. I looked absolutely stupidly out of date in them. I have seen fucking dolls dressed better. Mandy looked splendid in his uniform and robes and Manch [the Duke] looked stunning as always. We arrived at the abbey around 730. I was seated next to Viscountess Younger of Leckie. It was a splendid moment. We latter [sic] returned home and had dinner. The fucking footman spilled the food. Mandy's allergies were made worse by the ermine on his robes.

Nell's diary entry after attending the coronation of King George VI said much about her attitude to society and its fashions, as well as her fearless use of language. She may have felt uncertain in the first years of her life as a viscountess, but by the mid-1930s she could hold her own in any company.

In London social circles Nell stood out as a fun-loving Australian with a sense of fashion, a penchant for dancing and little or no filter. Unlike her mother-in-law, Helena, who had spurned the Manchester jewels, Nell adored wearing them in public, favouring big drop pearls, emeralds, diamonds and precious stones that she would match with coloured shoes, starting something of a trend, as reported by the *Evening Standard*: 'On this occasion Lady Mandeville's dress was white, fastened with a large jade plaque. Her bracelet was set with emeralds and she wore jade green shoes.' Such was the fuss that a bodyguard was sometimes hired for the evening, for protection in case of any robbery attempt.

Although Nell didn't seek them out, her circle of friends included some Australian women who had married Englishmen of influence, in business or society. Most notably, she was friends with the Rani of Pudukkottai, formerly Miss Molly Fink of Melbourne, whose romance with the Indian Raja Martanda Bhairava Tondaiman had echoed Nell's own love story with Mandy.

Like Nell, Molly had been a student at Lauriston Girls' School in Armadale. But when her father, a barrister and Shakespeare scholar, died suddenly in 1915, she and her mother moved to the Blue Mountains in New South Wales. They were staying at the Hydro Majestic hotel near Medlow Bath when the Raja, who was visiting Australia, spied the twenty-one-year-old in the dining room and fell in love. They married six months later, but the mixed-race union was not welcomed by colonial government officials in India.

Rather than give up his wife, the Raja gave up his kingdom, the princely state of Pudukkottai in central India, and the couple decided to live in Europe, where they were accepted socially until the Raja died in 1928. Molly then returned to London, where she settled in Mayfair and in the early 1930s met Nell. The pair, bonded by their stories and both trying to save their husbands' legacies, were seen regularly dining together in restaurants around Mayfair, especially at the Café de Paris, the restaurant and dance club where the Charleston had been introduced to London.

There were twenty or so prominent Australian society women in Britain in the 1930s, which provided endless interest for the London correspondents of Australian newspapers and magazines like the *Australian Women's Weekly* and *Smith's Weekly*.

Sheila Chisholm, or Lady Milbanke as she was titled, was the most prominent of them. A close friend of Edward, Prince of Wales and his younger brother Albert, better known as Bertie, she was beautiful and charismatic and moved in the upper echelons of political and social circles. Enid Lindeman, Lady Furness, was another; the wife of a shipping magnate, she would eventually boast four husbands and two fortunes. Others included the Viscountess St Davids (formerly Doreen Guinness Jowett of Melbourne), Countess of Bective (Elise Tucker from Sydney), Lady Portarlington (Winnifreda Yuill of Adelaide), Lady Doverdale (Audrey Pointing of Sydney) and Princess Radziwill (Harriet Dawson of Sydney).

There was also an obsession with peer rankings and where each person fitted in, depending on whether they had married barons, viscounts, earls or dukes, and the year each title had been created. In 1938, as reported by the London *Daily Telegraph*, Lady Horlick, formerly Betty Murray of Sydney, scrambled onto the peerage list at number 28,212, having married a baronet. Likewise Lady Grey-Egerton, formerly Aimee Cumming of Melbourne, was at 27,010 and Lady Pyers Mostyn, formerly Margery Marks of Sydney, at 22,159.

Further up the rankings came the Countess of Jersey, Patricia Richards from Cootamundra, who was ranked 11,009, having married the Earl of Jersey. The Countess of Bective was at 8015, Lady Portarlington at 6119 and Lady Ducie (formerly Maria Bryant of Maryborough, Queensland) at 6180. The Countess of Darnley, formerly Florence Morphy of Beechworth—widow of Ivo Bligh, the Earl of Darnley and English cricket captain—ranked 6099 on the list. But highest of all was Nell Stead, who as Lady Mandeville was at number 4019. Her ranking would rise significantly when Mandy finally inherited the Duke of Manchester title.

Nell was not without society friends in high places—in particular Edwina, the Countess Mountbatten, and her younger sister Ruth, Lady Delamere, who were regarded as two of Britain's wealthiest heiresses. Perhaps her most controversial friendship was with the former Margaret Whigham, wife of businessman Charles Sweeny, who would become better known from her second marriage a decade later as the promiscuous Margaret, Duchess of Argyll. Nell and Margaret were regularly seen together at La Touquet, the French holiday destination frequented by society figures.

Gossip columnists found Nell a complete mystery—often serene, measured and reserved, and at other times known to enjoy letting her hair down. It wasn't just what Nell wore or who she was with, but how she sometimes behaved, such as on the night when she was out with friends having a drink at the Ritz Hotel. In a story recounted many years later by one of the attendees, Nell decided to leave the group and join Mandy, who was drinking at the Berkeley, then a grand hotel across the road. Rather than walk there, she commandeered a taxi and ordered the driver to drop her at the hotel's front door. He did so.

The Berkeley party carried on merrily and at some point she excused herself to go to the bathroom. When Nell didn't reappear, two of the women in the group went looking for her, only to find her locked inside a cubicle because the door's bolt had broken. Neither of the ladies could shift the bolt and open the door. Neither could Mandy, even with all his rugby strength. The attendant then called out to Nell that help was on its way.

'I've sent for a plumber,' he assured her.

'I want to come out through the door, not down the fucking drain,' she snapped back.

16

FETED IN AMERICA

For much of the nineteenth century, Park Farm at Kimbolton was considered one of the most prominent breeding properties for Shorthorn cattle in England. The herd had been established in 1849 by George, the 6th Duke of Manchester. A decade or so later his son William, the 7th Duke, enlarged it in scale and scope when 'fashion began to assert itself', as reported by the industry bible of the era, *The Shorthorn Herds of England*.

With names like Wild Eyes Duke, Lally of Leighton and Princess Silence, the Kimbolton cattle were not only noted for their flamboyant monikers but, more importantly, their 'good milking and feeding qualities'. With several of the farm's best bulls in stud, it would not be long before there was an established 'Kimbolton line' of shorthorns.

William was also known as a rural innovator, one of the first farmers in England to use machinery such as steam cultivators for his fields of clover and corn, and developing techniques hailed by the Royal Agricultural Society for turning old arable land into permanent pasture for his herds. But perhaps the 7th Duke's biggest innovation came in 1880 when he imported two prized merino rams and eleven ewes from a property in Victoria, Australia, to begin an experimental flock at Kimbolton. The arrival aboard the ship *Northumberland* created headlines around Britain as 'the first sheep sent from Australia to England for breeding purposes'.

But that changed in 1890 when William died and his son George, the 8th Duke, inherited the title. Relations between father and son had been tense for years because of the younger man's drinking habits; instead of moving into the castle and its farm, George turned his back on the estate and sold off most of the herd, raising £3000 as he scrambled for money to repay debts owed to his wife Consuelo's dowry. Such was the industry interest in what was billed as 'an important sale of pedigree cattle' that the highest priced bull, Oxford Helene, was bought by the Prince of Wales for £160.

In 1894 Mandy's father, the 9th Duke, finished the job by selling off the remaining cows when he lost interest in Kimbolton and headed for the bright lights of America. Park Farm had been largely ignored in the years since, and the pastures and crops let go. But now, almost forty years later, there was a renewed energy at Kimbolton Castle. Despite their slew of embarrassing family legal troubles, or perhaps because of them, by the early 1930s it seemed that Mandy and Nell were determined to turn a corner, return to the family's agricultural roots, and attempt to rescue the family's tattered and precarious financial fortunes.

There was a new, productive rhythm on the estate as Park Farm rejuvenated. Mandy began restocking the property with cattle—not with Shorthorns but Red Poll, a milking breed that had its origins in the muddy flats of nearby Norfolk and Suffolk. Charles Montagu, Mandy's great-uncle, the younger brother of the late 8th Duke, would take a lead role in managing the breeding operations, which they hoped would, in time, once again produce award-winning animals.

While his great-uncle kept an eye on the operations of Park Farm, Mandy concentrated on another area he felt would provide stable, long-term income—game birds. By the spring of 1937 he had almost four thousand pheasant chicks under care and let out to roam in verdant fields. Large patches of grass, planted by his great-grandfather, had been left to grow wild; these gave the young birds a place to hide from predators like foxes. Breeding coops were also moved around constantly to give nesting hens views of the sky and so warn them of impending attacks from above by hawks, rooks and jackdaws.

It was the attention to detail that would make the Kimbolton shoots among the best in England. So said *Country Life* magazine, which featured the property in a glossy profile in the early summer. Their three-page spread of lavish praise and sun-filled photographs painted a picture of rural serenity: the Viscount and his employees gathered in the welcome shade of spreading oaks to discuss the birds and their welfare, a gun leaning against the breeding hut to ward off rooks and jackdaws; sacks of corn and meal ready to be boiled in the cooker.

Mandy, workmanlike in trousers and short-sleeved shirt rather than a tailored woollen suit, was photographed alongside his head gamekeeper Frank Cowlard—a giant figure, standing almost 1.9 metres tall—who was in the garb of a hunter, dressed in tweed plus-fours, peaked cap and jacket, with a shotgun resting in the crook of his arm.

The close involvement in the operations of the Viscount and his wife, the Viscountess, made the difference, said the magazine. Far from being a gambling womaniser like his father and grandfather, Mandy was a man of the land—'his own agent, bailiff and farm manager', not to mention one of the best shots of the day, a former navy rugby player, fine golfer and heavyweight boxer. On top of these skills, he was also a keen zoologist and entomologist.

Nell, her husband's 'gunner's mate', was photographed gazing wistfully from the steps of the hut. She helped with the breeding operation and, given her background in rural Australia, had no qualms about swapping her fine dresses and heels for trousers and boots and getting her hands dirty, including preparing the feed for the pheasant chicks—a mix of biscuit meal, oatmeal, barley flour, boiled rabbit flesh and eggs. In doing so, she earned respect from locals as a rare example of a lady unafraid of manual labour.

'Lady Mandeville breeds dogs,' the article began. 'She is an expert gardener, an interior decorator with part of at least one great London hotel to her credit, co-partner in a silk and lingerie business and is a distinct and decorative asset to the landscape of Huntingdonshire.'

It was a rare occasion when publicity not only mentioned her looks as a 'decorative asset' but also noted that she had skills as an interior decorator and made contributions as a businesswoman. The lingerie business was called Juanne (Model Millinery and Lingerie), with its storefront at the corner of Princes and Swallow streets in Mayfair; it would run successfully through the mid-1930s until war forced its closure.

The Kimbolton publicity would continue when the shooting season began in earnest. Magazines like *The Illustrated Sporting and Dramatic News* visited to report on the progress, concluding: 'Kimbolton Castle . . . is easily among the best shoots in that very rural and unspoiled county, a county which still preserves the atmosphere of pre-war England when squires and farmers flourished and the horrible voice of the tractor was not yet born.'

Immediately after the photo shoot in the northern summer of 1937, Mandy and Nell with Lord Kim in tow left for a six-month tour of America and Canada. The couple's arrival in New York towards the end of March attracted immediate attention when they booked into the Waldorf Astoria. Columnist Maury Paul, who wrote under the nom de plume 'Cholly Knickerbocker' for the Hearst newspapers (and was best known as the man who invented the phrase *café society*), remarked on their choice of accommodation. 'Lord and Lady Mandeville must have had a financial windfall from somewhere,' he noted snidely, adding: 'Helena, Duchess of Manchester may have written history in the Montagu clan by loosening the strings wound so carefully around her purse.'

He then reminded readers of the family's celebrated connections in the city, including a lavish ball held in 1883 when the wealthy Vanderbilt family celebrated the completion of their mansion, Petit Chateau, on Fifth Avenue by hosting an event for George and Consuelo, then Viscount and Lady Mandeville, who had just arrived from London. The event cost $250,000, including $65,000 on champagne for a thousand guests. It was the moment when 'new money', built from investment in railways, was finally accepted into New York's 'old money' society. That shift was signified by the Vanderbilt family being invited to join the so-called 'Four Hundred Club' created by Caroline Astor, matriarch of the family known as 'the landlords of New York'.

A few weeks after their arrival, Nell and Mandy were guests at the iconic Sagamore Hotel in Bolton Landing, the millionaires' playground in upstate New York where Mandy was invited to play in an invitational golf tournament and impressed his hosts by reaching the semifinals. His opinion was sought for the upcoming America's Cup yachting battle off Newport, Rhode Island, which was pitting the US entrant *Ranger*, owned by Harold Vanderbilt, against the British entry *Endeavour II*, owned by Sir Thomas Sopwith. 'In my opinion, Sopwith has an excellent chance,' he declared after watching the boats in action. The American boat won 4–0.

But it was in California that Nell and Mandy were most feted. At times the newspaper commentary was gushing: 'Lady Mandeville is one of the piquant types,' one scribe began. 'Gracious, animated, vivacious—with sun-kissed complexion and soft brown eyes that sparkle, then dream.'

Their hosts were San Francisco's business and society leaders, among them industrialist Richard Heimann, tourism entrepreneur Paul Fagan, philanthropist Herbert Fleishhacker, and investment banker and patron of the arts Charles Blyth. They were entertained at the Bohemian Club, dominated by writers and artists, and the Pacific-Union Club, which counted billionaire newspaper publisher William Randolph Hearst Jr as a member.

An American city like San Francisco felt a more comfortable place to be socially than London, where Mandy had to face the inevitable comparison with his father and grandfather, his every financial action scrutinised and critiqued. America was new money, where a man was judged by his own actions rather than those of someone who had come before. Yet his title was also valuable because he was one of few rather than many; Americans would always be in awe of what they regarded as royalty.

Nell had even more reason to feel at home in America rather than England. She was a woman of the new world and did not easily mingle with established British society. She also struggled with cold English winters and wet summers, much preferring the climes of the west coast of the US, which reminded her of Melbourne.

And yet she had long since moved on from Australia. Her parents were dead and her siblings often visited her in England. David, in particular, had become a semi-permanent fixture in Kimbolton, and Erin had been several times in recent years with her husband. Even her youngest sister, Penelope, made the occasional visit.

The social whirl and accompanying media coverage did raise one sore point. 'No more interesting personalities could be found than Lord and Lady Mandeville,' wrote Susan Smith, a society columnist working for the *San Francisco Examiner*, before she provided her readers with a potted history of the Dukes of Manchester. Most important, she said, was the majesty of Kimbolton Castle and its significance in English history. Within its walls were some of the world's great art treasures, some of them once owned by Catherine of Aragon. Nowhere else could there be finer examples of Chippendale furniture.

Why, then, were Nell and Mandy still living in Brampton Park House?

William Montagu, the 7th Duke of Manchester, was not just a champion of innovative farm machinery and cultivation techniques. Soon after he inherited the title in 1855, William embraced new technology and installed gas lighting in Kimbolton Castle when the town became one of the first in Britain to open a gasworks. But by the time he died, in 1890, gas technology was ageing and broken and the castle's lighting and heating needed upgrading to the newfangled electricity, which was beginning to be installed in homes across the country.

Instead, the castle was all but abandoned as the next two dukes frittered away the family's money and legacy. First it was George, 'Kim', the 8th Duke, who had little interest in the castle, let alone modernisation; then Little Kim, the 9th Duke, followed his father's example by ignoring Kimbolton, other than as an occasional hideaway and place to bed West End actresses.

Janice Rudderham worked as a housemaid at the castle in the early years of the twentieth century, until she met and married the gamekeeper Frank Cowlard and started a family. According to notes of an interview she gave many years later and kept by the Huntingdon Archives, the job paid board plus 12 shillings a week. In the days immediately before the Great War, only a handful of staff was needed to keep the few usable rooms clean and to cater for the hodgepodge of visitors who came sporadically during the year.

Mandy's great-uncle Charles Montagu was the most regular, driving up from London most weekends and bringing with him his own chauffeur, butler and footman. Lord Montagu was a formal man who loved Kimbolton and his family's heritage, unlike his late brother and rebellious nephew.

Setting aside its romance, Janice remembered the castle as a dull and cold place, lit upstairs only by candles and warmed by fires fed with a constant load of firewood, chopped and carried in from the nearby forest. Mrs Bowyer was the housekeeper, and there were three housemaids, two kitchen maids and a pantry boy. The male servants slept in the old dungeons.

The castle represented a loneliness for Mandy during his childhood; he'd been sent away to boarding school at the age of eight and then returned each holiday to an empty home with only a tutor for company. His mother and sisters were in America and his brother, Edward, was more likely to be in London with their father. Yet despite his conflicted emotions about Kimbolton, when Mandy and Nell returned from their 1937 American trip, they decided that they wanted to reclaim the castle as their own.

The Kimbolton Castle project was daunting in scale and cost. It would be the first major works on the building since 1707, according to the records Mandy and Nell had found in the castle library.

They embarked on a program of adding central heating and electricity to the castle by installing a private plant that could light up the castle and provide enough power to heat half a dozen rooms. It would take more than a year. The finished project was revealed in an edition of *Country Life* magazine, and it boasted three hundred and fifty 'lighting points' in the castle and outbuildings. 'Although it would require an exceptionally large plant to provide heating for a building of this size, it has been found possible to arrange for a limited number of electric fires to be used in addition to the lighting,' the article explained:

> Actually there are eighteen power or heating points, but it is assumed that only six portable radiators will be connected,

> and these are in the nature of additional heating for small rooms. As is usual with a large country house, electricity takes a full share of those domestic devices which it can do so well. In addition to pumping soft water to a storage tank, an electric pump is used to circulate hot water in the central heating system. In the kitchen a small electric cooker has been installed for occasional use and a large refrigerator is operated electrically.

The renovation had been a fraught process and survey teams had resorted to using torches to complete their work before builders moved in and spent more than a year making part of the imposing building presentable, mostly on the second floor. It was a huge investment considering Nell and Mandy's limited money, and their attempts at the same time to rescue the estate's income streams through farming.

The usable layout consisted of rooms on the first two floors, as well as the kitchens and servants' quarters downstairs. To the left off the main entrance, which faced east, was the grand White Hall, adorned with paintings of former dukes and earls and their families, which continued through a series of drawing rooms and salons.

The dining room was to the right, dominated by a lengthy table that seated forty guests—a constant reminder of better times and days gone by. A cocktail bar occupied the north-east corner of the building while the giant library, with floor-to-ceiling shelves, ran most of the length of the eastern flank. There was a series of guest rooms in the western wing of the second floor while the eastern wing was used as the family retreat, with Nell's room in one corner, her late mother's portrait on the side-board overlooking the walled gardens she tended, and Mandy's in the other. Lord Kim's bedroom was between them, alongside a nursery. Nell was pregnant again.

17

MY OWN DARLING BOY

On 9 October 1938, as the vast green lawns outside her bedroom window became a sea of golden-brown leaves and thoughts turned to the grey winter months ahead, Nell gave birth to her second son, Angus Charles Drogo Montagu.

She had been in an unusually pessimistic mood in the weeks leading up to the birth. A junior staff member would recall many years later an unusual conversation with 'the Duchess', as she was called, a few days before the delivery. 'Do you ever think I will get back in shape?' Nell asked the young woman wistfully one morning, as she sat propped up on pillows. The housemaid was taken aback. Her mistress was always friendly but it came as a surprise that she would hold personal doubts, let alone bother to ask a mere servant their opinion. She stammered her assurances that all would be well.

Nell's question was about much more than her post-pregnancy waistline.

Mandy and Nell had moved into the castle in June, four months before Angus's birth. Even though the renovation work had not yet been completed, Nell, now aged thirty-six, was eager to have her baby in their new home. The work seemed to go on forever. Dozens of workmen still swarmed over the castle and its grounds; the final stages would take several months to finish.

But there were other worries. War with Germany loomed as a possibility, and the tingle of excitement at settling into a new home was dulled and confused by the uncertain future.

There had already been preliminary discussions with authorities about what would happen to large stately homes if there was conflict, and Mandy had committed Kimbolton Castle to the cause even though it would mean losing their home. Instead of comfort, there was insecurity: a mother with a newborn baby and a husband who would almost certainly return to sea.

The arrival of a second child meant little in terms of ancestral lineage and would normally not have attracted any media interest beyond a simple birth notice—*Second son born. Mother and child doing well.* Angus was akin to his uncle Edward and his great-great-uncle Charles—men without meaningful titles, estates and money, unless their older siblings died 'without issue'. But the birth came barely a week after British prime minister Neville Chamberlain had returned from Munich to declare 'peace for our time', in the misguided hope that the appeasement of Adolf Hitler would stop his march across

Europe. Perhaps because of the timing, Angus's birth attracted a few extra news reports, some of which held a hint of ugly nationalism.

'There is a good deal of blood that is not English in Lord Mandeville and his son,' observed a columnist penning 'A London Letter for Women' in the *Liverpool Daily Post*, before listing the foreign-born duchesses of Manchester—beginning with Louisa, the German-born Double Duchess. The saving grace, according to the writer, was that the new arrival's mother was from Australia—a British colony and ally.

Angus's baptism was even less elaborate than his older brother's had been, more than nine years before, although it was performed by the Bishop of Ely (Cambridgeshire) rather than the local vicar. Charles Montagu stepped in as godfather, and there would be no town celebration and concert band. Neither was there a bonfire at Tandragee, where the cheers were polite.

But there was one special element to the ceremony. It was held in Kimbolton Castle's private chapel, where Catherine of Aragon would have prayed, and beneath the vivid, majestic Giovanni Pellegrini murals that had been added in the eighteenth century. This was the first time the chapel had been used formally for several centuries, and it pointed to Mandy and Nell's desire to once again make the castle the dynasty's real home.

There was one close family member missing. Baron Kimbolton, 'Lord Kim', aged nine, had just begun his new school year and was boarding at Hawtreys Preparatory School at Westgate-on-Sea, on the Kent coastline near Margate. Mandy had been to the same school, then followed the family path to Eton and Cambridge University before the navy called him.

It was important that the eldest boy followed the same tradition, although young Sidney was missing his mother. She missed him too, as is clear from reading the short, loving missives written by Nell in the late autumn and early winter of 1938. The young boy kept them and they would be among the papers held in the family archives almost a century after they were penned.

My own darling love bud,
Still you have not told me you are pleased about your little brother. Mandy and I will come down on the weekend of the 19th to see you which I am longing for. Will send you chocolate and cakes. God bless you my darling boy.
Nell xxxxx

My own darling boy
Hope you get the chocolates safely—we will be down next weekend to take you out and see you play football. Will telephone you before we arrive and let you know what time. Tons and tons of love sweet one and God bless you always.
Nell xxxxx

My own darling Love Bird,
I am writing the way you asked me to. We both miss you so much. Yesterday Mandy and I spent all day . . . at Kimbolton. Mandy is shooting today with Hugh and tomorrow if it is not

raining. We are going over to plan some gardening. Frank, Miss Carter and everyone were asking after you and everyone misses you very much but not so much as I do my own baby. Your blue trousers and shirt have arrived and I will send them to you. I know you will look divine in them. There are hundreds of workmen at Kimbolton so it should look very different when you return. Just tons and tons of love and xxxxx my darling.
Nell

Although the family took great pride in their titles and formality when they were addressed by others in public, once behind closed doors they dropped all convention as Nell tried to counter any feelings from her son of abandonment or neglect by being sent away to boarding schools. Some children thrived in the boarding-school environment but many more did not.

Nell's feelings are laid bare in family photographs, including a study of Lord Kim asleep at home a few hours before he was due to leave for boarding school, the photo capturing not only his innocence but a mother's misgivings. Another page contains photos of a November 1938 reunion, probably the one she mentions in her letter, in which she hugs her son close as they walk on a beach near the town of Sandwich, rugged up against the winter cold.

The castle renovation had been difficult and cost more than had been anticipated as the hidden secrets of Kimbolton were slowly revealed. More than £14,000—squeezed from Mandy's trust fund, against the better judgment of trustees and the indifference of his father—had been pumped into the construction alone. Mandy, unhappy with the pace and standard of some of the work, had changed personnel on several occasions.

One of his grievances targeted a firm of London surveyors that had charged him £75 to comb through the castle and ensure that planned structural work would be safe. The bill made him furious because he felt the work was taking too long, and had cost too much.

When he refused to pay the bill, the company sued. This led to a rash of newspaper stories about the claim and, more sensationally, the state of the castle. The headline in the *Evening Standard* was typical, if exaggerated in its estimate of the size of the building: 'Castle had 350 rooms but only two baths'. The case was fascinating and not just because of the apparently paltry amount of money involved, but also because it enabled readers to peek behind the gates of one of the country's most famous castles.

Everyone agreed that the project had needed a quantity surveyor to carefully map the shuttered rooms and crumbling corridors, ensuring that the building was safe and that the work to install lighting and heating could be done.

'It was uninhabitable,' Mandy conceded when he took the stand to defend his decisions. 'The last renovation was done in 1707 so there were no modern conveniences of any kind.'

The judge, Sir Mordaunt Snagge, was intrigued. 'How do you know that the last work was done two hundred years ago?'

'Because the men found a full set of plans dated 1707 when they were exploring some locked rooms,' Mandy replied. 'I don't think anyone had been in those rooms since.'

The judge hadn't finished: 'If there was no electricity, then how was the castle lit?'

'Candles,' replied Mandy. 'The men had to use torches as they moved through the castle.'

Sir Mordaunt Snagge laughed. 'Or cigarette lighters,' he suggested, conjuring up images of surveyors clambering around ancient stonework by the faint light of Zippo lighters, which had been sold in the UK since the mid-1930s.

But Mandy had become frustrated by their slowness in producing their report and he eventually sacked the firm. He was shocked when the bill arrived and complained, like his father, that he was being charged extra simply because he was an aristocrat. Twelve pounds would have been a reasonable charge, he insisted, and was backed up by a rival firm that gave evidence that a competent assistant and a junior should have been able to draw up plans within a week.

The judge spent some months mulling over his decision, arriving at a compromise figure of £58 as a fair price under the circumstances, bearing in mind what the surveyors would have paid for food and lodgings while in the town.

Mandy and Nell's legal problems kept mounting. Not long after he grudgingly paid the surveyor's disputed fee, the Viscount found himself in court over the theft of personal items by his new valet. The tale was instant fodder for the newspapers, which looked for every opportunity to write the next chapter in the Manchester family's travails.

Mandy and Nell had hired a man named Joseph Kennelly in November 1938, one of several new staff employed to cope with the growing household. The forty-one-year-old Kennelly presented well and had solid experience, which was detailed in references from well-known households in London. But the couple soon regretted the decision. Mandy had shown Kennelly his wardrobe and mentioned that his wife sometimes went through his clothes and discarded unwanted suits, which were sent to local jumble sales for charity.

Kennelly, whose references turned out to be fake and who had a string of convictions for burglary and stealing while working as a servant, saw this as an opportunity. He began carefully pilfering clothes so they wouldn't be missed, later insisting, when caught, that he had been given permission, even encouraged to take three suits, gloves, socks and riding breeches, among other items.

As his audacity grew, Kennelly began stealing other items, including a silver cigarette case emblazoned with the Montagu crest, a silver travelling clock, a set of ashtrays and a table cigarette lighter. A camel-hair coat owned by David Stead also disappeared.

Kennelly would claim later in court that they were gifts from the Viscount, who had handed him the cigarette case, even though he had only been employed at the castle for a week. 'Keep it if you like,' Mandy had allegedly said.

Mandy scoffed at the suggestion.

Kennelly's tenure at the castle lasted only a few weeks. He was not sacked for his thefts, which had gone unnoticed at the time, but because of an altercation with a footman. Mandy had found the two men arguing loudly near the kitchen pantry and, after hearing their explanations, dismissed Kennelly on the spot, giving him a week's wages in lieu and telling him to leave the castle immediately.

In a fit of pique, Kennelly had gone back to Mandy's wardrobe before leaving and taken another coat, insisting later that he had done so in anger at being dismissed unfairly. A month later he claimed he had written to the Viscount, admitting to the theft and offering to return the coat if he was paid the wages he felt he was owed.

Neither Mandy nor David Stead recalled receiving any letter. It was only when Stead went looking for his coat that he realised it had been stolen; suspicion immediately fell on Kennelly. He was tracked down to a flat in Chelsea, where police found not only the coat but Mandy's clothes and silver valuables. When he was confronted by police about the thefts, he held out his hands and said, 'Well that's the end of that.'

The jury dismissed Kennelly's stories as fabrications and found him guilty within twenty minutes of retiring; the judge sentenced him to eighteen months' hard labour, after revealing that he had nine previous convictions for crimes ranging from stealing to immoral behaviour and forgery.

'The evidence admitted of no doubt whatever,' he told Kennelly.

> Your record is a very bad one. I have seldom seen a worse one and you seem to have indulged in more varieties of crime than most men who belong to the criminal classes. Dishonesty, bigamy, coining and living on immoral earnings. Then you obtained situations in respectable houses by false references. Unless you mend your ways long terms of penal servitude are your certain fate. You are a pest to society.

Kimbolton Castle, ancestral home of the House of Montagu since 1615, now home to a private school. *Jim Osley*

Prometheus Bound by Peter Paul Rubens, held by the Montagu family for centuries before being sold off with other family treasures in 1949 to pay debts. Now part of the collection of the Philadelphia Museum of Art.

Tandragee Castle in Northern Ireland came into the Montagu family estates in the nineteenth century. *GreyHobbit*

Kylemore Abbey, part of Kylemore Castle, Ireland, acquired by the Montagu family in 1903, shortly after Mandy's birth. *Sabine Holzmann*

The achievement (coat of arms) of the Dukes of Manchester.

Consuelo Yznaga, Duchess of Manchester, Mandy's grandmother and wife of the 8th Duke.

Helena Zimmerman, Duchess of Manchester, Mandy's mother and wife of the 9th Duke. She is wearing the Manchester tiara, made by Cartier in 1903 for her mother-in-law with more than one thousand brilliant-cut and four hundred rose-cut diamonds—once worn by Nell and now housed in the Victoria and Albert Museum.

Clyde Girls Grammar School, 1919. Nell Stead is in the centre of the middle row.
Courtesy of Geelong Grammar School archives

The Galle Face Hotel, Colombo, Ceylon, in the 1920s, where Nell and Mandy first met by the swimming pool.

Nell, Mandy and their dog Biscuit in 1927 with their Bentley they called Stephanie. Pure luxury. *Courtesy of Nicholas Hodgkinson-Montagu*

Nell with Lieutenant Viscount Alexander 'Mandy' Mandeville (later the 10thDuke of Manchester), clearly besotted on the day of their wedding at Kimbolton, 5 May 1927. *Courtesy of Nicholas Hodgkinson-Montagu*

Nell on her wedding day with her new father-in-law, William 'Manch' the 9th Duke of Manchester. *Courtesy of Nicholas Hodgkinson-Montagu*

The wedding party: the officiating bishop is top left next to the Duke of Manchester; Mandy's sister, Mary, is at front next to Nell and Mandy in centre.
Courtesy of Nicholas Hodgkinson-Montagu

Duchess Nell with her first child, Sidney Arthur Robin George Drogo Montagu, Baron Kimbolton. Born in 1929, he would later become the 11th Duke of Manchester.

Brampton Park House, a magnificent eighteenth-century mansion near Kimbolton, and Nell and Mandy's primary residence in Britain. Mandy is at right with two friends. *Courtesy of Nicholas Hodgkinson-Montagu*

Mandy and Nell enjoying a drink in the Brampton Park House bar. *Courtesy of Nicholas Hodgkinson-Montagu*

Nell, Mandy and friends stop for a roadside picnic and booze-up near Stonehenge in 1936. *Courtesy of Nicholas Hodgkinson-Montagu*

Mandy and Nell (second and third from left) at a duck hunt in October 1936. 'The bag at lunch time—final bag 288 ducks.' Mandy's close friend James Wentworth Day is fourth from left and Babe Barnato is fifth from right. *Courtesy of Nicholas Hodgkinson-Montagu*

Mandy (left) with his gamekeeper Frank Cowlard and Nell at rear. *Courtesy of Nicholas Hodgkinson-Montagu*

Mandy hunting with his dog. *Courtesy of Nicholas Hodgkinson-Montagu*

Hunting birds was a key source of income for the Kimbolton estate and a passion of Mandy's (third from right). He was 'Easily one of the twelve best shots in England'. *Courtesy of Nicholas Hodgkinson-Montagu*

Nell's son, Sidney, 'Lord Kim', setting off to board at Hawtrey's Preparatory School aged nine. Nell's brother David is beside him. *Courtesy of Nicholas Hodgkinson-Montagu*

Nell's sitting room in the refurbished Kimbolton Castle, 1938. *Courtesy of Nicholas Hodgkinson-Montagu*

The birth of Nell and Mandy's second son, Angus, in 1938. *Courtesy of Nicholas Hodgkinson-Montagu*

Nell and Mandy in Egypt in 1940. *Courtesy of Nicholas Hodgkinson-Montagu*

Nell and Angus in Ceylon during the war. *Courtesy of Nicholas Hodgkinson-Montagu*

Nell as a Red Cross volunteer in the 1940s. *Courtesy of Nicholas Hodgkinson-Montagu*

Nell and Mandy's farm and homestead, Kapsirowa, in Kenya, which they bought after the war aiming to revive the family fortunes through farming. *Courtesy of Nicholas Hodgkinson-Montagu*

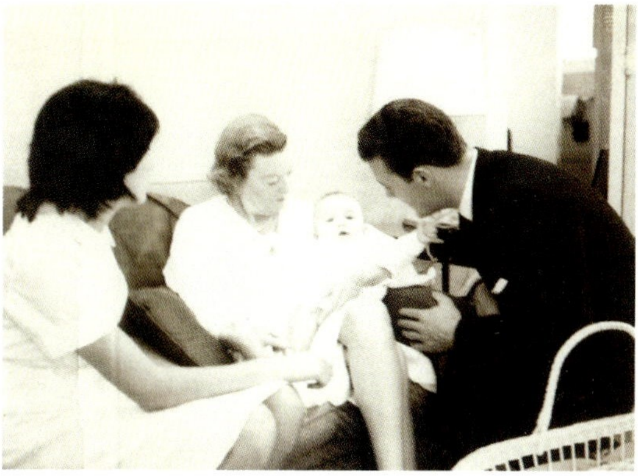

Grandmother Nell with Angus and his baby son, Alexander, now the 13th Duke of Manchester. *Courtesy of Nicholas Hodgkinson-Montagu*

Lord Kim competing in a rally in Kenya, 1963.

Nell, suffering from the melanoma on her eye which would later claim her life, with American friends in the 1960s. *Courtesy of Nicholas Hodgkinson-Montagu*

Nell being shown a koala on her final trip to Australia in 1965.

Sidney as the 11th Duke Manchester in 1981. *Allan Warren*

Angus as the 12th Duke of Manchester outside Kimbolton Castle, 1989. *Allan Warren*

18

A CASTLE REBORN

In the European spring of 1939, a mild-mannered but adventurous American businessman named Chester Woodward decided to 'go vagabonding' around the globe, knowing full well that the world could plunge into war at any time. Having canvassed opinions among colleagues and friends, the sixty-three-year-old set off for Japan, declaring, 'I have come to the conclusion that your guess or my guess as to what will be the outcome is as good as anybody's.'

Money was no object for the pharmacist-turned-banker who had ploughed much of his money into good civic works around his home city of Topeka, Kansas—schools, a library, a hospital and the Scouts. But for all his Americanness, Woodward loved England and its culture. He collected art and rare books, which he housed in a grand, Tudor-style mansion he had designed and built in the centre of the city. Here he reputedly kept a library of six thousand books, including a first edition of Shakespeare's *A Midsummer's Night Dream*, a leaf from the Gutenberg Bible and an inkwell used by Charles Dickens.

In recent years he had turned his own hand to writing, publishing a well-reviewed book about his travels through Europe, Africa, Asia and South America titled *Out of the Blue: Essays on Books, Art and Travel*. This current trip would provide the material for another book, *Lanterns Alight: Journeys to Far Places*, in which he concentrated on his journeys through the Orient. But he also included a chapter about an unplanned visit to Kimbolton Castle, just as Mandy and Nell were trying to recapture the grand life of the ancestral home.

Woodward spent a month in Japan before making his way to China and Hong Kong. He went through Malaysia and across the Bay of Bengal to Ceylon before sailing up the coast of India and on to Aden and Egypt. Next he took a ship across the Mediterranean to land at Marseilles, from where he made an overland trip to Paris and later caught the train that meets the night ferry to England.

He had made arrangements to do a summer literature course at the University of Cambridge but first spent a week in London, catching up with old acquaintances, in particular Lord Mottistone, the former Secretary of State for War, whom he had met on a previous visit to South Africa. He was hesitant at first about making contact but penned a note anyway, not expecting a reply, then was surprised when Lord Mottistone readily agreed and suggested they meet at his club, the famed Athenaeum in Pall Mall. The notion that he could meet and mingle with important men seemed a fantasy for someone like Woodward, who regarded himself in this company as 'a little nobody'.

A few days later, Woodward fell ill with what he believed to be a 'minor ailment', but he called the house doctor at the hotel where he was staying just to make sure. After the consultation, the pair fell into conversation, during which Woodward mentioned that he was a keen antiquarian.

'You should meet my friend Viscount Mandeville,' the doctor told him. 'He has one of finest libraries in Britain at his castle Kimbolton. It's actually quite close to Cambridge.'

Woodward scoffed at the idea of an aristocrat opening his castle to a stranger, but the doctor insisted. 'He's coming to see me tomorrow. I will raise the matter with him,' he promised.

Woodward thought no more about the doctor's promise until he arrived at Cambridge a few days later—when, to his surprise, the Viscount telephoned him as he was settling into his digs, inviting him not only to visit but to stay for lunch. Woodward delightedly accepted, hired a car and driver, and set off the next day for the 45-kilometre trip, marvelling at the lush green countryside as he tried to imagine what he was about to experience—a grand castle occupied by an elderly duke and duchess who would, by definition, be cold and aloof. 'I expect to be politely dismissed in a short space of time,' he noted in his diary.

The sight of Kimbolton Castle did not disappoint, as he recorded:

> When at length we arrived at the grand entrance of the estate, my heart fluttered with excitement. Through the gates the winding road led up a long avenue of fine old trees through which presently I caught a glimpse of the castle in the distance. Before me rose an immense stone building with its battlement parapet etched against the sky. Kimbolton Castle! Built in an immense square around a courtyard, at first sight it seemed the magnitude of Buckingham Palace.

To his delight, a liveried butler appeared when he rang a doorbell installed beside the huge entrance door. He was ushered through a series of rooms with ceiling frescoes and walls covered in gold-framed portraits—'I felt like I was walking through the Palace of Versailles'—to a salon with a bar and a fire glowing in the hearth, where the butler loudly announced his arrival. So far, his expectations had been accurate.

'Hello Woodward, what are you going to have to drink?'

The voice arrived before its owner. Not a pompous, red-faced lord, as he had expected, but a man in his mid-thirties with, dare he say, the look of a Hollywood leading man. Viscount Mandeville, square-jawed, hair swept back and finely dressed in a double-breasted suit, appeared from an adjacent room and strode to the bar, where he waited for his guest to order.

'Scotch and soda, thank you,' Woodward eventually replied.

Drinks in hand, the two men sat in front of the fire, as was required inside a thick-walled building in the midst of an English summer, and chatted about their hobbies—both loved old books, photography and travel—before Lady Mandeville joined them. Woodward was effusive in his praise for Nell.

'I could rave about this young woman for pages, but suffice to say, she is one of the most charming, intelligent and beautiful young women I have ever met.'

Lunch was called and served by sedate butlers. The Viscountess's brother, David Stead, joined them for the meal, where the conversation was dominated by the expectations of war. The recent German invasion of Czechoslovakia, fears for Poland and failing diplomatic efforts at appeasement made conflict seem inevitable, and that meant sacrifice at home.

Even though they had only just finished renovating the castle, arrangements were already underway to turn it into a major hospital in the event of a cross-Channel invasion. In fact, Nell and Mandy had made the offer to the government six months previously, 'just in case steel begins to fly'.

Lady Mandeville was in the throes of planning the details of the transformation. She was matter-of-fact about the likely, if temporary, loss of their home. A building, even a castle, needed a use to be of worth, she insisted, and duty and patriotism were far more important than luxury and pleasure. Besides, her husband would go back to serving in the navy and she would find a wartime role—perhaps as a nurse—to fit in with being a mother of two young boys.

With lunch over, Woodward and the Viscount toured the castle, ending in the great library, which housed an astonishing 16,000 volumes, all in the process of being catalogued for the first time. During the renovation, workers had discovered a secret panel in one of the library walls behind which were three copies of rare medieval prayer books. They had also discovered a fine copy of the 1632 Second Folio edition of collected Shakespeare plays.

The Viscount excused himself and left Woodward to examine the prayer books. 'I sat alone, spellbound, turning the leaves of these treasures before me. They were twelfth, thirteenth and fourteenth century French manuscripts, exquisitely illuminated and done on the finest vellum I have ever beheld. The leaves were as thin as tissue and after 600 years still as white as snow. The superb illuminations were as bright and fresh as in the days they were made.'

Mandy returned and ushered his guest away from the volumes to tour the castle's art gallery. Woodward was gobsmacked. He had been told about the castle's art treasures but they took his breath away:

> It was like a private viewing at a goodly section of the Louvre. There were five fine examples of Van Dyck, several Holbeins, the immense Rubens' *Prometheus Bound*, a Mabuse, a Titian, a Rembrandt and examples of Reynolds and Lely, to mention only a few of them. It grew more difficult every minute to realise that I was in a man's home as his guest, and he was modestly showing me some of the works of the world's greatest artists.

The tiny chapel behind the gallery held another dizzying artwork. Above the wood panelling, mellowed by time, were the eighteenth-century frescoes by Giovanni Pellegrini, as well as the ceiling painting above the grand staircase. They were mesmerising.

'Can you tell me something of the history of Kimbolton Castle?' Woodward asked his host, prompting a quick history lesson from its beginnings as a Norman keep to the Earl of Essex building the first castle, King John's frequent visits and Henry VIII's treatment of Catherine of Aragon.

'Do you see that hill yonder?' Mandy asked, pointing out of a window. 'On top are the ruins of an ancient abbey, and it is said that Catherine had an underground passage made from the castle so that she might go to the abbey secretly to Catholic worship.'

Woodward's tour paused as Lady Mandeville returned carrying the couple's younger son, nine-month-old Angus, before resuming again with a walk through the castle gardens. Here the pear and plum trees, and grape vines, were trained up the high walls so the bricks, warmed by the sun, would help ripen the fruit during the dullest of English summers. This was Nell's domain—more than 5 acres (2 hectares) devoted to flowers, fruit and vegetables, and a lake where white swans glided elegantly.

'I counted twelve gardeners at work and probably there were many more,' Woodward wrote. 'We went into the glass hot-house filled with tropical plants and vines of every description. My host of many interests modestly told me, "As I travelled about the world I have brought home these tropical things and in here they invariably grow as luxuriantly as in their natural habitat."'

As he said his goodbyes to the couple, the Viscount invited him to return for the pheasant season. 'We have wonderful sport and the birds are plentiful,' he offered. Woodward did not record his response, but he glanced at an old trunk that sat against the staircase in the entrance hall. 'Did that, by any chance, belong to Catherine of Aragon?' he asked.

'Yes indeed,' the Viscount said proudly. 'It was her dowry trunk when she came from Spain to marry Henry.'

The American shook his head in wonder at the history he'd just witnessed:

> As I drove away down the avenue of trees, the Mandevilles were out on the portico waving a last goodbye. I turned and looked out over the long stretch of green lawns flanked on either side by heavy forests and it all seemed like a beautiful dream come true. But I knew it was real and I knew that the Mandevilles were real—the kind of people Kipling meant when he wrote of those who could 'walk with kings—nor lose the common touch.'

Further satisfying his desire for grandeur, Woodward recalled: 'My chauffeur told me on the way home that evening that he had lunched with three butlers, a pantry boy, the cook and four housemaids.'

Two months later, as he passed the Statue of Liberty on the way into New York Harbor, Woodward thought of Kimbolton again. War with Germany had just been declared, which meant the Mandevilles' castle dreams had been dashed. The building would now be requisitioned by the Royal Army Medical Corps; it was subsequently used throughout the Second World War to set up field hospitals and store medical supplies. He wondered if their world would ever be the same again.

Unbeknown to Woodward, Nell and the two children had arrived in New York the day before him, aboard the ocean liner *Queen Mary*. The future was hard to predict, but Nell and Mandy had come to the conclusion that war was inevitable and they would have to abandon Kimbolton Castle—at least for the time being. Lord Kim would be taken out of harm's way by placing him in an American school until it was safe. She would stay with a family friend while a school was found, then return with the baby to Britain. What would happen after that was uncertain.

19

LIFE BELOW STAIRS

Sybil Cooke was one of the servants on duty the day Chester Woodward visited Kimbolton Castle. The teenager was the daughter of a railway signalman from Catworth, a village 6 kilometres north, and had left school in 1935 to take up a household position at Brook House, home of a local politician, on the outskirts of Kimbolton.

A year later she jumped at the chance to take a job at the castle when Lord and Lady Mandeville began hiring extra staff as the renovations were being completed. She would stay for three years until war intervened, when she moved to the northern city of Huddersfield to find employment.

It would be seven decades before Sybil returned to Kimbolton and the castle. In 2006, when she was aged in her mid-eighties, she made the nostalgic journey with her family and was given a tour through the rooms she had once tended, recalling the names as she wandered through—the Coote Room, White Hall, King William Gallery and Popham Gallery among them. Her memories and observations of people and events had remained vivid, as she explained in an interview with castle historian Nora Butler, who would collate an article featured in the Kimbolton Local History Society's journal.

The downstairs household and retinue of servants had been much smaller in Sybil's day than in earlier centuries but, even so, Sybil recalled as many as two dozen staff on hand twenty-four hours a day to respond to the wants of the Mandevilles and their guests.

Sybil had been one of four housemaids among a female staff headed by the lady's maid, Mrs Gutteridge, who tended to the Viscountess's personal needs and scurried down from her attic bedroom whenever Lord Kim, at home on holidays, called out cheekily for 'Mrs Guts'. Mrs Walsh was the senior kitchen maid, while Mrs Finnemore was the cook and housekeeper, assisted by a scullery maid. Winnie Dobney needed four maids to run the laundry. The male household included a valet for the Viscount, four butlers, two footmen, an odd-jobs man who was referred to as 'the pageboy', and a large staff of gardeners, headed by Mrs Gutteridge's husband, Josiah. The gamekeepers were headed by Frank Cowlard, who lived in the gatehouse cottage.

The reopening of the castle and return of the Montagu family to live in situ had provided not only welcome employment for the townsfolk of Kimbolton but an important focus for the community, most of whom lived in cottages owned by the

Duke and so were beholden to the family for work and shelter. There was excitement when Nell walked down the high street.

It would be another decade before Mandy and Nell would formally assume the titles of Duke and Duchess of Manchester but, from the moment the couple and Kim, then aged eight, moved back into the castle, the townsfolk referred to them as such. The arrival of baby Angus only added to the relief that a new sense of maturity had settled over the family.

Mandy's warring parents had long abandoned their aristocratic roles and left the responsibilities to the next generation. Six years after her divorce from the 9th Duke was formalised at the end of 1931, Helena remarried, this time to career soldier Arthur Keith-Falconer, a decorated veteran of the Boer and Great wars. More important to her was his title, the 10th Earl of Kintore. Although she had stepped down a peg in the peerage, Helena Zimmerman was still a countess; she returned from the US after the war to live in Keith Hall, a palisaded Norman tower in Aberdeenshire.

She had little interest in the affairs of Kimbolton, other than ensuring that her former husband kept his hands off the fortune designated for their children, who were now scattered across the globe. As a demonstration of just how tangled the British aristocratic lineages could become, her new husband's late mother, Lady Sydney, had been the daughter of George Montagu, the 6th Duke of Manchester.

Meanwhile, the current duke had remained a prominent figure around London and in America, where he had published his entertaining if factually questionable autobiography, *My*

Candid Recollections. He too had remarried. This was a decision that surprised many, considering his predilection for multiple relationships, although his choice, a thirty-four-year-old West End actress named Kathleen Dawes, was less of a surprise.

The rare occasions when the Duke visited Kimbolton—a handful of rooms were maintained specifically for guests at the hunts and weekend parties—usually resulted in mirth and astonishment among the staff. Suddenly they would have to respond to bells ringing in the middle of the night because the Duke had somehow made his way from London, giving himself an alibi to avoid the consequences of a police raid at his club.

On one occasion, a maid knocked on his door the next morning and entered the room: 'Good morning, Your Grace,' she said, as she walked across the darkened room to pull back the heavy drapes and fill the room with sunlight. A voice called out from behind her: 'I shall need more cups.' The maid turned to find the Duke in bed between two women. One of them was the American actress and socialite Tallulah Bankhead.

The actress told a different version in her 1952 book *Tallulah: My Autobiography*: 'I slept fitfully at Kimbolton, the haunted castle in which Henry VIII locked up Catherine of Aragon. I was the house guest of Lord Mandeville, son of the Duke. Mandy six times offered to make me a Lady. My nays were gentle but firm.'

Could both be true, or did Tallulah, known for her hedonistic ways and frequent love affairs, mix up father and son?

The maid's version seems the more likely of the two. Her name was Alma Waite, an older colleague of Sybil Cooke. She was married to the warrener, whose job was to manage rabbits on the estate, and the couple lived with their daughter, Dawn, in a timber-framed cottage built on the escarpment behind the castle. Dawn had once asked her mother how she had responded to the Duke's request: 'In those circumstances you just got on with it,' Alma had replied simply.

Sybil Cooke agreed. She'd had her own experiences with lusty guests, who usually left tips or thank-you gifts such as chocolate for staff who had to clean up after their amorous adventures and be discreet about their behaviour. The exception, as she recalled, was the Russian Prince Galitzine, who had a habit of chasing and bedding married women while at Kimbolton. 'He was mean. He never left tips,' Sybil remarked tersely as she inspected the four-poster bed that still stood in the King William Gallery on the first floor.

Sybil had lived in the staff quarters on the ground floor with her husband, who was a gardener on the estate. She would begin her working day at 6.30 a.m., dressing in a blue-and-white uniform that identified the morning shift, during which she was responsible for lighting the fire in the nursery and helping to serve breakfast trays to the family and any guests. The timetable was strict as the staff, having completed their initial set of tasks, ate breakfast together in the 'Still Room' downstairs at 8.30 a.m. as the 'Duke and Duchess' ate upstairs. 'We ate well because the servants always ate the same food as the family,' she recalled.

Life below stairs had its own hierarchy and sense of formality. The senior butler, Broughton, was at the top of the pecking order, insisting that Sybil, one of the youngest, had to make his bed each morning after breakfast because she was the only one who did it properly—a backhanded compliment that was more about power than admiration.

After lunch downstairs in the housekeeper's room, the maids changed into coffee-coloured uniforms to signify afternoon duties which, for Sybil, included changing the sheets each day on the Viscountess's bed. She was also tasked with spending time with Lord Kim while he played in the walled garden and drove his toy electric car around the pathways, or was taken into the town occasionally to visit Maye's Sweet Shop in the high street.

After hours there was occasionally a time for levity, when the footmen would entertain their colleagues late at night by donning old castle armour; after attending the town's annual fete, some of the staff would take delight in sneaking back into the castle in the early hours of the morning. But over time Sybil, because of her role with the children, struck up a pleasant acquaintance with the Viscountess. Nell was 'very friendly and approachable' and had insisted that Sybil take food from the castle kitchens whenever she took time off to visit her family. The Viscountess's informal manner belied their relative social positions.

By contrast, Sybil's interactions with 'the Duke' were limited. Her strongest memories of him were the days during the hunting season when she had to clean the white carpet in the cocktail bar after Mandy and his friends had stomped inside from a hunt to mix themselves a drink while still wearing their muddy boots. She regarded the task as irksome and the men selfish, but she suffered it in silence.

Sybil fondly remembered the christening of Lord Angus in 1938, the only time she recalled the castle chapel ever being used, at least formally, and she treasured a photograph of herself sitting on the nursery window seat with Angus, aged eight months, on her lap. She carried this photo with her when she returned to the castle—it was her last memory of the castle before war broke out.

20

A HERO

As the threat of war turned from probable to a reality, Lieutenant Commander Alexander Mandeville joined the crew of the HMS *Eagle* in October 1939, his aristocratic title meaning little among a crew of more than eight hundred men and officers.

The *Eagle* had begun life as a dreadnought battleship for the Chilean navy before she was bought at the end of the Great War by the British government and converted into an aircraft carrier. The transformation took seven years before, after a series of trials, what was then the world's largest aircraft carrier entered service sporting the motto *Arduus ad solem*—soaring to the sun—to embrace its role as warfare entered a new phase of aerial combat.

The *Eagle*'s twenty-two aircraft—Swordfish biplane torpedo bombers—were integral to helping seek out and run down

German battleships, like the *Admiral Graf Spee* that had taken refuge near Montevideo in December 1939 after limping, damaged, from the Battle of the River Plate, the war's first naval confrontation.

Logbooks show that the *Eagle* steamed more than 56,000 kilometres in the first six months of the war. Its planes covered more than 1000 square kilometres conducting searches, each armed with a 110-kilogram bomb strapped to its fuselage.

In mid-March 1940, the *Eagle* was helping to escort Australian troopships on their way to Suez when she was diverted to investigate a suspicious vessel. On the morning of 14 March, as the ship approached the Nicobar Islands off Sumatra, aerial patrols were sent off to scour the area. As each plane returned it was secured, and its bomb struck down, boxed and defused in one of the below-deck bomb rooms.

It was just after 2 p.m. and most crew were on their afternoon break when there was a loud explosion from Bomb Room D on the starboard side. Smoke billowed out of the hangar on the quarterdeck and a flash of flames vented through a lift shaft, igniting the wings of a plane.

One of the bombs had exploded while being stowed. It had ripped through the bomb room, where a dozen other devices that were lying ready for storage had somehow remained intact. A board of inquiry later concluded that the explosion probably occurred because the bomb's safety device had been damaged when the plane carrying it landed heavily.

The thirteen men closest to the bomb were blown apart; others, in a nearby mess room, were injured, among them

Mandy. But rather than escaping the area, Mandy began helping the other injured servicemen to safety.

Sub Lieutenant Alexander Mitchell Hodge had been on the main deck when the explosion occurred and immediately rushed downstairs. He joined Mandy, who was wounded and bleeding, and the two men entered the bomb room to search for survivors.

Inside the bomb room, the two men found the bulkheads near the blast area had been bent like paper; the heat and smoke were overwhelming. It was hard to see in the blackness as they searched the room, acutely aware that one or more of the other bombs could explode at any moment. They had to move quickly because the automatic sprinkler system had been activated and seawater was quickly flooding the room to douse the flames and quell the heat.

Most of the men in the room were dead; those who were still alive were helped to safety. One man was pinned beneath two unexploded bombs: Mandy and Hodge managed to move the shells and drag the man free before escaping themselves so the door could be shut.

It took two days to drain the bomb room, and collect the bodies and body parts. These were then put in bags and buried at sea as the ship headed to Singapore for repairs and for the injured men to be hospitalised.

Mandy was back at sea five months later when word came through that he had been awarded an Order of the British Empire 'for outstanding courage and enterprise . . . and for persistent devotion to duty in searching for wounded, although himself injured'.

Hodge would be awarded the Empire Gallantry Medal, his citation concluding: 'Sub-Lieut. Hodge did not go on deck until he had satisfied himself that no one was left alive below. Throughout he showed outstanding courage, enterprise and resource, without any thought for himself. He saved all the lives he could though, for all he knew, further fatal explosions might have occurred at any moment.'

Mandy's honour was noted by the British press—'Gallantry of wounded duke's son'—though was almost lost amid mass coverage of the daily attacks and losses as the Battle of Britain shook the nation. Some of Mandy's friends believe that he should have received the ultimate award for bravery, the Victoria Cross, given that he was wounded when he helped rescue other soldiers and could have been killed at any moment.

Mandy would spend another eighteen months aboard the *Eagle* before he was reassigned to the naval headquarters in Colombo. It was a fortuitous promotion because on 11 August 1942, just six months after he had left the ship, the carrier was sunk, hit by four German submarine torpedoes off the southern tip of Majorca while delivering fighter aircraft to Malta. More than a hundred and thirty sailors lost their lives as the ship sank in less than four minutes.

Back in Kimbolton, the castle's head gamekeeper, Frank Cowlard, had become Mandy and Nell's eyes and ears, watching the castle as it was transformed for military use while still preparing for the winter hunting season. He would write every few months to update them on both. He was normally a man of few words, but added an enthusiastic note of congratulations to his boss at the bottom of his report dated 5 November 1940.

Mandy replied in early December, after returning from six weeks at sea in the Mediterranean, where the *Eagle* had been sent after repairs. His letter focused first on questions about the approaching game season before recounting recent skirmishes with German and Italian vessels.

His response to Frank's congratulations about his award was a succinct, almost embarrassed postscript, which suggests that he felt it was an honour that might have been shared with other shipmates: 'Many thanks for your letter of congratulations. I was very lucky to be the one picked on.'

Kimbolton townsfolk would wonder in years to come why Viscount Mandeville put so much faith in his head gamekeeper. Some took offence at the relationship, uncomfortable when Frank appeared in one of the local pubs, as if he was spying on behalf of his employer. Small-town gossip aside, the reason seemed quite simple: Frank managed the one aspect of the family's estate that provided an income, and would perhaps offer a financial future, when the war was finally over.

Certainly their correspondence, which Frank kept in his personal records, was dominated by discussions about hunting seasons and whether it was too wet or dry or hot or cold. Mandy bemoaned the floods of 1941, which drowned thousands of rabbits ('we'll have to go to Australia to restock'), and celebrated what he was told had been a 'fine show' of pheasants in 1942 that made him homesick. He cursed the impact of petrol rationing which made hunts difficult because 'no-one can drive anywhere' and worried about the physical impact of a US airbase being built on the estate.

Nell was managing the estate house staff via correspondence with a strong-willed woman named Miss Carter. In their letters both Mandy and Nell complained bitterly about how little people were paying for the privilege of hunting for game and questioned why some neighbours, like Major Reuben Farley, should get free access rather than pay their way while they were sitting out the war.

It seemed unfair to them that people were taking advantage of their absence to shoot free of charge and that some men of the area were not made to sign up: 'I am surprised that a fellow like Herbert has not been made to join up. On what excuse do they get off?' Mandy wrote about a neighbour. 'The shooting at Kimbolton is of a quite high enough standard to be bringing in a revenue instead of costing me money, while I am at sea, for the amusement of such people as Major Farley. It seems to me unfair that I should have to pay shooting accounts for people who are sitting at home.'

Neighbours like Farley and Hugh Duberley seemed to think they could roam the estate at will, actions that Mandy considered poaching: 'It infuriates me to think that gentlemen who I take to be my friends should behave as they do while I am abroad. It has to be stopped, even if Captain Duberley is a prospective candidate for Lord Lieutenant of the County and Major Farley is a magistrate.' But Frank couldn't bring himself to confront the men.

When he wasn't writing about the hunting, Mandy pondered the war and its likely conclusion. Never once did he contemplate defeat; quite the opposite. There were moments when he hoped it might finish quickly—'at the rate Hitler is going at present it is possible that he will blow up all of a sudden', he wrote at the end of 1940. Three years later he was again optimistic: 'The Hun seems to be having a pretty poor time of it so it may not be so very long before we are shooting at Kimbolton again.'

But at other times he was downbeat, lamenting in a 1941 missive about how he had left behind at Kimbolton a young dog he'd named Snug—'I am sure he would have made an absolutely perfect retriever for me but he will no doubt be an old gentleman by the time I get home.'

A year later Mandy had grown impatient: 'One never knows what is going to happen next in this war. I only wish that it would hurry up and finish. In the meantime Frank we will just have to go along as economically as possible and when this damned war ends it won't take long to work up a shoot again even if we have to start from where we did before.'

Frank Cowlard was a man whose formal education would have been limited. Despite this, he kept meticulous books. The well-worn pages of his various diaries were scrawled with columns and numbers totting up wages for a dozen or more men; the cost of moving pheasants from rearing fields to the woods and watching over them at night, food for the hounds, and rabbit guides; and payments made to 'beaters', the local boys who earned 6 shillings each to make noises in the river rushes to scare the pheasants and make them fly.

He even included the 7 shillings he spent buying cigarettes for German prisoners of war, who were housed in the estate's stable block and the gatehouse late in the war, and occasionally filled in as beaters during the pheasant season.

The prisoners worked 'up the hill' at Park Farm, where they were given sacks of potatoes to 'fatten them up' and paid with tokens to exchange at local shops for food which they cooked themselves. At first, they were treated with suspicion by wary townspeople but, as time wore on, they were accepted and paid with money, allowed to ride bicycles (because there was no sense in attempting to escape), and even send postcards home to their families.

Nell was unlike most wives of servicemen. Even though the family had been forced out of Kimbolton Castle, there was no reason why she couldn't have settled back into Brampton Park House and sat out the war with her children in relative comfort. She also had the option, after dropping Lord Kim at his American boarding school, to remain in the sanctuary of the United States with her mother-in-law, Helena. It might have even made sense for her to return to Melbourne, where she would have enjoyed the social status of being a future duchess and the support of her sister Erin.

But no. Instead, Nell chose to follow her husband, first to Singapore in late 1939, where the Royal Navy was based until its fall to the Japanese, and then to Colombo, where life in a sheltered compound on the edge of the city was far from safe or luxurious. It was a far cry from the luxury and romance of her first visit to Ceylon fourteen years before, when she and Mandy had met at the Galle Face Hotel swimming pool.

Now she lived among the locals, rather than being separated from the trials of daily life, and endured the incessant sticky heat and damp, the swarms of insects, the snakes and rats that invaded homes, and the constant fear of disease.

That fear was real; Mandy was struck down with diphtheria and hospitalised for months in 1943. The following year he gashed open his leg while coming ashore in a motor launch and the wound quickly became infected. 'Luckily, they gave me a course of treatment with this new drug called penicillin otherwise I am told I would probably have had my leg off,' he wrote to Frank.

Domestic help was no longer a swathe of uniformed servants but a single nurse to watch over Angus. Neither was there a glamorous social life of gambling clubs and restaurants; rather, Nell was one of only a handful of British wives in Colombo and joined the others in volunteering with the Red Cross as a nurse.

Mandy and Nell's one social release was the occasional drive out of Colombo to the other side of the island for a shoot—mainly duck and snipe. The experience was made exciting by close encounters with pythons and crocodiles, usually while in a boat—a vastly different experience from the fox hunts and pheasant shoots of Kimbolton.

While Mandy was at sea aboard the *Eagle*, often for weeks at a time, Nell fielded questions and corresponded with Frank Cowlard. 'I want you to fully understand His wishes and Mine,' she wrote, making it clear that they were a couple who made joint decisions. But she also showed her sense of humour, commenting disparagingly on her skills as a markswoman: 'I have managed to get a few days snipe shooting and seem to be hitting them fairly well. I have come to the conclusion that either I am improving or, more likely, that our snipes don't fly as fast as your pheasants.'

Life changed in April 1942 when the Japanese raided Colombo. The Imperial Japanese Navy had expected to find the British Eastern Fleet at harbour when they raided on Easter Sunday but naval intelligence had warned of the approaching armada of five aircraft carriers, so most of the warships put to sea before the attack began.

The three vessels still in harbour were sunk while a ferocious air battle was fought overhead and thousands of Colombo residents fled in fear to the jungle. Out at sea, Japanese aircraft carriers hunted down two British navy cruisers, the *Dorsetshire* and *Cornwall*, which were sunk with the loss of four hundred and twenty-four men. The Allied forces had taken a beating but their aircraft had prevented a rout. Most of the fleet survived and would be relocated to East Africa.

Mandy downplayed the situation—'we gave the Japs a very unpleasant surprise'—and he was right that it would be the first and last attack on Colombo during the war. But it also showed how vulnerable the Allied forces and the citizens of the city were.

Much of the work for Red Cross volunteers like Nell was at places like HMS *Mayina*, a jungle transit camp 8 kilometres from Colombo, where all naval personnel were sent on arrival to Ceylon. The camp consisted of Cadjan huts, made of interwoven leaves of coconut palms that were not only highly flammable but a natural nest for insects. Disease spread quickly. The men frequently came out in boils and skin rashes; some even suffered deafness caused by insect bites. Their health was not helped by their basic diet: bangers and red lead (sausage and tomatoes) for breakfast, pot-mess (stew) at lunch, and corned dogs and onions for supper.

Letters home would always say that Nell and Angus were well and content. But it was a veneer of happiness, as Mandy once admitted: 'I am glad to say she is very well though she dislikes this part of the world as much as I do,' he told Frank.

Angus was a toddler when he arrived in Colombo with his mother, fast to walk but slow to talk—'he certainly makes weird enough noises which her Ladyship and nurse say "there you are, he's saying so and so"', as Mandy told Frank. But he quickly showed a liking for motor cars, which pleased his father no end.

Years later, Angus would tell his friends fantastical stories about his experiences in Ceylon, the tales so wild that there seemed to be an element of truth in them. 'So improbable they might be true,' one friend, Charles Lousada, told author Marcus Scriven.

According to Angus, at the age of two he was left in the care of Catholic nuns by his mother while she went to Alexandria, where she was a nurse when his father was off fighting the war.

This was partly true, although Mandy told Frank Cowlard that Nell only spent a few months in Alexandria in 1941, where she was indeed photographed in her nurse's uniform before 'returning to join Lord Angus', who had been left in the care of his ayah (nurse), Missy.

In another story, Angus claimed incorrectly that Mandy was governor of Ceylon. 'I didn't like the nuns because they beat you,' he would claim in a newspaper interview many years later. 'They weren't very pleasant people. They used to make these dummies of the baby Jesus and because I had tight blond curls they used to cut them off and use them for the dummies, so most of the time I was bald. I objected to that.'

According to one of his stories, Angus was peering over the walls of the school run by the nuns one day when he saw a group of local Ceylonese boys riding by on elephants carrying logs. Over a period of weeks he managed to befriend the boys who 'helped him escape' the school and he disappeared into the local community, where he was given an elephant and forgot how to speak English. At the end of the war, when his parents returned to collect him, Angus did not even recognise his mother. He was so upset that, when she gave him a tin car, he threw it back at her and ran off. His father, a stern, distant man, got hold of him and gave him a good thrashing.

The unlikely sequel to this story would come years later when Angus returned to Colombo to do his national service, during which time he claimed to have been reunited with his elephant. As he walked into the enclosure, he said, the animal recognised him and lifted the young man onto its back.

Of course, it was all pure fantasy, as family photo albums attest. He was a golden-haired boy who enjoyed the attention of his parents. At the time he was supposedly running away with the elephant boys, Angus was photographed cuddling his mother, who was dressed in her nurse's uniform.

One album page, titled 'Angus September 1940–March 1941', displays a dozen or more photographs of the cherubic toddler with his parents nearby. He is carrying a bucket and spade on the beach, and around a Christmas tree; playing with other young children; and even riding a pony, which his father jokingly insisted was his Australian genes at work. On later pages, he is aged five or six: dressed in a suit, the pageboy at a wartime wedding, and in costume for a child's cowboys-and-Indians party. By his side is Nell, who would describe her son as 'a wild little devil but very sweet and lots of fun'. Far from being isolated, it seems that Angus enjoyed the full attention of his parents in a time and place fraught with worry.

If anyone was impacted by the war it was his older brother, Lord Kim, who was cut off from his parents and who struggled to fit in at American boarding schools. Nell immediately regretted the decision, even as she left him—'I miss him dreadfully,' she wrote to Frank Cowlard as she was on her way to Ceylon. Mandy, by contrast, was optimistic, reporting in his letters that his eldest son was doing well, though he offered no details—other than that Kim had spent one summer at a mountain camp: 'I hear that he is very well and has grown very big.'

Significantly, Kim had kept all the loving letters sent to him by his mother when he was at Hawtreys but kept none of the missives sent during the war. The separation would contribute to a tension between the brothers that was never really healed. Both believed the other was favoured by their mother, whose frequent enthusiastic adoration of her children was open to misinterpretation by these two young men. Both would struggle to find their place in a world of ever-changing fortunes.

21

KAPSIROWA

> SS *African Star*
> At Sea
> 8 May 1946
>
> Dear Frank,
> We are now on our way to East Africa and in fact at the time of writing are just about on the Equator. The purpose of our visit is to buy an estate in Kenya.

The letter from Mandy would have come as a shock to Frank Cowlard. After years of wartime correspondence, in which all the Viscount and Lady Mandeville ever wanted to discuss was the future of Kimbolton and how to resurrect the hunts, the two of them were not even coming home. At least not for now.

The move was, indeed, out of the blue, born of conversations with other scions of landed gentry who were frustrated by the political aspirations of the Attlee government, which came to power in 1945 in a landslide victory promising economic and social recovery. Attlee pledged to nationalise public utilities and industries, establish a national health service, maintain full employment and launch a series of sweeping social reforms—all of which would mean higher taxes.

Africa, and in particular Kenya, suddenly appealed as an established British colony—the East Africa Protectorate—with cheap land and labour that had been stripped from the Kenyan tribes. The so-called 'White Highlands' promised an agricultural boom and social wealth.

The idea that Mandy and Nell could run a profitable farm and visit Kimbolton and London when it suited them seemed like the best of both worlds. After all, Frank and Miss Carter were managing Kimbolton well in their absence.

But the reality would prove far more complicated than the ideal, and the political consequences of the exploitation would eventually explode.

Nell's brother, David, was back at Kimbolton. He was supposed to have told Frank Cowlard about the diversion to Africa but had not done so. It was typical of the man, who some believed lived like a parasite off his sister and brother-in-law, staying rent-free at Park Lodge while they were absent and not even paying for his shooting. It had been a constant source of disquiet in recent years. Nell was furious. Because of their absence, it was left to Frank to fix, but an employee asking for money from a member of his employer's family was not an easy task.

But this latest development was worrying.

After Mandy was demobbed at the end of the war, he and Nell had gone to America to fetch Lord Kim, now a strapping seventeen-year-old with his father's stocky build and his mother's eyes. Their arrival in Portland, Oregon, in mid-1946 had caused some attention—the arrival of an aristocrat always did—and they posed for photographs alongside the ship's captain for the local papers, talking about business plans and 'much shopping'. Mandy looked commanding and Nell somehow glamorous in a beret and overcoat.

The 'shopping' turned out to be a car—a station wagon, of all things—which they then shipped with them to Africa. 'We will motor from Mombasa about 450 miles [725 kilometres] to Nairobi and stay in a hotel there while looking for places we have heard about,' Mandy told Frank in his letter. 'At present there are some lovely properties going at very reasonable rates. But I am convinced that in a very short time a lot of people coming out of the services will come to the same conclusion with the result that the price of land in the colonies will rise tremendously.'

Driving to Nairobi alone seemed full of danger. It was on a mostly dirt road through the middle of the wilderness, surrounded by herds of wildebeest, buffalo, elephants, ostriches, giraffes and lions, all of them seemingly unperturbed by the presence of a motor car. But the Mandevilles were in a hurry, driven by concerns about Attlee's plans to increase taxes on landowners to raise funds for Britain's postwar rebuilding.

'I am afraid that with the present government, things are going to get worse instead of better for the poor unfortunate landlord, and I think it is wise to be prepared in case they clamp down on us even more than they have done already,' Mandy wrote.

But buying another estate when they could hardly afford the upkeep of Kimbolton seemed risky at best. One line in the letter in particular worried Frank—'There is a considerable amount of money to be made in farming.' It echoed the harebrained schemes of Mandy's father, who had not been seen at Kimbolton since his son and daughter-in-law left seven years before.

All the promises of rejuvenating Park Farm and re-establishing the hunts seemed to have been cast aside by this crazy idea. 'I'm not yet sure when we will get back to England,' Mandy wrote, 'but will let you know after we've seen various properties.'

It would be August 1946 before Frank heard again from the Viscount. This time the letter was headed not by the name of a ship but the name of a property—Kapsirowa. They had found and bought a property.

'I have been meaning to write to you but find there is so much to do here that it is hard to find the time to sit down and write letters,' Mandy began. 'Mr Stead has no doubt told you that we are not going to leave here until next June so will not be at home for this shooting season.'

It seemed that, yet again, David Stead had not passed on information and that the couple had bought a farm—high up in the Kenyan highlands, near a town called Hoey's Bridge (later Moi's Bridge). 'As things are, according to the papers, I think we are better off out here,' Mandy wrote.

Out here. To Frank Cowlard it seemed that the next Duke and Duchess of Manchester had been seduced by the romantic notion of Africa and its beauty and freedoms. Indeed they had been. They arrived around the same time as an American writer and adventurer named Negley Farson, who was touring Kenya for his book *Last Chance in Africa*. 'Most of the post-war settlers have been put down on farms around Kitale, one of the most beautiful bits of Kenya,' he would write:

> It lies at from 6,000 to 8,000 feet [1800 to 2400 metres] across the Nzoia River and around the slopes of the towering Mt. Elgon. Here is Kenya, the real thing, such as many people must have pictured in their dreams. To get there from the grassy Molo Downs you pass through mountains deep with belts of creepered, indigenous cedar and podo forests; grey forests, where the towering trees and their dangling parasites seem locked in a static combat, and the black-and-white colobus monkeys swing from branch to branch, travelling in their own world high over your head. There are forests of feathery bamboo on the highest ridges . . . And then you drop down past the saw-mills, to come out on the vast, golden, seemingly empty plain of the Uasin Gishu Plateau . . . It seems that you can go on here for mile after mile without seeing either man or beast.

> Just the dark islands of the wattle plantations standing on this feathery sea. Then you come to the town . . . the road leading in and out of it, flanked for a mile or so by flowering gums; the beautiful Nandi-flames, with their dark green leaves and vermilion blossoms; the long side avenues when you get into town of hyacinth-blue jacaranda trees.

Mandy and Nell had bought 10,000 acres (4050 hectares) from Arthur Cecil Hoey, a British sailor and hunter who had arrived in the area after the Great War and taken up farming, first at Sergoit Rock and then in the Cherang'any Hills, where he established Kapsirowa, about 20 kilometres from Kitale. There he grew maize and sisal, and bred Friesian horses. He later built a bridge to drive his oxen teams over the Nzoia River, hence the name of the town that grew up around the crossing.

Hoey was selling Kapsirowa for health reasons—'defeated by altitude', he reckoned—and moving further down the mountains.

In fact it was the second property Mandy and Nell had considered, first inspecting a hotel and ranch near the town of Nanyuki, 390 kilometres to the south-east and regarded as the gateway to the land around Mount Kenya in the centre of the country. It was beautiful, but they turned it down because they feared there was not enough land to make it viable as a farm.

Kapsirowa was much bigger and established. 'This really is the most amazing place and it is the perfect climate,' Mandy wrote to Frank. 'We have just finished the rainy season which while it lasted was very heavy. Now, however, it is lovely and although we are right on the Equator it is nice and cool. We have to have big fires every evening. As we are at 7,000 feet [2130 metres] it makes you puff and blow climbing up and down the hills but I am getting used to it.'

His enthusiasm continued in a letter a few weeks later. They had views for what seemed like hundreds of kilometres in all directions; there was bush thick with birds and butterflies, and a river from which he could pluck trout at will for breakfast. The one frustration was bushbucks and baboons trampling his abundant grain crops, and leopards and hyenas killing his cattle. At least it was good for keeping his shooting skills sharp. 'Or you can get a small black boy for 5 shillings a month so one does not have to go out and shoot these animals unless you want something to eat,' he added.

There were other benefits, like not being overrun by government regulation: 'I am my own master. If I want roast beef for lunch on Sunday I'll kill a bullock and that is all there is to it.'

By December 1946 they had brought in their first wheat crop—'an absolute bumper'—and work was underway on expanding the existing mudbrick farmhouse. 'We are off to Nairobi tomorrow where we are going to stay for a few days while we wait for Lord Angus to arrive. You can imagine how excited Lady Mandeville is. Even if I hadn't got to go down to have the car overhauled and my hair cut, I don't think I could have kept her up here.'

Both boys were based at Kimbolton temporarily. Angus, aged eight, had been sent back for schooling while his parents settled into Kenya. Kim, now seventeen was about to begin a stint of national service.

Despite their joy about Kenya, Mandy was still insistent on protecting the Kimbolton hunt, which had endured a damp and largely unproductive season in 1946. Costs were going up, particularly clothing and wages for keepers, as well as traps, shotgun cartridges and licences. Even the beaters were demanding more money, which meant that more of the game birds killed needed to be sold rather than given to the hunters.

In desperation Mandy had devised a plan to create shooting syndicates, each consisting of seven 'guns', for which members would pay £150 each for the year. In return, the men would get access to the property for the shooting season, organised shoots, a brace of birds (two), luncheons, and 'beer, when available'—an obvious reference to postwar supply difficulties that would hamper the nation's economic recovery for years.

Mandy was at pains to be seen to be even-handed in his dealings with fellow shooters: 'Should I be at Kimbolton at any time during the season I will take two guns and pay for them at the same rate as other members of the syndicate.'

No one would be allowed to shoot without payment, although there was one exception to his rules. George Whitby—a 'great friend', who with his wife, Gill, had chaperoned Nell on her first visit to Ceylon—was due to spend a few days at Kimbolton. 'Take care of him,' Mandy told Frank Cowlard. 'He was the gentleman who originally introduced Lady Mandeville to me years ago in Ceylon.'

There was, however, one other thing bothering Mandy. In one letter he implored Frank to tell him and Lady Mandeville the truth about what was happening at the castle. 'As I have told you before, anything that you tell me will be treated as strictly confidential,' he wrote. 'Both Lady Mandeville and I rely on your judgment and information to know what to do at Kimbolton.'

Dear Diary,

Well, it's been a busy day. We have been to Kimbolton and it's in a rather sorry state. The Soldiers have trashed it plus have taken all my clothes including my panties. Furniture is trashed everything it's so sad and this is our home. I am still trying to establish where my Mothers sideboard is. I hope it's not lost.

There was another reason for Mandy and Nell's reticence to go home to Kimbolton. The Royal Army Medical Corps was now long gone, but the impact of its five years at the castle was devastating, as Nell's diary entry revealed in her own style.

The Queen's Room on the eastern side of the building was locked and unusable. The ceiling in the Green drawing room, once draped in Italian damask, was propped up by telegraph poles and holes had been hacked into its wood panelling. Some portraits of family ancestors had even been used as dartboards. Soldiers had ransacked the wardrobes where clothes had been left; much of the furniture had disappeared, stacked up in the chapel and the stables.

This was wartime vandalism at its worst, and the time and money invested in the castle's renovation by Mandy and Nell was now virtually worthless. Outside, the lawns were unkempt and the row of grand fir trees at risk; the rides through the woods were overgrown.

The army's only attempt to maintain some order had been the use of some captured German soldiers who had been kept in England after the war. Herbert Gabler was one of them. Conscripted into the German Army on his eighteenth birthday in 1944, Herbert was captured by the advancing Allies in France soon afterwards and taken to a prisoner-of-war camp in Ireland, where he saw out hostilities with several hundred other captured soldiers. But instead of being repatriated, the men were moved to England and ordered to work on farms for the next two years.

Herbert found himself at Kimbolton, where he and three others lived in the gatehouse, and worked in the castle grounds and Park Farm doing general maintenance. As well, he served as a beater on occasions during the pheasant season. He would remember the experience not with bitterness but fondness because, at the behest of Nell and Mandy, he and the other men had been treated with kindness by other staff and the villagers. He also felt some attachment to the beautiful but empty castle, although the only time he saw the family was the day he watched the two boys, Kim and Angus, riding on a tractor when they returned for a few months in 1946.

Nell and Mandy were in a dilemma about their return. It was becoming more and more doubtful they could go back to live in the castle, not just because of the cost but because of the Attlee government's decision to keep wartime restrictions in place. That limited what sort of work could be done on properties like the castle, with men and equipment in short supply. The impact on property prices was devastating, and large country houses across the country would be demolished over the next decade at a rate of almost one per week.

If the thought of facing a derelict castle wasn't reason enough to stay in Kenya, then taxation certainly was. As Mandy predicted, tax rates were on the rise as the government attempted to save a nation on the verge of bankruptcy.

But there would soon be a compelling reason to return to England. Their lives were about to change dramatically.

22

AUSTRALIA'S FIRST DUCHESS

> The Duke of Manchester is desperately ill (maybe near death) at his home in England.

The sentence was squeezed into the 'Cholly Knickerbocker' social column published by the *New York Journal-American* on 4 February 1947, as if it was an important, last-minute news item. There were no other details, but clearly the Duke's name still meant something in a city that had been equally amused and appalled by his excesses and antics over four decades.

But not so thousands of kilometres away in the English town of Seaford beneath the spectacular chalk cliffs of the Sussex coast, where 'Little Kim' had retreated during the war. Here he was almost anonymous, just an old, ruddy-faced man as he puffed along the street on the rare occasions that he ventured outside. Ill health had dogged him throughout his life, even preventing him from enlisting in the Great War, and he was now in rapid physical decline. The Duke had suffered two heart attacks in recent years, but this latest illness was due to an advanced stage of diabetes. He was near death. It was just a matter of time.

Mandy was already on his way from Kenya by the time the newspaper column item appeared, prompted by a telegram from his stepmother, Kathleen Dawes, who was still by the Duke's side. He had not seen his father since 1939 and wanted to make it to England in time to see him before he died.

But he was too late. On 9 February 1947, a few weeks before his seventieth birthday, the Duke drifted into a coma and passed away. Mandy's flight from South Africa arrived the following day.

There was no time to settle and little to mourn. Just two days later William Angus Drogo Montagu, the 9th Duke of Manchester, was interred next to the ancestors he had often regretted publicly in the family vault at St Andrew's Church in Kimbolton.

Most of the Kimbolton townsfolk turned out along the streets to pay their respects as the hearse passed by, but it was a muted response for a man who had so often disavowed his own heritage and, more importantly to them, ignored responsibilities that went with the title. His gallivanting ways meant he had no time or interest in maintaining the estate and its farms, which might have earned him a level of community respect.

Although he had largely disappeared from public view in recent years, the Duke had popped up twice in the media in recent months on both sides of the Atlantic. The stories fed nicely into the round of obituaries that followed the Duke's death, which confirmed his notoriety and his panache. He may have been 'England's most notorious spendthrift' but he was also a 'titled cosmopolite' who was prone to delightful exaggeration and fireside tales that played to the American vision of the British aristocracy as wild eccentrics.

First, there was a court case in London, in which he was accused of defrauding an art collector of two supposedly expensive paintings—a purported Veronese and another said to have been painted by Rembrandt. He was accused of taking possession of the paintings and then disappearing but the case was eventually dismissed. For once, there was 'not a shred of evidence' against him. However, applications to the judge made it clear that he was not well enough to attend the court hearing.

Another news item was a New York story about a colourful anti-mafia police detective and celebrity bodyguard named Jack Cannon, who always carried an ivory-handled Colt .38 and wore a white carnation in his buttonhole. The Duke was mentioned in passing as having given him both the gun, in gratitude, and the nickname 'Dasher Jack', in reference to his sartorial elegance—even in shootouts he wore the carnation as a lucky charm. Cannon would often greet people by drawing the weapon menacingly, Clint Eastwood–style, and growling, 'Let me show you something nice.'

There was no end to the stories: from American business scions promising him millions to marry their daughters, to duels with German princes and lucky nights at Monte Carlo roulette tables. The Duke always seemed impervious to embarrassment, once hiding in the ladies dressing room at a society ball after his skin-tight trousers tore open. In his bid to escape attention, he went through the wrong door and found himself, trouser-less, in the middle of the ballroom.

An Indiana Baptist Church had once even seen fit to quote the Duke while advertising its Sunday school. Its newspaper advert read: 'The Duke of Manchester once said, "I believe that the energy expended by a society woman in one year is enough to lift Buckingham Palace nine inches off the ground and hold it there for 43 seconds." A good deal of energy is expended in our Sunday school to lift the morale of our children.'

The US coverage was typified by New York's *Daily News*, which heralded 'Rakehell Duke dies; Don Juan knew Palace, hockshop and jail' before detailing a life of exciting excess and including a rather sad quote: 'My trouble is that I have been a mug. I am not quite sure that I am glad I was born a duke.'

English papers took a more sombre tone about a man whose life was about seeking a fortune that was always just beyond his reach—at various times as a prospector, a gambler and even a filmmaker—while wasting his own legacy. Some acknowledged the Duke's early achievements as a Privy Councillor, and Captain of the Yeomen of the Guard under the prime ministership of Sir Henry Campbell-Bannerman, but it was impossible to ignore his own words about being a failure.

The Times was a little more considered about his potential and understated about his flaws: 'He had personality and a certain ability, and his firm mouth and jaw betokened qualities which might have brought him distinction had he not also been curiously lacking in judgment. Though he had at times a great deal of money, he was frequently in financial difficulties.'

It would take a few months to finalise, but the Duke's will laid bare the reality of his desperate financial situation, with an estate of just £257. He had bequeathed all his guns to his oldest son, but even this was not a simple process. Many had been taken by the Irish Government from Kylemore during the rebellion of 1916, and others had been confiscated by the government of Northern Ireland from Tandragee Castle during the Black and Tan rebellion of 1921.

In the end, the Duke had been truthful—he had nothing left.

Mandy was the only one of the Duke's four children to attend the quiet service after his death. Their mother, Helena, now wife of the Earl of Kintore, did not make the journey from the couple's home in Scotland.

Edward was in Mexico, about to marry his third wife. He was back in the news: first being jailed for a month in Canada after passing a worthless CA$250 cheque while negotiating the purchase of a yacht—'a stupid mistake'—and then being involved in a messy divorce from his second wife, Dorothy Peters, in America.

Alice, who had spent the war years in America, would soon follow her brother's marital trek to Mexico.

At the time of the Duke's death, Louise was in India. Her marriage to Martin Hofer had not lasted through the war years;

Hofer decided to spend them in America, while Louise had remained in Britain and became a poster child for the aristocratic war effort. In November 1941 she had been interviewed by the *Evening Standard* as part of a newspaper feature on 'disguised royalty doing the heavy work', about titled women working in factories for the war effort:

> Lady Louise is one of the best skilled workers in the shop. For four pounds sixteen shillings a week, she finishes patterns for the manufacture of bullets. She is billeted with other women employees and, like them, works eleven hours a day, six days a week, with two weeks on day shift and two weeks at night. 'I don't see why we should have any flag-waving or do any shouting because we happen to have titles in front of our names. I like machinery and decided this is the best place for me.'

In the meantime, Hofer was running up gambling debts and eventually ran afoul of the New York police. Details of his dubious personal and business life began to leak out as Maury Paul—'Cholly Knickerbocker'—took an interest. He was revealed as having had two previous marriages, one of them to a New York socialite. He was prone to haunt the casinos of Deauville in France where, in the summer of 1935, he was heard 'plotting a third marriage to the Duke of Manchester's younger daughter, Lady Louise'.

Louise and Hofer divorced in 1944, and Louise married Major John Shairp in August 1945, when the war was coming to an end. Major Shairp had remained in the army after the war and in 1947 was posted to British India, where officials were grappling with how and when to divide the country into two dominions—India and Pakistan. Louise, now aged thirty-nine, went with him, and the couple hoped to start a family.

Nell and the boys were waiting in Nairobi when Mandy arrived back after two months in England trying to sort out his father's affairs. 'He looked very tired,' she wrote to Frank Cowlard. 'What a dreadful time his Grace has had trying to fix everything up but I am sure he will be happier now the boys and I have met him at the plane. But you wouldn't know he was the same person after even one week in this wonderful climate.'

Mandy was more confused than ever about their future. Kimbolton Castle was a mess, its future uncertain even if they had the money to fix it—again. Perhaps they could rent the castle and make Park Lodge their base when visiting England. But their commitment to England was now sorely tested. The weather had been appalling during his visit; wind and snow and floods made things look far worse than they perhaps might have been. And he had little interest in a political career, or even taking his seat in the House of Lords.

By contrast, they had begun building their new home on the hillside at Kapsirowa using bricks made on the property. Rather than rescuing something old that belonged to a bygone era, he and Nell felt like they were creating something new, unencumbered by the past.

The design—a bungalow built of local stone and roofed with a mix of tiles, thatch and tin—would become known as 'White Highlands architecture'. At either end of the structure there was a room with a bay window; one was the main bedroom and the other a sitting room designed to take full advantage of the majestic view to the Cherang'any Hills in the distance. The morning sun washed through the building, 'a daily and palpable sense of the African Frontier', as Mandy told Frank.

'We can see for miles in every direction over the jungles which are as thick as anything and very hard to walk through right down to the plains and [west] across to Mount Elgon 100 miles [160 kilometres] away,' he wrote. 'The birds and butterflies have to be seen to be believed. There is a big river running through the place. I get as many trout as I want.'

Mandy and Nell had fallen in love with the freedom of Africa as much as its beauty. Not only were they not constrained by government, but labour was cheap and taxes were low. Back in England, inheritance tax rates had jumped from 60 to 80 per cent. More assets would have to be sold, including 500 acres (200 hectares) of crop and grazing land around Tandragee and twenty of their houses.

But there was some bright news. Kimbolton's Red Poll cattle had won several awards at the local county show. Some of the herd were about to be shipped to Kenya. Mandy had not given up entirely on reversing the family fortunes, although he was becomingly increasingly excited about his prospects in Kenya and downhearted at political developments in England.

'It is good news to hear that the season has hopes of being

fairly good,' he wrote to Frank. 'I hear that all the guns have paid their subscriptions to the syndicate and this means that any game that is sold will go as profit to the estate. When listening to the news at night, it makes one wonder what is ever going to become of England and whether there is any chance of getting back to the mode of living that we used to have before the war.'

'First Australian Duchess', the headlines proclaimed, and the story made spectacular reading in the households of postwar Australia. The *Australian Women's Weekly*, which boasted a circulation of more than seven hundred thousand, led the media charge to celebrate Nell's ascension as Duchess of Manchester. There had been numerous examples of Australian women marrying an assortment of British and European aristocrats, but never a duke.

It had been two decades since the initial excitement about her marriage. This latest development was the realising of that potential and there was a new generation of readers excited by the aura of the British aristocracy. Little did they know about the challenges of a titled life.

The magazine feature was full of glowing prose about 'our beautiful former Melbourne socialite', accompanied by photographs of the couple arriving in America before the war, Mandy shooting on the estate and a handsome recent portrait of Nell.

'Slim, with red-gold hair and a lovely smile, Australia's Duchess of Manchester will be the mistress of three of Britain's finest old castles,' the piece began, before listing their properties—in the

UK and Africa, and forests in Canada—and indicating how they planned to divide their time between Kimbolton Castle and their wheat-and-cattle estate in Kenya. Mandy was described as a handsome rugger-playing sportsman and war hero, and Nell had 'a vivacious personality' that was 'well known to the gay Mayfair set and London cafe society of the early thirties'. The Ceylon love story was revisited but there was no mention of their troubled family history or money worries.

The rest of the Australian media would roughly follow suit with stories that concentrated on the importance of the 'ancient title'. There was mention that the Kimbolton estate, once 70,000 acres (28,300 hectares), had now dwindled to barely 4000 acres (1620 hectares) thanks largely to a 'blight of taxation' but it was offset by stories of the family's art collection hanging on the walls of Kimbolton that had remained intact, including works by Van Dyck, Titian, Holbein, Reynolds, Rubens and Lely.

Some questioned why Nell had only been to Australia twice as a viscountess, but the truth was there was little reason to travel back. Her life had changed dramatically several times since she had left. At first she had been thrown into the social whirlpool of aristocratic England and village life as a viscountess; then there was motherhood, a war that effectively lasted six years, and now a new life in the wilds of Africa.

Both parents were now long dead and she had kept in touch with her sisters, and even hosted them at Kimbolton before the war. Both were now married with families, Erin to John Grimwade and Penelope to the prominent surgeon John Somerset.

Brother, David, was closer to hand, still at Kimbolton and now causing tongues to wag by becoming involved with an American woman, Mrs Jeannette Sclater-Booth, the estranged wife of the 4th Baron Basing. David and Jeannette had moved in together into one of the estate houses, Kimbrook House. 'I presume they are still "living in sin" or do you think Mr Stead is going to make an honest woman of her?' Nell pondered in a letter to Frank Cowlard.

Now there was a trip on the horizon. 'My wife and I are looking forward to going out to Australia again as soon as possible,' Mandy told the *Australian Women's Weekly* reporter who had found him at Kimbolton in the days after his father's funeral. 'We want to revisit our old friends and particularly my wife's sisters in Melbourne.'

They would make it back to Nell's homeland, as promised. In the meantime there would be more tragic news for the family.

Lady Louise was dead.

In the aftermath of the Partition of India in 1947, conflict erupted over the disputed Kashmir region, trapping Louise and her husband, Major John Shairp, in the coastal city of Karachi. On the night of 30 August 1948, Indian aircraft dropped bombs on a residential area of the city. John survived, but Louise was killed.

23

A CASTLE CRUMBLES

In 1531, as King Henry VIII was declaring himself the head of the Church of England, a humble schoolroom was being opened in an outbuilding on the grounds of St Andrew's Church behind the castle at Kimbolton, where Catherine of Aragon would soon come to live and die.

More than four hundred years later, the school had moved premises but still thrived. By the early twentieth century, the school was in a building on the western edge of the town with a sports-mad headmaster named William Ingram who, over the next three decades, would inculcate the importance of physical health in the development of students.

As a sign of his belief, Ingram convinced his friend Harold Abrahams to make Kimbolton the base for some of his training for the 1924 Olympic Games, where Abrahams would win the 100 metres sprint, immortalised in the film *Chariots of Fire.*

Abrahams and Ingram even had a race down Tilbrook Road one day, Abrahams winning a close race even though Ingram was driving a high-powered car.

Eventually Ingram would retire and in the first few months of 1947, the board of Kimbolton Grammar School, as it now was, began to interview applicants for the headmastership, conscious that the school faced new challenges as England emerged from the war.

There were two hundred and ten applicants for the now prestigious job. Among them was Cyril Lewis, a senior history master at The Leys School in Cambridge, who happened to visit Kimbolton on the day of the funeral for the 9th Duke of Manchester. He noted that the castle had been largely abandoned since the war had ended and the Royal Army Medical Corps moved out. Far from the pride of the community, its lawns were overgrown and gardens withered. Heavens knew what it was like inside.

Lewis would eventually win the job, but he faced his own set of problems when he took over. New classrooms were desperately needed and the school kitchens, built seventy years before, were now so inadequate that meals had to be prepared offsite and trolleyed in three times a day on what became known as the ghost train. The married staff were living in a converted ablution block of the nearby wartime airfield and the boarding houses needed renovation. The boys had to take turns using Headmaster Ingram's old bathroom which, for some reason, had two baths. He had left them a note: 'Boys, please clean the bath after use.' Extra premises needed to be found or money raised to repair and improve the existing buildings.

Lewis struggled through his first year as principal and the problems were only worsening as the school year drew to a close on the cusp of summer 1948. The day after the last students left, he was invited to visit the new Duke and Duchess, who had returned from Kenya and were staying at Park Farm. Other than the fleeting visit to attend his father's funeral, it was the first time Mandy had been back to Kimbolton since 1939.

The purpose of this meeting for Lewis was not only to formally introduce himself but to explore any properties on the estate that might be suitable to help the school cope with its growing demands. Lewis found the couple very relaxed and open about the dilemma they personally faced. They did not want to abandon Kimbolton, but for tax reasons they couldn't maintain a residence in England. Their official residence would have to be in Kenya, but they planned to visit during the English summers for several months at a time. Lewis also sensed that the problems of maintaining Kimbolton were a hurdle, and that the ancestral home of the Montagu family had become a millstone rather than a jewel.

As Lewis prepared to leave, the Duke had an idea. Perhaps the sprawling Park Lodge would be suitable as a school, he ventured. Not only was it large inside but it came with substantial grounds that would be suitable for student activities. Lewis stayed a while longer as he viewed the house with fresh eyes.

Afterwards, Lewis met Canon Powys Maurice in the high street, where they had a discussion. The lodge wasn't suitable,

Lewis told Powys Maurice, who chaired the school governors committee. 'I just don't see how it can be adapted for school use.'

'Have you thought about that?' Powys Maurice asked, pointing back at the castle.

Lewis was taken aback. He hadn't even considered the castle, especially having seen its deterioration during his previous visit. 'Besides,' he added, 'buildings like the castle lack heat, light and modern plumbing.'

'Well, the castle has all three,' the clergyman replied. 'The work was completed just before the war.'

That night Lewis called the Duke, who agreed to arrange a tour of the castle. Two days later he had what he thought was a solution to the school's long-term future. Although tired and in need of a paint job, the main rooms had largely survived the war years. There were plumbing issues, but they were not insurmountable. The castle, if available, would make a perfect school—and a prestigious one.

A few weeks later, Lewis addressed the school governors at a meeting. He would write later that he was so worried about his audacious castle plan that he had not written a report or told anyone beside his closest advisors. 'I was afraid that it might sound such an absurd plan that the Governors would be unwilling even to consider it before I had a chance to put my arguments fully. I therefore broke it to them at the meeting. I have never seen a body of men so stunned.'

By the end of the meeting, Lewis had won over the board, which agreed to formalise a plan to put forward to the Ministry of Education. If it was approved, they would then take it to the Duke and the trustees of the Manchester estate.

> 6 October 1948
> Dear Diary, Manch [the late 9th Duke] went through the majority of the money . . . I don't want to sell but Mandy says its [sic] likely going to happen. Perhaps we could start off with leasing the castle. Kimbolton will likely be bought by some company in London. I am very distressed.

Negotiations about the school had stalled because Mandy and Nell still had doubts; they were undecided about their future and reluctant to part with Kimbolton Castle, as Nell's diary made clear. Kenya may have been calling but giving up the castle and the family's history, however fraught, was difficult to accept.

Instead, Mandy proposed a long-term lease and asked how much rent the school was prepared to pay. The school governors offered £105 per annum on a ninety-nine-year lease. The Duke and his trustees countered at £500 per annum over twenty-one years, and there the matter stayed for the next year, a stand-off in which the school board hoped to wear down Mandy's resistance, and Mandy hoped Kenya and a bumper hunting season or two might right the sinking ship.

Behind his hope Mandy was keenly aware of the reality facing dozens of his aristocratic contemporaries. The newspapers he read frequently detailed the travails of blue bloods with no cash and no future. 'Death duties have sown ruin among the aristocracy and brought some of the proudest lineages in Britain to bankruptcy,' groaned the *Daily Telegraph*, before going on to detail the trail of woe.

The Duke of Sutherland, the Earl of Harewood, the Earl of Euston, the Earl of Crawford and Lord Plympton had all recently sold mansions to keep a tiny portion of their estates. When his estate was sold off, the Marquess of Winchester decided that all he had left to earn a living with was his name, which he offered for a fee to London companies to put him on their board as a 'guinea pig director'. Fourteen companies took up his offer.

Unable to sell his one-hundred-room home, Packington Hall, because of a legal quirk that meant the title had to go with the property, the Earl of Aylesford cut down his forest to pay his tax bill. Packington Hall, filled with ancestral paintings and tapestries, simply rotted away. The Earl of Crawford moved out of his home, Haigh Hall, and into rooms above the manor house office, while the Countess of Loudon handed over her estate to creditors, who then granted her just three guineas a week to live off.

Some had taken menial jobs to survive. Lord Langford was a farm labourer and odd-jobs man, and the Earl of Mayo was a film extra and a bricklayer. Others simply declared bankruptcy, including Lord Victor Paget, Lord de Clifford, the Earl of Kinnoull, Baron Lisle and Baroness Kinross.

Mandy's frustrations with the Attlee government and its taxation policies were clear in his letters to Frank Cowlard:

> When we listen to the news at night it makes one wonder what is ever going to become of England. In fact, it seems that the six years we spent at war to get rid of dictatorships has had the reverse result and there are more in the world today (including England).

Taxation wasn't the only regulatory complication that Mandy and Nell faced. The government had introduced the Town and Country Planning Act in 1947, intended to help coordinate the postwar rebuilding of Britain. Now landowners did not have the absolute right to develop their land without planning consent, and authorities were also given the power to compulsorily acquire land and buildings if it was deemed to be in the public interest. On the face of it, Kimbolton School, as a publicly funded institution, appeared to have the right to solve its problems by compulsorily acquiring the empty castle.

It was Cyril Lewis who spotted the opportunity. The county council agreed with his interpretation and in February 1949 the school governors wrote to the Duke's solicitors: 'The property is rapidly deteriorating and accommodation for tuition and boarders is urgently required. Unless his Grace is prepared to give the Governors the opportunity of buying the property or acquiring a long lease we will be compelled to approach the County Council in the interests of the school.'

The Manchester estate trustees were given a month to consider their position but, inexplicably, made no reply and forced the hand of the school, which took the issue to the county council and won. Kimbolton Castle, home to the Manchester family for more than three hundred years, would be compulsorily acquired.

It would be June 1950 before a valuation was finalised. The castle and 50 acres (20 hectares) of land around it was worth just £12,500, and its purchase would be financed by a thirty-year government loan for the school. It was devastating news for Mandy and Nell—an unbelievably low valuation given the £14,000 they had spent renovating the building just a decade before. But it reflected Britain's flattened postwar economy, and took into account the cost of repairs and renovations to transform a castle into a school.

'Almost as we go to press the news has arrived that the Castle is ours,' announced the Kimbolton School magazine in July 1950. Emergency work began immediately, though the sale would not be formalised until the middle of the following year, when the school was able to report that the castle's transformation was well underway:

> The Castle again resounds to the hammering and sawing of workmen's tools. The caretaker's flat is almost finished, and work has begun on the dormitories we hope to use next term. We plan to have fifty senior boarders in the Castle, with Mr. Gibbard living in ducal splendour as their Housemaster. The main floor should also be almost complete by September, but we have not yet started on the dining hall, kitchen and changing-rooms that we hope to install in the stable block before another school year is over.

> The grounds at the Castle are already much improved. The west lawn is being slowly brought back to its pre-war condition, and the courtyard is a joy to behold. The avenue to the Bedford Road is being levelled and will be re-sown with grass; it is to be known by its old name 'The Mall' . . . The tennis courts and field on the south are being ploughed and will be levelled and sown in due course; we hope to have here our 1st XI cricket field. The swimming-bath will be built on the north side—when we can obtain a licence!
>
> Kimbolton Castle is part of the heritage of England, and the Governors have always intended that it should so far as possible become an asset to the community as well as to the School.

The castle had gone, but the Montagu family would keep a financial interest in Kimbolton. There were still almost 3500 acres (1420 hectares) of farmland around the town and another 600 acres (240 hectares) of woodland. The estate also owned six tenanted farms and eighteen cottages. Kenya might be Mandy and Nell's principal address, but Kimbolton remained the Duke's ancestral home.

24

FIRE SALE

An estimated four hundred grand homes were demolished across England in the decade between 1945 and 1955 as struggling landowners quit their estates to meet unpaid taxes or because they couldn't afford the upkeep. Hundreds of others were sold for reuse, their contents scattered like confetti across the world at gloomy onsite auctions.

But the Kimbolton Castle clearance sale in July 1949 was like few others. It would take four days to sell more than twelve hundred lots, from the paintings and books to furniture, silverware, glass, carpets, china and linen. Even the 'motor mower' used to cut the lawn had to go. It was a bizarre combination of fine auction-room finesse and a car boot sale.

Grandly written newspaper adverts had begun appearing in June: 'By direction of His Grace, the Duke of Manchester OBE . . . Kimbolton Castle important sale of English period furniture.'

There were sets of Chippendale chairs, Georgian serpentine chests and lattice bookcases, Queen Anne bureaux, a William and Mary gilt suite, Hepplewhite four-poster beds, the state bed canopy of King William III, and, of course Catherine of Aragon's dowry chest.

Some of the most prestigious treasures were already gone. Auction house Christie's had visited in June, taking silverware given to the first Duke of Manchester by William of Orange, including two silver candlesticks that had once sat on the altar in the chapel, each over a metre long and weighing more than 12 kilograms. They sold at auction for £4513.

In early July the adverts changed, focusing on the famed artworks that framed the walls. 'Comprising paintings by or attributed to Van Dyck, Mytens, Veronese, Claude, Bassano, Correggio, Tintoretto, Canaletto, Hudson, Zoffany, Ramsay, Jordaens, Lely, Kneller and others,' it read. In this moment of reckoning there was some doubt about family legends. Were the attributions authentic, or the product of assumptions and fables? After all, this was the first time they had ever been catalogued and assessed.

Such was the optimism about the sale that on the first day, 18 July, a bus service had been laid on to ferry buyers coming from London to and from the railway station at the nearby town of Bedford. The visitors mingled with Kimbolton locals, some hoping to buy a cheap souvenir but most simply intrigued by the passing parade and fading world of privilege. The reality hung heavy as the rooms began to fill with potential buyers making their choices.

At 11 a.m., the large crowd in the White Hall settled as the auctioneer rapped his gavel to open proceedings. Nell sat next to him, scribbling notes in pencil in the margins of her catalogue. She would sit in the same seat each day, recording the sale price for every item that went under the hammer.

The paintings would be the first two hundred and forty-seven lots, beginning with a portrait of Oliver Cromwell seated in a chair with the inscription *Sigillum Reipub Angliae* (Seal of the Republic of England) and attributed to nineteenth-century British painter Charles Lucy.

'What am I bid for this Cromwell?' called Mr Coleridge, who would be the first of six auctioneers to conduct parts of the sale. Here was the first test of authenticity. Lucy had indeed painted portraits of Cromwell, who was born in Huntingdon, and this version, painted in 1857, had been exhibited at the Royal Academy. Yet there seemed little interest and the painting was snapped up by the governors of Kimbolton School for just £15. It was a portent of things to come.

The sixth lot of the day was another test, billed in the catalogue as *Prometheus Bound*, said to have been painted around 1612 by the Flemish Baroque artist Peter Paul Rubens in collaboration with Rubens' compatriot Frans Snyders.

This time there was no doubt that the giant canvas—2.7 metres long and 2.4 metres wide—was genuine. It was referred to in a 1687 inventory of the castle's artworks and had hung above the fireplace in the great dining room at Kimbolton for almost three hundred years. The price would reach more than 3000 guineas before the hammer fell. It was bought by a Mr Bernard, who quickly sold it to the National Gallery for a tidy profit. A year later the gallery on-sold the painting to the Philadelphia Museum of Art. Although the price was not disclosed, it was said to be £30,000—ten times the auction price.

But the Rubens sale did not spark a frenzy of bidding. The next painting in the catalogue was the portrait of Elizabeth, 4th Duchess of Manchester, and her son, George, as Diana and Cupid, attributed to the great English portraitist Joshua Reynolds. It went for just £100.

The morning trickled on but the bidding remained subdued even when a number of works attributed to Anthony van Dyck, the Flemish Baroque artist who settled in London in 1632 under the patronage of Charles I, came up for sale. Van Dyck was in constant demand among the aristocracy, so the half-dozen or so paintings of seventeenth-century noble families, including the countesses of Rutland and Sutherland, seemed more than plausible. Yet the paintings only fetched between £21 and £50 each and another, titled *Lord Kimbolton, Gentleman of the Parliament Force of Charles I*, made £80.

The afternoon continued in the same vein. Portraits of Sir Henry Montagu, the 1st Earl of Manchester, by Dutchman Daniel Mytens went for £20, and another of his son, the 2nd Earl, by Sir Peter Lely for £26. Names like Godfrey Kneller, Louis Desanges, Willem Wissing, James Swinton and Jean-Baptiste-Camille Corot failed to ignite the room, their paintings rarely reaching more than £30. It seemed that buyers were not so much concerned about authenticity as by the sheer number of works. As it was a fire sale, there were no reserve prices to protect their value.

Everything was a bargain, including works attributed to the great Venetians. Giovanni Canaletto was named as the painter of a sprawling work titled *The Grand Canal Venice showing the state barge with innumerable gondolas, figures and buildings,* which attracted a £150 bid. Tiziano Titian fared even worse when £105 was paid for a portrait of the 1st Grand Duke of Tuscany.

A giant canvas attributed to Paolo Veronese was knocked down to £30, as was a Jacopo Tintoretto work. It took a little longer to settle on £200 for a grand Venetian scene showing the arrival in 1707 of Charles, the 4th Earl of Manchester and British ambassador, perhaps because it had been exhibited at the Art Treasures Exhibition in 1857 and was painted by another Venetian, Luca Carlevarijs.

Many pieces went for a few pounds each, meaning dozens of local people unexpectedly were able to take home a piece of their local history. One man was photographed trying to strap down a full-length portrait of the controversial sixteenth-century politician Sir Henry Sidney to the top of his Vauxhall sedan. He'd bought the painting, by Flemish artist Paul van Somer, a leading painter in the court of James I, for just £30.

The Kimbolton School board of governors, still negotiating purchase of the castle, bought several dozen portraits, mostly of Manchester family members but also monarchs like Queen Anne and William of Orange, who had visited Kimbolton in 1695. They acquired works by Kneller, Lely, Lorenzo Barlolini, Wissing and Mary Beale, one of England's first female portraitists. What better way to decorate the walls than with a painted reminder of the building's history?

Among the crowd on the second morning was Frank John Bly, an antiques dealer from the town of Tring, an hour or so south of Kimbolton. He had spied what he regarded as an important piece of English furniture: an ornate cabinet designed in 1771 for Elizabeth, wife of the 4th Duke of Manchester, by the neoclassical architect and furniture designer Robert Adam.

The oak-and-mahogany cabinet was built not for function but as a way of displaying eleven Florentine *pietra dura*, depicting romantic seascape and mountainous pastoral scenes, made by famed Italian craftsman Baccio Cappelli. They had been bought in the first years of the eighteenth century by Dodington Greville, wife of Charles Montagu, the 4th Earl and 1st Duke of Manchester, during a Grand Tour of Europe.

The panels had been put away on their return to Kimbolton, the Duchess seemingly unsure of how to show off her purchases, and then lost for several generations until discovered in 1771 by Elizabeth, who then hired Adam to solve the puzzle. Adam's ingenious design arranged the marble and stone panels as false drawer and cupboard fronts. The only real doors were at either end, and inside was empty space. Its construction was also sublime—the satinwood and rosewood marquetry was by Ince and Mayhew, one of the most prominent cabinet-making firms of the day, and the gilt-bronze mounts were by Birmingham metal manufacturers Boulton and Fothergill.

The finished cabinet, almost 2 metres tall and 1.8 metres wide, stood in the bedroom of successive duchesses for almost two centuries, until 1939 when it was carried down into the castle cellars and stored, with dozens of pieces of furniture, when the castle was taken over by the Royal Army Medical Corps. It was still there, half-hidden in the shadows, when Frank Bly visited a few days before the auction a decade later to view the lots, his seven-year-old son, John, in tow.

'I know what that is,' he told young John triumphantly as he threw back the cover to reveal the cabinet, which was incorrectly described in the catalogue as 'an antique Italian satinwood and rosewood marqueterie cabinet'. It seemed that two well-known London auction houses—Knight, Frank & Rutley, as well as Christie's—had both failed to recognise what would come to be regarded as one of the most significant pieces of furniture in English history, highlighted in the authoritative reference book *The Dictionary of English Furniture*.

John Bly, who still runs the family business in Tring, recalled his father returning home and arranging a bank loan of £500: 'It was a huge amount of money in those days. You could have bought five thatched cottages in Buckinghamshire for that sort of money but he was determined to buy the cabinet. He knew its value, not only as a beautiful object but its importance in history.'

Frank Bly's estimation was spot-on when it came up for sale early on day two, which concentrated on the vast swathes of furniture that had been collected over the centuries. The cabinet was lot number 314 and still in the basement, so only those who had ventured down the stone steps into the cellars had any real idea of what it looked like, let alone its story.

Although there was a scattering of interest among the London dealers, Frank realised that there was only one other serious bidder in the room—a young man he didn't recognise—and the pair traded bids until he trumped his rival and bought the cabinet for £470. He went home happy and told his anxious wife not to worry about the bank loan. Two days later, after the sale had ended, he returned to the castle with his son to pick up his trophy. 'I remember helping to load her onto the truck, her legs in the air,' John recalled.

But there was a twist. Frank had bought the cabinet to on-sell at a tidy profit, but it was so rare and expensive that it could only really be sold to a museum, and the obvious place was the Victoria and Albert Museum in London. He waited a few days before phoning the museum's curators to inform them that he had an object they would be interested in acquiring, only to be told that the museum had been the underbidders, having sent an office boy to the sale so their interest would remain hidden.

Now he had a problem. Not only were the museum's executives still miffed at being outbid and in no mood to be hustled, but they refused to issue him with an export licence to sell it overseas. 'They made him wait a month before relenting and agreeing to buy the cabinet for a tidy profit of £680,' John said. He added that the cabinet was probably now worth up to £12 million.

It would take two days for three auctioneers to make their way through hundreds of items of furniture from a house so large that it had eight telephones. Yet again, prices were lower than expected, reflecting not only the apparent desperate nature of the sale but the depressed prices postwar.

A Thomas Chippendale dressing table was the most prized, selling for £600, but eighteenth-century furniture seemed a dime a dozen. Three suites of William and Mary high-backed chairs were taken for less than £400; a Louis XVI walnut settee for £16; a Regency sofa table, £54; a pair of Georgian mirrors in carved gilt frames, £75; a Queen Anne walnut bureau, £55; and a Thomas Sheraton armchair, £19. A canopied four-poster bed attributed to George Hepplewhite was sold for £80, while the canopy of William III's state bed in ruby velvet and gold thread made just £52.

And what of the dowry chest of Catherine of Aragon? Would it end up in a museum or a private collection? The answer came as a surprise to many. The chest, sold at the beginning of day three, would remain at Kimbolton and be placed in the Montagu Chapel inside St Andrew's Church, after Mandy and Nell decided to trump the highest bid of £750. 'There is much rejoicing in the town,' a local newspaper reported. 'Efforts had been made to acquire the national treasure by other bodies but it is very fitting that some link with the Manchester family, in whose custody the coffer has been since the Queen's death, should be perpetuated in Kimbolton.'

The media coverage of the auction, which eventually raised more than £19,000, was a mix of surprise and disdain. Reporters were amused by the variety of objects sold, including an American pinball machine called 'Pearl Harbor', rare because the game had been banned in the US since the war. It sold for £3, and a nobleman's coach with armorial crests made for William Montagu, the 5th Duke of Manchester, who served as the governor of Jamaica, went for just £100.

'Nell Stead Manchester and her husband, the Duke, whom she first encountered in that friendly bathing pool at the Galle Face Hotel, haven't done so well out of the sale of their art treasures from Kimbolton Castle,' sniffed 'Andrea', London correspondent for the Sydney *Sun*. 'Some of the prices they got hardly merited the trouble of getting the stuff into the auction rooms.'

But others saw it from a wider perspective. The *Harborough Mail* in Northamptonshire lamented the auction as an example of what it called the chill blasts of the postwar world sweeping noted families out of the great houses:

> When you see an auctioneer's advertisement offering a great house for sale, raise your hats to the passing of an era. It is all part of the biggest social revolution in a thousand years. All over England now you can watch it as it sweeps onwards, emptying the halls and mansions of great families with their roots in the past. It is not the purpose of this article to discuss whether this far-reaching change is for better or for worse. Political platforms will give you that answer. But in the county of spires and squires, the spires are still there but the squires are dwindling. Make your way up the tree-shaded drive and ring

> the bell at one of the mansions. It does not follow, as it did fifty years ago, that after a discreet interval a footman will appear and inquire your business. You may find the great house split into flats. It may be a school with pupils at prayer. It may be a hotel, a youth centre, industrial offices or even partly a factory. Or it may be empty and deserted, with nettles growing in the forecourt and uncurtained windows blankly reflecting the sky.

Many, of course, celebrated the demise of the landed gentry, and the loosening of the grip on power and wealth of the few at the expense of the many. In many ways, it mirrored the fracturing of the British Empire, and decolonisation, over the same period.

Mandy and Nell were among the more industrious of the family descendants who tried to survive and put right the poor management of their immediate forebears, their rearguard action stymied by unfortunate timing in terms of a collapse in postwar land values. Had they held on for another decade or so, the story could have been very different.

History would later show the financial resilience of the upper classes. Although severely dented, there remains a solid rump of aristocratic families who retain a level of financial and political influence seventy-five years after the fire sale at Kimbolton.

25

BROTHERS IN ALMS

Angus Montagu was almost seven years old before he got to know his older brother.

Up until then, circumstances had kept the boys apart for all but a few months of Angus's life. He had been a baby in 1939 when the war broke out, forcing the family to abandon Kimbolton Castle. Angus ended up in Ceylon with his parents, while Sidney—Lord Kim—was deposited at the first of a number of schools he would attend in America.

By the time the hostilities had ended six years later, Angus was almost seven, a young boy with no experience of having an older brother around the house—or indeed any other family members, apart from stories told and photograph albums meticulously kept by his father. Among the pages there was a picture of the former duke with Angus, a grandfather he would not remember, and another in which a worried-looking dark-haired boy—Kim—was holding him awkwardly on his lap when he was a few months old.

Normal family life did not resume after the war either. Instead, he was sent back to Kimbolton, alone, in 1946 while his parents fetched Kim from America and searched for a property in the wilds of Kenya.

The boys were finally reunited in 1947 when Kim joined him at Kimbolton for a few months while the purchase of Kapsirowa was being finalised. It was a notable moment for locals when the brothers were spied together on the back of a tractor. Kim, then a young man in his late teens, was at the wheel with Angus, half his age and size, clinging to the back.

Education was problematic for Angus, because of both the haphazard opportunities given to him and his own personal challenges. His academic struggles were almost certainly exacerbated by an undiagnosed dyslexic condition, as well as something akin to what would be known years later as ADHD (attention deficit hyperactivity disorder). To compound matters, he was overweight as a child, courtesy of the Montagu stockiness, which led to unkind nicknames such as 'Butcher's Boy'.

Nell did not want to send him away from Kenya to an English boarding school, as she had Kim. Instead, she brought a British tutor to Kapsirowa, but he proved to be a drunken layabout in her eyes and was sacked. She tried homeschooling him herself; though he made some progress, she gave up, realising he needed proper instruction. Attempts to fit in at the local school also failed.

His mother was out of ideas and in 1949, aged ten, Angus was again sent back to England where he lived at Park Lodge—his parents' first matrimonial home—under the care of a cook, a housemaid and a man named Aubrey 'Skipper' Butler, the local scoutmaster who doubled as Angus's tutor and guardian. Although admired as a scouting leader, Skipper's skills as a tutor were limited and Angus struggled, unable to spell or even read fluently. It seemed remarkable that the child of a duke could fall between the cracks.

Angus was an enigma to the local village boys. David Whiteman, speaking to author Marcus Scriven for his 2009 book that would draw attention to Angus's troubled life, said, 'Today you would call him hyperactive. He was always . . . a bit scatter-brainish . . . would never do anything correctly.' Whiteman recalled the day that Skipper took the Scouts to swim in the moat at Major Farley's house, Wornditch Hall. 'Angus wouldn't go in the water proper. He would just roll about in the mud to get as ridiculously filthy as he could. He did seem to be a penny or two short of a shilling at times.' On another occasion, Angus climbed onto the roof of the new Scout hall and refused, despite Skipper's pleas, to come down.

Neil Sclater-Booth, who was the son of David Stead's mistress and would later become the 5th Baron of Basing, was a few months younger than Angus and a frequent childhood companion. Reflecting on their relationship years later, he thought Angus probably suffered from ADHD. 'I could never know what he would do next,' he said. Bill 'Tiddler' Ewens agreed: 'He needed a bit of looking after'; he added that Angus always seemed to be hungry. 'He seemed to be almost ignored. My mother would feed him.' John Mayes, another playmate, remembered being dazzled by Angus's enormous toy-train set, which could fill an entire room, whereas his own was a modest figure of eight. And yet Angus was never happier than when the two of them raced homemade carts.

To the adults in his life, Angus seemed to be missing a firm hand, difficult to control and somewhat lost in the strange life in which he had found himself. Skipper found him impossible; Olga Welton, who read to him when he was aged ten, thought he was a 'horrible kid', as did Grey Duberley.

Hawtreys Preparatory School, which his father and brother had attended, was not interested in taking him as a student. It was only when he was accepted (via a family friend) into Trearddur House, a boarding school on Holy Island, Anglesey, that Angus began to get a formal education. By then he was aged eleven, a long way behind the other students, and still barely able to read or write.

There was another piece of good fortune when, in 1953, Major Farley convinced the headmaster of Gordonstoun—the spartan school in Scotland that would become home to the Duke of Edinburgh Awards—to take the boy, who had settled somewhat and was now 'civil and apparently tractable'.

The educational philosophy of Gordonstoun's founder Kurt Hahn, a German-Jewish educator who had escaped Nazi Germany, was to create leaders with a social consciousness. Among his educational aims were self-discovery, learning to accept triumph and defeat, training the imagination, sitting with silence for reflection, self-effacement for the common cause and making competitiveness important but not predominant. Hahn's desire was to 'free the sons of the wealthy and powerful from the enervating sense of privilege'.

Angus Montagu seemed to be perfectly suited to such a regime. Gordonstoun's ethos of 'experiential therapy' also suited a boy whose achievements would never be in the classroom but outside, where his physical abilities could shine through. Seamanship and rock climbing were among a raft of outdoor activities in a school that championed cold-water showers and a run for students before breakfast. Angus seemed to thrive on the discipline.

There were no passengers here and no one left behind, not even Angus. He responded well to involvement in the school fire service and was always the first out of bed if the drill siren went. His physique, endowed to him by his family's genes—thickset and strong—made him perfect for weight training, rugby and shot-put. A photograph taken during fire drill shows Angus on the hose, standing awkwardly; while the classmates around him seem to be focused on the task at hand, he is transfixed by the camera.

For the first time in his chaotic life, Angus was truly liked by his peers. There was a mix of boys at Gordonstoun, including locals from fishing villages, the sons of professionals, and a few on merchant-ship scholarships. Angus was among a 'sprinkling' of aristocracy who would attend the school, the most famous of whom were Prince Philip and his oldest son, Charles, the future king. There were no luxuries to speak of and even the nearest town, Elgin, where they would sometimes go, offered only fish and chips and a cinema.

Former classmates would speak kindly of him when tracked down by Marcus Scriven. 'I never remember seeing him depressed or down or grumbling,' Fergus Rogers recalled. 'He was always immensely polite, and always cheerful. He was already the size of an eighteen-year-old when he arrived, a big lad, heavy—much larger than us little shrimps—but he was never a bully, always very kind. Nobody had any trouble with Angus. He was liked.'

Angus often spent term breaks with his paternal grandmother, Helena, Lady Kintore, who lived at Keith Hall in Aberdeenshire. She adored her grandson so much that, when he lost a gold watch she'd given him, she simply replaced it with another.

For holidays he flew to Kenya, where he felt out of place. Lord Kim, having finished his national service and who was studying in Africa, was now working with Mandy on the property and they had little time for a bumbling boy. It was significant that none of Mandy's letters to Frank Cowlard had inquired about Angus. The apparent distance between father and son was commented on by some, although others thought there was a simpler, less offensive explanation: that Nell doted on her youngest son while Mandy had developed a natural, practical relationship with the older boy who was now a young adult.

Nell certainly worried about her youngest child and missed him, as she told Frank Cowlard one Christmas: 'We are off to

Nairobi to meet our baby tomorrow. I am just thrilled and know we will see a big change in him. Nine months is a long time. I hope he is nice and fat because I will want to eat him.'

Nell's language could be guileless at times, particularly about children—and not just her own. She adored having them around her, according to Kapsirowa neighbour Patsy Bowles, who said Nell once asked her if she could 'borrow' her young son; on another occasion, clearly missing Angus, Nell offered another woman money to 'buy' her son and bring him up. 'She had a thing about little boys; I don't think in a salacious way. She liked to have a court around her.'

Children liked her. Huw and Mark Boyce, whose father, Gerry, managed Kapsirowa in the mid-1950s, remember a kind, down-to-earth woman who always had marshmallows as a treat, and who kept Mandy's old cigar boxes for Huw and white spider marbles for Mark. 'The Duchess was thoughtful,' Huw recalled. 'I didn't ask her to keep the boxes; she simply knew that I liked them.'

The way Patsy Bowles saw it, Nell had adored Lord Kim when he was young, as her letters written to him while he was at Hawtreys clearly showed, but once he became a young man and turned his attention to women of his own age, Nell seemed to switch her focus to Angus, whom she spoiled with attention. As another Kapsirowa neighbour Mary Fox attested: 'She would always say Angus was so wonderful . . . It was always "Angus, darling, do you like what I'm wearing? Do you approve?"'

It was why she tried using the local school and then a private tutor for his education, before giving up and sending him back to Kimbolton and ultimately boarding school. But, despite his later improvements, Angus would leave Gordonstoun in 1956 without any formal qualifications, his learning problems confirmed. All he had was his name, and that could make him or break him.

National service led Angus into the Royal Marines, joining at Lympstone for basic training in January 1957 where, once again, he stood out as different from the others. He was one of only three publicly educated young men among the forty-seven young recruits on Squad 911, and the only one with a title.

Lord Angus Montagu quickly became 'Monty' and admired for his physical abilities. A hefty lad and a fine water polo player, he also enjoyed a pint—but he struggled academically and never attempted to become an officer. At times he could appear aloof, flashing a £5 note around among recruits who were paid 26 shillings a week, and once offering a colleague sixpence to press his khaki and two blue uniforms.

Things changed when he was assigned to the frigate HMS *Loch Fyne*, where he seemed to relish becoming one of the crew with no expectations other than to perform what was required, including scrubbing deck floors. The ship travelled to Mombasa, the Seychelles and Colombo where, thanks to his wartime childhood years, he was a man who had contacts everywhere. Having learned his lesson at Lympstone, Angus shared rather than flashed his family wealth.

But some of the poorer family traits were emerging. He was careless about repaying debts and an unabashed 'skirt chaser', once turning up at Kimbolton in a sports car with a woman who a friend outrageously described as 'a whore on the bonnet with her legs astride, waving her garter belt in the air'.

If Angus was the son who suffered from a disjointed education, Kim was the one who missed out on family life. Mostly alone from the age of eight, when he was sent to boarding school in America through the war years, he was finally reunited with his parents as an seventeen-year-old.

Like Angus, he struggled at school and would be relocated several times from one school to another, although he did not have Angus's level of learning disability and social awkwardness. After returning to the UK to do his two-year national service stint, Kim joined his parents in Kenya, where he ran the farm alongside his father and developed his management skills through an agricultural college.

His other connection with Mandy was motor racing, a passion they shared. Kim became a prominent rally car driver, particularly on the African circuit, and performed credibly in the East African Safari Rally, which had first been held to celebrate the coronation of Queen Elizabeth II in 1953. As an international contest, it was regarded as one of the most difficult in the world.

Just finishing the four-day, 5000-kilometre race through Kenya, Tanganyika (later Tanzania) and Uganda was considered an achievement. Described as pitiless, it demanded that participants climb to heights of 2700 metres on rough mountain tracks, and combat humid coastal roads and dusty flatlands—all of which combined to choke most engines and destroy most chassis. In 1961, just as the event was being launched on the international circuit and attracting some of the best drivers in the world, Kim and his co-driver William 'Bill' Fritschy finished a close second. In 1966, just nine teams out of eighty-eight crossed the finish line, but they included Kim and his co-driver.

He was regarded as a character, as noted by famed Irish rally driver Paddy Hopkirk in his memoir. In the 1960 rally, he was paired with Kim and they led the race until the car's differential failed in the harsh conditions. 'He was the son of the Duke of Manchester and an excellent co-driver,' Hopkirk wrote. 'But he was a serious boozer, and kept a bottle of brandy in the car, under his seat.'

Kim was also fearless, bordering on foolhardy at times, on roads where one misjudgement on a curve could mean plunging a kilometre down a mountain. Elephants had right of way and rivers could flood in a matter of minutes. During a sponsorship trip to America, Kim recounted to the press one particular drive on a moonless night:

> We came around a corner and headed down a long hill, the car going as fast as it could—perhaps 75 miles an hour [120 kilometres per hour]. At the bottom we noticed lights along the road which was rather weird. We couldn't have stopped so I pushed past the lights. Then it felt as though a huge hand

grabbed the car, practically stopping it. The headlights went out. Blackness. The lights, we discovered, had been other drivers trying to signal that a river had flooded the road. We were going fast enough to go right through. The lights came back when we came up from beneath the water on the other side of the river. The car behind us tried the same thing and was swept away.

It would come as no surprise to friends and neighbours that as they grew older, a divide would emerge between Kim and Angus, who were vastly different characters. Angus was outgoing and amoral, according to those who knew him. Careless with money, he was also seemingly unaware that there was a need to repay personal debts. It was an attitude not unlike his grandfather's, as his solicitor told Marcus Scriven: 'He had a marvellously cavalier attitude that said: "If you've lent me money, I'll pay you back when I feel like it."'

Kim, by contrast, was regarded as an honest man who would always repay debts and who had little taste for the social high life of London, preferring the quieter life of Kenya and, later, South Africa. Once asked if he would consider living in America, he replied: 'I have often given some thought to living here, but the pace would be quite beyond me.'

26

KIMBOLTON REBORN

Patsy and Roger Bowles had been on their way to Nairobi from the coast at Mombasa one afternoon in late 1949, taking their time along the dangerously pitted dirt road, when they spotted the Duke and Duchess of Manchester stopped on the verge.

Mandy stood at the back of the car, reaching into the boot. Nell sat nearby on a folding chair, next to a small table tucked up against the dense jungle foliage that edged out onto the road. Were they in trouble?

They both seemed relaxed. Nell looked as if she was waiting for something, but caution was always best in the middle of the Kenyan bush. Patsy tapped her husband on the shoulder: 'Let's pull over, darling, to see what they're doing.'

Nell looked up at the sound of the approaching car and waved as she recognised her friends: 'Hello Patsy,' she called out as the car halted alongside. 'Come and have a drink with us.'

Far from being in trouble, the Manchesters, as they would come to be known among the other settlers, had simply paused for refreshments on their long journey back to Kapsirowa. Other travellers might have taken sandwiches and poured tea from a thermos, but Nell and Mandy preferred gin and tonics served from a minibar built into the boot of their car.

Patsy and Roger joined them as the sun began to set, the silence broken only by the occasional call of a bird or rustle of an animal making its way through the spear grass. The world seemed at peace out here in the African bush, barely a hundred kilometres south of the equator.

The tranquillity was suddenly broken by the sound of a whistle in the distance. The Mombasa–Nairobi rail line ran adjacent to the road, carved from the bush at the turn of the twentieth century as the white settlement of Kenya gained momentum. A few minutes later, a train thundered past.

'You see those last couple of coaches?' Mandy said, pointing with his half-empty glass. 'That is all my furniture going to our new house.'

That was an understatement. In fact there were three carriages filled with their possessions, including a mix of their favourite furniture that had been plucked from Kimbolton before the auction catalogue had been finalised. There were also some unsold lots; bringing them to Kenya seemed better than leaving them to rot in the Kimbolton cellars. Other items had been sent for auction as far away as Australia, where there was a better market for period furniture.

Among the load were a giant silver mantelpiece and most

of the great library—the sixteen thousand or so books that had caught Chester Woodward's eye. Children who visited Kapsirowa over the years would recall being offered first-edition copies of classics like *Tom Thumb* and *Alice in Wonderland* to read. There were rolls of fine silk Aubusson rugs, ancient wall tapestries, delicate silverware, fine china, gilded mirrors, marble busts and statues, as well as dozens of artworks—harbour scenes, landscapes, and portraits by the likes of Holbein and Van Dyck of kings and queens, politicians and aristocrats spanning three hundred years. Medieval England was being transplanted into an African setting.

The main house at this time had only just been completed. Although relatively modest in design, compared to their English and Irish castles, it was tended by fourteen male servants, known as houseboys. Built into the hillside over two storeys, with polished timber floorboards, the house was a maze of rooms, including six bedrooms, each initially with its own colour theme—a nod to Kimbolton's Green, White and Red drawing rooms—although this would change over time.

Their arrival had caused a stir, as neighbour Nellie Grant later wrote in her diary about a visit to the property:

> All over the Uasin Gishu plateau now are signposts *Manchester* which gives the plateau quite the industrial tang. After tea we went up to the Manchester abode. It is quite fantastic. The Duchess has fifty-three dresses still unpacked—she simply hasn't the time between gins. Her drawing room is virginal white, with tables all glass or silver chrome. Beautiful flower

> arrangements, straight from Constance Spry [the doyenne of British floristry], everything defoliated so that even quite heavy sprays of honeysuckle look slender.

The flowers came from the house garden that Nell had created. She had done the same during the renovations at Kimbolton, but this time she had a team of twenty gardeners to help her turn her grand floral visions into reality. One flowerbed near the house was filled just with white blossoms, while others championed the blooms of Kenya. There were numerous varieties of orchids, Kenya's unofficial national flower, which flourished in the temperate climate; there were fields of Alstroemeria lilies alongside succulents like the desert rose while sprays of gypsophila contrasted with the spiny sculpture of eryngiums. In a nod to England, there were also beds filled with varieties of roses and carnations.

There were four fish ponds stocked with tilapia, perch, trout, carp and bass, and a vegetable patch that supplied the busy kitchen. The orchard featured pixie oranges, Bearss lemons, grapefruit, limes, Kara mandarins, satsuma tangerines and avocados.

The compound would take six years to complete as the operation grew, supplied with water pumped from the river that ran at its base. The property was dotted with machinery sheds and workshops run with onsite generators. Visitors drove past immaculate horse stables, kept clean by dozens of staff and whose operation was controlled by a system of bells.

It was an investment that rivalled the money they had spent renovating and trying to save Kimbolton, not just to create a new life but in the hope that success would keep alive the last vestiges of the Montagu estate. It had dwindled over the years to acreage around the castle, woodlands and the estate's Park Farm.

'I'm down to my last castle,' Mandy would say with a smile when asked about his holdings, making light of the situation by adding, 'It's hard to keep staff, even though the place isn't haunted.' He was referring to Tandragee, not Kimbolton, although how long he could keep paying for staff to manage a castle with no occupants and few visitors was debatable.

By 1948 the Kapsirowa farm was up and running with crops of wheat, maize and coffee, the operation supported by a staff of up to two hundred local men thanks to pay rates of just 5 shillings a month. In addition to their pay, the workers received weekly goods rations of ground maize (known as posho), sugar, tea and occasionally meat. They kept their own small plots of land with chickens, banana trees and vegetable patches.

Mandy was ecstatic, having spent twelve hours a day on a tractor himself while the farm was being redesigned to suit his plans. In a letter to Frank Cowlard, he was desperate to convince his Kimbolton loyalist of his solid financial returns, but he also revealed some naivety about seasonal challenges

> Lady Mandeville and I are loving this place. It's not only beautiful from a climate point of view but everything grows with the

> greatest of ease. You should see my wheat crop. It would make your mouth water . . . At last I have finished the harvest and it is an absolute bumper one. In one field we got more than ten, 200-pound bags to the acre. You can work out how many quarters to the acre that is better than I can.

Mandy had remained in touch with his trusted gamekeeper about managing what was left of the farming and game-shooting operations at Kimbolton, and also about arranging for some of the cattle to be transported to Kenya in the hope of repeating in Africa his success in England. His plan was to eventually run two and a half thousand head of cattle. 'I had a cable from my manager in Kenya the other day to say that six of the Red Polls [are] on their way out,' he wrote in another letter while on a trip to the US. 'I am looking forward to getting them as I think they will do well and improve my stock a lot.'

The move of cattle was noticed back in Kimbolton and reported in one of the local papers, *The Bedfordshire Times*. It was another sign of the family's decision to move away from the district and many wondered how long their commitment to the town would last. After all, it had only been a few years since the then viscount had been buying animals to boost his stock postwar, setting a Red Poll Cattle Society auction at Ipswich alight by paying more than £1300 for eight animals, including a bull for £280.

The future had looked promising for Park Farm, although it was a long road back economically. The property had been largely abandoned during the war and the new manager would need at least a year to get it back in order. Mandy's pleas for government financial support to help repair rural properties from war damage had also been rebuffed. This added to his frustrations, given that Brampton Park House had also been taken over during the war years, by the RAF, and was in need of repairs.

There were problems ahead in Kenya as well. Mandy and Nell were still in New York when their cattle arrived in Mombasa. A heifer named Ranksborough Brush had died from a parasitic infection, anaplasmosis. 'She was gone in an hour. They couldn't save her,' Mandy wrote of the animal, which had been one of his expensive investments. She had been eight months' pregnant and the male calf died with her.

And now his prized homegrown bull, Kimbolton Pelican, had gone down with redwater fever. 'I very much doubt he will live,' Mandy wrote. 'The other cattle, as far as I can make out, have done very well but it is a shame that the two best should get knocked out like this.'

It was a frustrating beginning to their new life, to add to the uniquely African problems of leopards and hyenas constantly killing and taking calves, and in one case a fully grown cow, while baboons and deer rampaged through the Kapsirowa crops, and birds like the red-billed quelea feasted on his grain.

The agricultural challenges had changed from the soggy, genteel English countryside, with its rabbits and foxes, to a landscape more akin to Nell's home in Australia. Managing difficult countryside in harsh surroundings had been the speciality of Sidney Stead; now his daughter held the keys to the future of the troubled Dukedom of Manchester. Even her confidence with horses was an asset.

Mandy had once confessed, when writing to Frank Cowlard, that horses were something he feared. 'I hear Lord Kim is very good on a horse,' he wrote about his oldest son learning to ride. 'It must be his Australian blood as I am surprised that any son of mine would dare go near a horse.' And yet in Kenya, being on horseback and patrolling his estate became a major part of his persona among the workers, who regarded 'Mendy and the Duchess' as benevolent if colonial employers.

George Wanjala Simiyu was a small boy in the mid-1950s and remembered picking mushrooms one day with his sister when the Duke appeared on horseback. They tried to hide, worried that they were trespassing and in trouble. But when Mandy saw the children, he dismounted. Instead of running them off the land, he picked a handful of mushrooms and offered them to George. Then he smiled and walked back to his horse to carry on his journey. 'He was always smiling,' George told researchers from Mount Kenya University many years later. 'His labourers talked well of him.'

George visited the property often over the years because his uncle was a groundsman who worked for the Duchess. George was taken by the gardens and the grandeur of the 'great mansion.' He also admired the management approach, under which teams of workers were supervised by a series of foremen, and by a manager who oversaw the whole operation, particularly when the Duke and Duchess began travelling frequently. Their trips were not between Kenya and England as much as to

America, and in particular to the San Francisco area where they had established a new coterie of friends.

The bulk of the Kapsirowa workforce came from nearby towns and villages; many workers had families. Their young children had to travel on mountain roads to attend a school in the town of Kitale, established by Roman Catholic priests almost two decades before. As an alternative, Mandy and Nell set aside land to build a school to teach the children of their workers. At its peak there would be more than one hundred students.

Giles Remnant was in his late teens when he met Mandy and Nell. It was the early 1960s and his father, Harry, had taken over management of Kapsirowa.

> They had begun to split their life between Kenya and San Francisco, which meant my father ran the operation, and when he flew Dad back to London for a gall-bladder operation I took over.
>
> It was predominantly a cattle ranch but they also grew maize and coffee, which I think was a pretty good money-spinner for them. As well as the school there was a rudimentary medical centre, which was important when you had a staff of two hundred or more, because there was bound to be some injuries along the way. For anything more serious, we took them to the hospital at Kitale, which was about 15 miles [24 kilometres] away.

Years later Mandy would recall that he and Nell had to act as doctors on occasions, treating wounds caused by farmyard accidents and even delivering babies. On one occasion, a worker was bitten by a deadly puff adder: 'I cut the wound open and asked some of the Africans to suck out the poison,' Mandy recounted to an American newspaper. 'None of them would, so I did it myself. The fellow was in hospital for three months but he lived. He was killed later on in a raid by the Masai.'

It was typical of the couple who, Giles Remnant said, were down to earth in spite of their titles. 'People in his social circle called him Mandy but most of us called him "Your Grace". He liked it, not because he was pretentious but simply because he had been used to it all his life. Nell was the Duchess. As a young man you tended to look up to someone like her but she was not aloof.'

It seemed that—by accident rather than design—Mandy and Nell were recreating a form of the feudal system they had left behind in Kimbolton: a community was being built around the walls and in the shelter of a castle (in this case, a grand house), where they were protected and given work and security in exchange for loyalty. For the moment, at least, the Manchesters were enjoying a peaceful and productive entry into Kenyan colonial life.

27

SWILL TIMES

Well Kid, how is your sex life?

If ever there was a line that summed up Nell Manchester, it was this opening sentence in a letter to Patsy Bowles in 1954. At least Patsy thought it did, so much so that she kept the missive, even though it was much folded and faded. It had been written by Nell while she was on her way back to London aboard ship from New York; in it she complained that the ship's captain was making passes at her—'a mad play Boy. B. awful'.

Her manner of writing had not changed since her days as a young mother, when she had penned loving notes to her oldest son, concerned that he was lonely at his boarding school. She used minimal punctuation and tended to overuse capital letters to place emphasis on a word. Ordinary grammar could not accommodate her rush of ideas and emotion, sprinkled with uninhibited independence of thought. Nell was a woman unafraid to express herself; in her letter to Patsy she added that the food aboard ship was awful and there was a strange, dank smell.

Patsy did not hold back while discussing her close friend with author Marcus Scriven. The two women had often swilled pink gin when Nell made the long trip to Nairobi to go shopping and escape the isolation of Kapsirowa. They usually met at the Muthaiga Country Club, on the outskirts of the city, a haunt for idle aristocrats and foreign businessmen passing through. Members' needs were tended to by an abundance of 'impeccable domestics' dressed in tasselled tarbooshes and white cotton robes called kanzus, tied with cardinal-red cummerbunds. The head waiters wore braided bolero jackets, to distinguish their seniority, and prided themselves on having the next drink ready and delivered silently just as a member drained their glass.

'She was very attractive and extraordinary with a very good figure. Very well dressed,' said Patsy, recalling that Nell's favourite outfit was a leopard-print raincoat and a 'shamelessly large' emerald.

Nell had a tendency to misbehave after she'd had a few drinks—'a bit shhtupid', insisted Patsy—although never to the point of being unfaithful. Mandy was grateful that another club member, Norman 'Nocky' Marsh, regarded himself as Nell's protector. There was nothing in it sexually, Patsy added: 'They were just good chums and Nocky ended up being an executor to her will.'

What Patsy failed to mention was that Nocky lived at Kapsirowa for a number of years and had his own house near the front gates. He was an old friend of Nell and Mandy's from Ceylon, a retired Far East director of the shipping company P&O Lines, who also invested money when Mandy and Nell later expanded their farming operations.

Nell could also be unfiltered at times, according to Patsy, who was with her one day at the club when she pointed to a woman named Bridget and remarked, 'Dreadful fat woman; she's only a countess.'

Bridget was the wife of Gerard Vernon Wallop, the 9th Earl of Portsmouth, who arrived in Kenya in 1952 for much the same reason as Mandy and Nell—hoping to save his family property by making enough money in Kenya to balance his tax losses back in the UK. This was a common refrain among several titled men who arrived in the years after the war.

Patsy did not explain Nell's derisive comment, but it had little to do with their respective titles and more a personality clash in a small community. Even so, it is worth noting that the Countess travelled from Nairobi to be among the mourners at Kimbolton when Nell passed away many years later.

It is difficult to understand why Patsy told such stories about Nell, given that she regarded herself as a close friend and was, by admission, a frequent drinking companion. Giles Remnant laughed at the drinking reference: 'Gin was their drink, a way of life. Nell Manchester was no better or worse than any of the others. They all went from bottle to throttle'—meaning they all drove their cars while drunk.

And Patsy was hardly in a position to throw stones, given that her own private life was full of scandals. She had arrived in Kenya before the war from London; as an aspiring actress fresh from a messy divorce, she quickly found herself a new—and titled—beau in Roderick Ward, second son of the Earl of Dudley. They would marry in 1928 but, by the time Patsy met Nell Manchester, she would be on her third marriage, to Dr Roger Bowles.

Patsy's flamboyance made it easy for her to fit into the so-called Happy Valley set, the group of British aristocrats who settled in the Rift Valley between the 1920s and 1940s with an appetite for decadence, drugs and promiscuity. She was a close friend of the insatiable Idina Sackville and a regular at the infamous parties held at the Muthaiga, where evenings frequently descended into debauchery. As Karen Blixen had noted, 'The Muthaiga was always replacing its chandeliers and parties tended to denigrate towards dawn.'

It was here on the evening of 23 January 1941 that Patsy had been enjoying a drink with Josslyn Hay, the Earl of Erroll and former husband of Idina, who was with his married lover Diana Delves Broughton. The next morning, Lord Erroll's corpse was found; he had apparently been shot while sitting in his car. Sir Jock Broughton, Diana's husband, was later put on trial but was acquitted. The murder remains one of the most intriguing mysteries of the time.

The Muthaiga was a four-hour drive across the Rift Valley from Kapsirowa, so it was only an occasional venue for Nell and Mandy who, in Nell's words to Frank Cowlard, were 'practically self-contained' while settling into farming life: 'We occasionally go and visit our neighbours for a game of cards or a drink, but the nearest is ten miles.'

Most of their socialising was done in Kitale, the closest town to Kapsirowa, where they would become prominent members of the Kitale Club, even finding cash to help the club rescue its golf course, which had been abandoned during the war, and to expand it from nine to eighteen holes.

The American author Negley Farson described the club in his memoir *Last Chance in Africa*, published in 1949, at the time when the Manchesters were establishing their new lives. 'Kitale has one of the most delightful little clubs I have ever been in . . . where colonels are clustered like grapes,' he wrote. 'This is an Englishman's paradise. The club, with its golf, dancing, the happy-go-lucky chatter over a sundowner in the bar, the happy foregathering of old friends at luncheon on market day who are laughing all the time about the gay jauntiness of their lives!'

Nell and Mandy were members of the Nairobi Race Club, which featured the Duke of Manchester Cup on its calendar (and still does), and the Malindi Fishing Club, where Mandy would serve as captain and patron, helping to launch a renowned international billfish festival.

He and Nell would also join the Mt Kenya Safari Club, billed as the most prestigious club in Africa, built on the property near Nanyuki that Mandy and Nell had initially considered buying before choosing Kapsirowa. It was opened in 1959 by a prominent trio—eccentric American oil baron and gambler Ray

Ryan, Swiss entrepreneur Carl Hirschmann, and Hollywood actor William Holden. It quickly became a place 'where even the insects dress for dinner', as one member put it.

As a local celebrity, Mandy was among a handful of charter members of the club, who included Winston Churchill and Clark Gable. Other Hollywood celebrities quickly joined, including Walt Disney, Bing Crosby, Bob Hope, John Wayne, hotelier Conrad Hilton, press baron William Randolph Hearst, and Lord Louis Mountbatten.

The club sat in 90 acres (36 hectares) of fertile land at the foot of Mount Kenya where streams were filled with trout, rose gardens bloomed and waterfalls tumbled. There were heated pools and clipped lawns where peacocks, storks and ibexes strolled. Salt licks placed carefully around the property attracted big game, including elephants and antelopes, as postcard backdrops. The gardens seemed to stretch forever around cottages that all had sunken marble tubs, parquet floors and fireplaces lit each evening for ambience. By the early 1970s it would have three hundred millionaire members and be described as the most exclusive club on Earth.

It seemed that out here in Africa the name Manchester was one of prestige, rather than the social embarrassment it had become in London caused by the misbehaviour of Mandy's father and grandfather. History meant little in an environment in which everyone was building something new, rather than resting on the foundations of past generations.

Nell and Mandy were firmly ensconced in their new life although Kimbolton Castle, or at least what remained of its farming land and forests, was still in family hands. There were hopes that they could keep a foothold in England, which they visited each year, but they rarely strayed outside London. Visits to Kimbolton were brief and they avoided the castle altogether, as if the memories of its loss were too painful.

But life was about to change once again, bringing with it a new threat to their lives that threatened to tear up the roots they had carefully planted and nurtured.

28

THE UPRISING

On the morning of 1 November 1952, a herdsman living in one of the outer huts at Kapsirowa woke to find that four of the cows from the herd he was supposed to be protecting from predators had been taken.

It didn't look to be the work of animals, rather of poachers who had snuck in from the forests. Concern became alarm when one of the animals was found nearby speared to death, its stomach slashed open and entrails left to spill out in a bloody, oily pool. This was no ordinary theft but a message to the Duke and his family: it wasn't his livestock under threat, but their lives.

A few weeks before, when Mandy celebrated his fiftieth birthday, the colonial government had declared a state of emergency in the wake of growing violence by the Kenya Land and Freedom Army. The insurgent group known as the Mau Mau had mounted a concerted and violent campaign to reclaim land confiscated by British authorities and given to white settlers, and rebels had begun sneaking into farmhouses to capture and kill farmers in the most horrific manner.

A police operation, on the day before the Kapsirowa raid, had rounded up more than one hundred suspected Mau Mau hiding in the jungle of the Aberdare Range, a few hours south-east of the farm. Behind the scenes, three battalions of the King's African Rifles had been brought to Nairobi as a backup force to the Kenyan police, and a battalion of the Lancashire Fusiliers would be flown in from Egypt under the cover of darkness to bolster 'home guard' troops, who expected armed resistance as they tried to flush out the rebels.

Several European farmers had already been killed, hacked to death with machetes and pangas—long heavy blades used to till the soil—in overnight attacks on isolated properties. The details made gruesome reading, particularly the killing of a family on their property at Kinangop, where farmer Roger Ruck, his pregnant wife, Esme, and their six-year-old son, Michael, were butchered by the Mau Mau. The gang included two members of the Ruck family's own staff. It was shocking, not just in its brutality but because the Rucks were popular among the local tribespeople. Esme was a doctor who treated Kenyans for free, and yet they were murdered.

More attacks followed in the first months of 1953. Charles Fergusson and Richard Bingley were neighbours who had been staying at each other's houses overnight for protection. On New Year's Day they were called into Fergusson's dining room by his houseboy for dinner only to find a gang waiting for them. Their bodies were mutilated and each gang member made a cut in the corpses, like a signature.

Eric Bowyer, a neighbour of the Ruck family, was found slashed to pieces in his bath. Ian Meiklejohn carried a revolver, but it did him no good; he was killed, and his wife, Dorothy, was severely maimed.

The attacks always followed the same pattern: they were on lonely farmhouses located next to dense forest so the assailants could approach, unseen, after dark. The Mau Mau recruited the target's African staff, who were either willing, swearing a blood oath to the cause, or forced to aid in the ambush on pain of death.

It was hardly surprising that the Manchesters felt vulnerable, with little or no security on a property that was surrounded by jungle, and with no close neighbours they could call for help. Nell took to carrying a gun and travelled with armed guards but the dangers lurked inside as well, the couple later learning that two of their principal servants had taken the first oath of the Mau Mau.

Mandy was a poster boy for the European settlers—a prominent aristocrat who had established good relations with local Nandi, Cherang'any and Marakwet peoples. 'I am a blood brother in the Maasai. I admire them; they are men,' he said in one interview. And yet his good intentions only made him a more obvious target in a sophisticated campaign that combined physical terror with propaganda.

The Kikuyu were the largest component of the Bantu ethnic group within the Mau Mau membership, but those Kikuyu who remained loyal to the Kenyan colonial government were cut down in far greater numbers than whites as the rebels tried to divide the population and force fealty to their cause. In the village of Lari, just north of Nairobi, more than eighty African inhabitants, mostly women and children, were herded into their thatched huts, which were then set on fire. Anyone who tried to escape was hacked to death.

It was war of a different kind and it would force the Manchesters to choose between defending their land and fleeing. Nell and Mandy seemed doomed to repeat the disappointments they had experienced at Kimbolton, when their attempt to reclaim family history had collided with the social upheaval of the Second World War. And now, after more than five years of toil to turn Kapsirowa into a home and a financial resource, their efforts might once again have to be abandoned.

They were not alone. There would be a mass exodus of English settlers in the coming months but Nell and Mandy would not be among them. Instead, Mandy joined the police reserve and took a command position, including leading regular patrols to seek out the insurgents in their jungle hiding places around Mount Kenya. It was reported that Mandy had even raised a private army in the earliest days of the campaign, such was his concern about the Mau Mau threat. He dislocated his hip during one operation, but he didn't realise the seriousness of the injury and it would leave him with a permanent limp.

In April 1953 he stood guard at the door of a schoolroom courthouse in the town of Kapenguria, 50 kilometres north of Kapsirowa, dressed in the uniform of a police reservist, checking passes, while an officer armed with a submachine gun guarded the magistrate. Nell sat in the public gallery with other wives. It was a show of defiance at a trial of six Africans, including Kenya African Union president Jomo Kenyatta.

All were found guilty in what would later be shown to be a flawed show trial, with Kenyatta unfairly accused of being the uprising's mastermind. He would be imprisoned until 1959 and then put under house arrest for another two years.

But while defending the colonial government, Mandy would also have regrets. In an interview in July 1956 with the *San Francisco Examiner*, with Nell by his side, he conceded that the administration had treated Africans poorly and that their land claims should have been addressed earlier. 'I think basically the trouble started from our not recognizing the Kikuyu tribe as soon as it should have done,' he said. 'They are an intelligent people. We should have appreciated them and given them more rights—as we are doing now. I don't think the trouble will happen again if we take advantage of what we have learned. There's no question that we'll have to have a multi-national government.'

Despite the danger, Nell continued to entertain guests at Kapsirowa, including friends from America, some of whom made light of the danger they faced. As visitors drove the ever-dangerous roads between Nairobi and Kitale to reach the estate, they did not realise that Mandy had placed lookouts on surrounding hilltops and used an intercom system to communicate in case of an attack.

Their house guests were varied, from movie star Joan Fontaine to lawyer Peter Kriendler, who would later serve as a special prosecutor in the Richard Nixon Watergate scandal. As well, there were numerous friends from their growing connections in San Francisco and Hollywood.

One group of golfers that made the trip lunched at Kapsirowa and then gawked at the Van Dyck painting of Charles I in the main lounge room. A journalist named Fred Vincent would later write of their trip for *The Times Herald* in Michigan: 'It takes a strong character to come out here, buy a farm miles from your nearest neighbour, fight the Mau Mau, the weather and the pests. If they make the grade, they are usually heavy drinkers and good golfers,' he quipped.

By now the house was a shrine to the colour white, not as a political statement but chosen rather for its elegance. Nell adopted the style of famed interior designer Syrie Maugham to show off the flowers from her garden and the spectacular Kimbolton antiques on the walls. There were two white cockatoos in matching cages on either side of the hallway entrance and a white Oldsmobile in the garage. Nell took to wearing white when entertaining and even used a white cigarette holder. Even her dogs were white, including two terriers named after drinks—Pernod and Pym (after the drink Pimm's)—and another named Fenzig after a headache tablet.

The Kenyan conflict did not curb the couple's travel habits. Most years they travelled first back to London where, in 1954, Mandy finally took his seat in the House of Lords, seven years after inheriting the title. *Hansard* noted his presence at roll call, alerting the media, which gave them an excuse to discuss his departure from Britain and to reveal the extent of the demise of the landed gentry.

'Poverty is a sign of real gentility in the Lords,' the *Daily Telegraph* concluded, adding that one hundred and sixty-five members 'keep the wolf from their drawbridges by opening their stately homes for the general public for half-a-crown a look'.

Many of Mandy's aristocratic contemporaries were faring badly: Lord Mowbray had a milk run, Lord Garnock ran a laundry and the Duke of Rutland was a publican. The younger generation, without the luxury of an inheritance, were employed in average jobs; Lord Louth was a beach photographer, while Lord Glenorchy played bagpipes in pantomimes. Unmarried daughters also struggled: Lady Blackwood was waitressing and Lady Rous, daughter of the Earl of Stradbroke, cleaned great houses.

Mandy and Nell would have their own tough financial decision to make. In June 1955, they quietly sold Tandragee Castle for £5000 to a group of local businessmen. 'It's too hard to find people to keep it running,' Mandy told a local newspaper. 'As sad as it is, we can't justify keeping the place going while we hardly spend any time here. I'm sure there are better uses for the town.' The Montagu family's last castle would be turned into a potato-chip factory for the company Tayto, which produced the world's first flavoured crisp—cheese and onion. Their slogan is 'Castle cooked since 1956'.

There would also be further personal tragedies. In 1954 Edward Montagu, aged forty-seven, died from heat exhaustion in a Mexico jungle where he had been travelling to the ruins of the ancient Mayan city of Yaxchilan with his fourth wife, twenty-six-year-old Roberta Herold Joughin. She buried him in the jungle near a temple, with a simple gravestone marked 'EM', and later wrote about the experience for *The Sun* newspaper, insisting that, although he was penniless, Edward was a genuine adventurer fascinated by the Mayan Indians and the ancient city of Yaxchilan:

'The world knew Edward Montagu as a scapegrace and playboy,' she wrote. 'I knew a different man, fine, gentle, thoughtful, brave: a man who had put the past behind and was trying to make good.'

Much less adventurous but equally tragic was Nell's brother, David, who in May 1959 had a heart attack and died as he sat in the back of a London cab on the way to have dinner with his sister. The years had not been kind to David, who was fifty-three when he died. Unlike Edward, he had never married; he spent the years after the war at Kimbolton working as a barman and keeping an eye on the Montagu 'sporting estate', as it was called, for his brother-in-law, while causing much angst. He was cremated and his ashes placed in the Montagu family crypt.

The Mau Mau atrocities were largely over by 1956 and the insurrection suppressed. But threats remained and would not be resolved for another five years, when the last of the Mau Mau were flushed from the jungles and self-government became a reality.

The farming business in Kenya was at a financial crossroads. The years of political turbulence had taken their toll on market confidence, and managing workforces in the face of violence and uncertainty had become problematic. There was also the fear that the new Kenyan government might confiscate their land.

Mandy and Nell had more than most to lose, having bought up two neighbouring farms abandoned by their white owners. The properties, named Pitman and Nelmanoc, would give them 16,000 acres (6470 hectares) in total and, importantly, access to land on the Nzoia River flats at the bottom of Kapsirowa. It made commercial sense, but only if they could make the three properties work in harmony.

In 1958 Mandy hired a local man named Gerry Boyce, a second-generation white farmer who had been managing a nearby property and agreed to take on what he called 'the big challenge' to make the three Manchester properties profitable. Boyce, who had lost a relative in the first days of the Mau Mau uprising and served as a volunteer with the Kenya Regiment, hit it off immediately with the Duke but, as he wrote many years later, would have reservations about the task ahead.

In his opinion, Nelmanoc in particular had been over-cropped—'flogged'—as far back as the Second World War and was in need of a new water source. The Duke had brought water-divining teams out from Nairobi to attempt to identify a new site for a bore-water hole, but without luck. As it stood, the acreage was only suitable for grazing cattle, otherwise it would be a complete waste.

By contrast, Pitman was in decent condition and had good access to water. But the property had been poorly managed, its potential for maize and coffee beans underutilised, and crops badly thinned. There was also potential for more livestock, mostly the local Boran breed rather than Mandy's favoured Red Poll cattle.

Mandy had also hired a 'top farm manager' named Bob Smith to oversee operations at Kapsirowa and report directly to Gerry Boyce. Bob was a likeable but feisty former jockey, aged in his late twenties and with a thick Geordie accent. He had pitched his credentials for the job partly based on the fact that he could speak Swahili with some proficiency. It was a valuable skill; Bob was hired and given his own house not far from the main house, where he insisted on practising the trombone in the evenings while sitting on his veranda.

Kapsirowa, as beautiful as it was, provided its own set of challenges. Because of its mountainous position, it rose almost 600 metres from bottom to top. The drive from the main gate to the main house was more than two kilometres along unsealed tracks that were frequently impassable, given the amount of rainfall in the region.

Gerry would recall with some amusement the night that Mandy and Nell got bogged as they drove home from a night out in Kitale. The next morning Bob Smith took a group of workers and a tractor to free the vehicle; but when they didn't return, Gerry became worried, particularly as they were in the middle of the coffee-picking season and all hands were needed to complete the work in a few weeks. He sought out the workers' headman, who said they'd been delayed because Bob wanted the men to search for the Duke's false teeth, which had fallen out into the mud.

'I knew that HG [His Grace] did not have dentures so I drove up to chat with Bob. It transpired that his Swahili left a lot to be desired in that he told the headman that the bwana had lost his *meno* (teeth) when he should have said *miwani* (spectacles).'

Bob's wasn't the only appointment that puzzled Gerry, who was surprised one year when Nell and Mandy returned from their annual trip to America and the UK with an English butler—a former soldier named Michael who seemed out of place in the rural setting. 'This was a very big surprise as there were no butlers in Kenya, just a retinue of native house staff, cooks and gardeners. The chauffeur, a Mauritian named Abdullah, was the only one who spoke English. My wife and I gave this some considerable thought. He would have to learn Swahili and what would he do with his time off? Where would he make friends?'

As Gerry would later learn, Michael's arrival was not so much because Mandy wanted a manservant (although he would travel overseas with them) but that he would be a bodyguard for Nell, who was concerned about the isolation, particularly when her husband was either away or late home in the evening. Most houses had metal security guards across their windows but in the darkness of the African bush, miles from the nearest neighbour and with bloody tales as proof of the potential violence, it was no surprise that Nell felt vulnerable.

Gerry Boyce was also coming to terms with a series of animal battles, the first of which was dealing with a troop of fifty baboons that sheltered in the river trees and raided the Pitman maize crops. Staff initially tried to scare the animals off by encouraging the farm children to rattle tins filled with rocks, but that only worked for a short time as the baboons, intelligent and aggressive, realised the children were no threat. Throwing rocks didn't work either.

Eventually an elaborate plan was hatched on the advice of a neighbouring farmer. They trapped a patriarch baboon in a wooden box and poured a weak solution of water and white-wash over his head, which Gerry was assured would wash off with the first monsoonal downpour.

'Tarzan', as they called him, was released after the paint solution had dried. He tried to rejoin his troop but, when the others saw the white apparition, they fled. The perplexed Tarzan followed, swinging through the trees and desperate to catch up; this just made the others flee faster and further. The baboon troop ended up several miles down the river and never returned.

Leopards were another problem. Without a way to scare them off, Gerry and Mandy established a herd system scattered over the three properties, with forty cows and one bull per herd. Each herd had their own grazing land and herdsman, who led them back to an overnight shelter strung with barbed wire and thorn-tree cuttings.

Just as concerning was the loss of several cows a week, found dead in the field with no apparent cause other than evidence of diarrhoea. The deaths went on for more than a month before it was realised that the cows were eating bracken, which was poisonous for them and had to be cleared from the boundaries of the property.

29

A FINAL TRIP HOME

'Am I still Aussie? Of course I am! This is my home.'

The Duchess of Manchester's eyes flashed. She was clearly indignant at the question fired at her by a journalist a few hours after disembarking from the passenger ship *Mariposa*. It was early March 1963 and the waters of Sydney Harbour were still and shining in the early autumn sunshine. Across the bay the foundations of what would become the Sydney Opera House were just emerging—a city on the move.

Just because this was her first trip home in twenty-five years, it didn't mean she was any less Australian than when, as Miss Nell Stead, she had left Melbourne in 1927 to marry into the British aristocracy. If anything, being away for so long had only entrenched her sense of being an individual—now a woman of almost sixty-one with a life story that few could dream of, let alone experience.

'Are you still an Australian?' was a barbed question that many adventurous Australians would face in the years to come for having the apparent audacity to leave their home shores and venture out into the world. The insinuation was that they were turning their back on family and 'the lucky country', as writer Donald Horne would title his iconic book, published the year after Nell's visit.

Those who knew her well would agree that Nell Manchester had remained unwaveringly Australian: first, in the face of the nitpicking English class system; then as a minority European in Kenya; and, lately, amid the new-world pressures of America and California in particular. She was a woman who lived alongside her husband, not behind him, and ensured that she had a voice. 'She and Mandy were partners,' Mark Boyce, son of Gerry, recalled. 'She had her role in their life, and when she wanted something she almost always got it.'

Nell had performed the role of a duchess with skill that few had thought an outsider would be able to summon. She had been unafraid to be herself in the demanding social whirl of London, helped drive and manage the renovation and rescue of Kimbolton Castle, and followed her husband towards the conflict of the Second World War to work as a volunteer nurse and ensure she was by his side. In the years since, she had helped them create a new life in the strange and at times frightening world of East Africa and was now exploring the possibility of yet another move, this time to San Francisco.

The reporter was intrigued to know why she had not returned in 1956, when her home city of Melbourne had hosted the Olympic Games. The couple had announced plans to do so and her sister, Erin, had even planned a welcome home party, which went ahead despite them cancelling a few days before boarding the ship in Southampton because of what they called 'the international situation'.

Nell frowned. Hadn't he heard of the Mau Mau revolt?

Eager not to upset the Duchess further, the reporter changed tack and asked about her life. Nell relented, the reporter forgiven for his impertinence.

'Kapsirowa is a beautiful place,' she began, spreading her hands as if to emphasise its breadth. 'The gardens are now over twenty acres [8 hectares] and we have as many gardeners to tend it. The main house was once mud and wattle but we can now accommodate twelve people comfortably, and often do. It can feel like a hotel at times.'

America now loomed large as their lives changed again. They were even toying with the idea of buying a house in San Francisco—a summer house, she called it. The Duke and Duchess had actually left Kenya almost a year before, intent on a world tour while Kapsirowa was being managed by Gerry Boyce.

The journey had begun with a sea voyage back to London (they both hated flying), then through Europe to America for the past four months before the journey to Australia. They would head back to the States after a month in Sydney and Melbourne; there they would indulge Mandy's motor-racing passion and watch the Indianapolis 500 car race, spend time in San Francisco before going on a three-week cruise to the Bahamas aboard a yacht owned by multimillionaire businessman Tony Hulman, a close friend and owner of the Indianapolis racetrack.

It all seemed very glamorous—the exciting places and high-powered friends—and disguised their constant concern about money. 'It's been a long trip,' the Duchess acknowledged. 'By the time we get back we will have been away from Kenya for eighteen months.'

The reason for the Australian leg was to attend the christening of their first grandchild. Angus's son Alexander Charles David Drogo Montagu had been born the previous December. Angus, after finishing his national service and being discharged from the Royal Marines, had spent a year in America before moving to Australia in 1959. There he had worked as a barman, outback jackeroo, rally driver and film extra—a job during which he was said to have wrestled a crocodile. By 1961 he was in Melbourne working in the menswear section of a department store, where he met Mary Eveleen McClure, a typist at a local newspaper. He was besotted and proposed to her within a few months.

The media lapped up the story—'Engaged to a Lord'—because family history was repeating itself as an English aristocrat chose a Melbourne girl for his wife. In response, Angus told the magazines that the reason he wasn't going to marry an English girl was 'because they are too blasé and put on too many airs'.

'Call me Mr Montagu,' he added. 'Mine is just a courtesy title. After all, I did nothing to earn it. Titles are becoming a thing of the past, you know. We want to live a normal life and have no ambitions to join the social set.'

The couple wed in late 1961 and baby Alexander arrived a year later. He would be baptised in a small church at Darling Point, sans the royal proclamation of his grandfather, after whom he was named. Little did they expect that father and son would, in years to come, both inherit the title of Duke of Manchester.

Jomo Kenyatta made a triumphant return to Nairobi in May 1963. He was elected as the country's first prime minister just as Nell and Mandy arrived in America after their Australian side visit.

The decade of violence was finally over but anxieties remained. Despite assurances in the months leading up to the elections, many feared Kenyatta's political ascension would result in retribution against the remaining European population in Kenya. In anticipation of that, whites were pulling out of the country at the rate of seven hundred people per month, threatening collapse of the country's agricultural economy.

Mandy and Nell were on tenterhooks as they checked into San Francisco's famous St Francis Hotel. 'The African situation is most annoying,' Nell grunted to newspapermen gathered around as their favourite bellman, Bob, took their bags. Mandy went further as he strode through the lobby: 'I fear that we are on a list of Europeans they want to get rid of, and we might have to sell the farm.'

It wasn't any physical threat that concerned them, but that Kenyátta would confiscate their land to return it to Africans.

This possibility was clearly playing on their minds as they began what had now become a serious search for an American base. If they were forced from Kapsirowa, then there was no choice but to leave Kenya and find a new place to call home.

America, and the west coast in particular, was the obvious choice given Mandy's familial links and the friends they had made over the years. Besides, both trust funds—his mother's and grandmother's—were managed by New York accountants and they provided the bulk of their income.

News that the couple was house hunting in San Francisco was greeted with excitement and unabashed adoration by the local newspapers. They couldn't believe their luck because crooner Bing Crosby also happened to be house hunting in the same neighbourhood. The appearances of the Manchesters with Hollywood celebrities at local restaurants were noted; Nell's fashion and style were scrutinised and praised. 'The duchess is in her early fifties—maybe,' the *Ventura County Star* wrote flatteringly of the sixty-one-year-old. 'She is tall with red-gold hair she combs back in a simple bob . . . Her clothes are simple and elegant, tailored and smart from her Capri pants to her jacketed cocktail outfits.'

A house was chosen within a month—a lavish property in the fashionable suburb of Hillsborough built by banker and antiques collector John Drum, and previously rented to US attorney general Robert Kennedy. A few weeks later, Nell and Mandy left for their Bahamas cruise with Tony Hulman before heading back to Kenya to face Jomo Kenyatta and make a decision about their future.

They were among a crowd of five hundred settlers packed into a hall in the city of Nakuru, known as the unofficial 'White Highlands capital of Kenya', in early August. Kenyatta had agreed to speak to them. The crowd was at first hostile and sceptical but then quietened down as he appealed for all sides in the conflict to bury the past. 'Stay,' he urged the white farming families. 'We want you to stay and farm well. Please believe me, that is the policy of my government. Kenya is large enough and its potential is great. We can all work together harmoniously to make this country great and to show other countries that different racial groups can work and live together.'

International news crews had also crowded into the room; photographs showed concerned faces as Kenyatta arrived and the relief after he'd spoken. The *Atlanta Journal* reported the farmers' collective response: 'The African cry welled up out of hundreds of white throats. "Harambee!" and the stately, turbaned black man on the platform grinned in pleasure. "Harambee!"—meaning, roughly, "We will pull together". It was the pledge—and equally it voiced the hope—of 500 white settlers in the Rift Valley applauding the man they once feared and hated more than any other.'

A few days later, a relieved Duke of Manchester declared that he and Nell were staying. 'There is no truth in the suggestion that we plan to leave Kenya,' he told journalists. 'If things remain as they are, we shall stay. You don't buy a piece of virgin Africa, as we did in 1946, build it up and then leave it just like that.'

British newspapers were also interested in whether the Duke and Duchess might return to Kimbolton, where Park Farm was still operating, if somewhat ploddingly. The answer was 'no', reported the *Sunday Mirror*: 'The Duke of Manchester will continue farming in a gorgeous homestead where giraffes crane their long necks through the casement windows to gaze at solid silver Loveday fireplaces and Aubusson tapestries.'

Nell and Mandy made their way back to America in the late spring of 1964 to check progress on renovations of the new house. Their return was noted by newspaper columnists, the couple now among the notable 'birds of passage' who migrated annually to the Golden State. The dinner and cocktail party invitations mounted as California's royals did the social rounds of San Francisco and the holiday playground of the rich at Lake Tahoe.

In July they flew west to Hawaii to mingle with tycoon and environmental philanthropist Laurance Rockefeller and his guests at the opening of his iconic hotel Mauna Kea. Then they headed back east to New York, where the latest fad was to be added to the list of clients allowed access to 'top tables'. The Manchesters were a natural fit on the royal station of tables at the famed restaurant La Côte Basque, where the Kennedys, Roosevelts and Hiltons sat when eating out.

In September they returned to Kenya via London, from where they made a nostalgic journey to Kimbolton. The castle was no longer owned by the family but there was some comfort in its restoration and care by the school. Dozens of portraits unsold during the fire sale in 1949 were again adorning the walls of the drawing rooms, which were now classrooms and offices.

But there were dark clouds on the horizon.

While they were in London, Nell arranged a health check-up. A melanoma was found on her right eye—cancer. History was repeating itself. Nell's thoughts turned to her mother, Lilian, whose death all those years before had paved the way for her visit to Ceylon and her meeting with Mandy.

This was a war unlike the others Nell and Mandy had faced together, and it was one that they could not avoid. They made the decision to pack up most of the Kimbolton artifacts at Kapsirowa and move them to America. They were moving out of their house not because it had been requisitioned or because they were under threat but because Nell needed consistent medical treatment that was available in San Francisco but not down the road at Kitale.

But they disguised their reasons for emigrating, blaming the move on continuing political uncertainty in Kenya. 'The Manchesters have dismantled many of the large rooms on their cattle and coffee estate and shipped them to their Hillsborough home,' the *San Francisco Examiner* reported. 'Things are so unsettled in the area that they are not certain how much longer they can remain and they are taking no chances on losing their valuable possessions.'

Before they left Kenya, there would be one last journey—a two-week safari in Land Rovers with several house guests. It repeated a journey they had made in the first months of their arrival in Kenya. The group travelled first to the Ugandan capital Kampala on the shores of Lake Victoria before travelling south into Rwanda, through bamboo forests filled with gorillas, and past the volcanic Mount Nyiragongo, which erupted the day after they passed it, sending lava flowing down into Lake Kivu. At Nyanza they encountered the Watusi, a tribe of towering warriors, and in the Ituri Forest near Lake Albert they met Bantu-speaking pygmy peoples. The journey continued past the snow-covered Rwenzori Mountains to the plains beyond, which teemed with game, and then back to Kampala and into Kenya once more.

It was hard to leave their home of nearly two decades, although the return to San Francisco and their friends helped soften the blow as they settled into their third continent as a married couple—this time without the grandeur, and with the knowledge that Nell's time was likely limited as her eyesight worsened. Their social calendar was still a whirl but there were signs of the cancer's progress. Photographs showed Nell wearing dark sunglasses and occasionally an eye patch. She was slowly losing her sight.

'The Duke and Duchess of Manchester missed the polo game but turned up to the cocktail party following the game,' the *San Francisco Examiner* reported, adding: 'They arrived with their host but remained at the party so briefly that the duchess didn't even take off her camel coloured coat.'

Nell was at their Hillsborough home with Mandy, Kim and Angus by her bedside when she passed away on 2 September

1966. Her death was announced in dozens of newspapers across four continents, such was the breadth of her life's experiences. She was farewelled with the three identities she treasured most: the Duchess of Manchester; Nell Vere Stead; 'a native Australian'.

30

AN ERA HAS ENDED

Mandy was eating by himself. The diners around him at Quaglino's in Bury Street, Westminster, were unaware of who he was, let alone his personal sadness. It was late September 1966 and he'd just arrived back in London to bury his wife, Nell, in the Montagu family crypt at Kimbolton.

His meal was unexpectedly interrupted by the arrival of a man carrying a bassinet, who loudly proclaimed that he had delivered a baby for the Duke of Manchester. Mandy looked up, unsure what was going on. The man handed over a letter in an envelope, placed the bassinet on the carpet and left without Mandy having the chance to say anything, let alone protest.

The child inside the cot was a fair-haired boy, aged no more than six months and dressed in a white matinee coat, dress, and bootees with a pink ribbon. He was covered by two blankets—one white and one blue. His name was Andrew.

Mandy was left staring into his soup, embarrassed by the incident and wondering what was going on. Thank heavens that Nell was not around to see it.

The letter raised more questions than answers. It revealed that the boy was a son of an Australian woman named Trixeena Bertine Stel who claimed that Angus was the father and that she couldn't afford to keep him. She had also changed her surname by deed poll to Montagu, as if it would strengthen her claim.

Angus, who was in a Mayfair bar with friends when the Quaglino's incident occurred, denied the claim. He had returned to London the previous year, leaving his now estranged wife, Mary, with three children: Alexander, now aged three, Kimble, aged two, and Emma, aged one. 'I don't even have enough money for a packet of cigarettes, let alone enough to feed three children,' Mary said when contacted by the media about the incident at Quaglino's.

The scandal was ignored two days later, when the family and Kimbolton townspeople gathered in St Andrew's to say goodbye to Nell. She may still have felt Australian but, after forty years away from Melbourne, her final resting place was with the Montagus.

There was some relief a month later when blood tests cleared Angus of being the father of baby Andrew, although not of having had some sort of relationship with Trixeena Stel. His marriage with Mary was effectively over, although the divorce would take some years to finalise. There were echoes of his paternal grandfather.

After the funeral, Mandy headed back to Kenya, where he found solace in the house on the hill that he and Nell had created together. He only ventured out into the world again six months later, to captain a team of Kenyan fishermen competing in a billfish tournament off Hawaii. He then returned to San Francisco.

The Hillsborough house, so much a part of his and Nell's plans for the future, now felt empty. One of the first to offer her condolences was Elizabeth Coleman Crocker, a widow who lived in a neighbouring fifty-three-room mansion called Sky Farm. Elizabeth had lost her husband two years before and, after an ugly court battle with the children of her late husband, had inherited Sky Farm as well as US$2 million. It added to a multimillion-dollar divorce settlement she had received a decade before when she and her first husband, a wealthy Texas oil baron named George L. Coleman, had split.

The condolence led to a friendship, which then blossomed into a romance; in February 1969, Mandy remarried in a ceremony held at Kapsirowa, followed by a blessing at the local church.

The union was greeted with some gendered cynicism by American society writers, among them the columnist for the *San Francisco Examiner*:

> Although the news came out of the blue, no one close to the principals was really surprised. The former Elizabeth Fullerton, who started her remarkable social career in Miami, Oklahoma, had no place to go but up. After bearing the names of one of California's first families, what else could she do but

> marry a title? Conveniently, there is a resident English peer in Hillsborough who is listed in the San Mateo county telephone book as 'Manchester, Duke of'.

Syndicated columnist 'Suzy', who had reported often on Nell and Mandy's American life, also had a warning: 'The motto on the Manchester coat of arms reads "By disposing of me, not by changing me". Maybe that means he plans to keep right on living in Kenya. The alluring new duchess, however, maintains an apartment in New York so, motto or not, they'll be spending some of their time here. One should never underestimate this bride.'

Motives aside, the relationship between Mandy and the new Duchess of Manchester—a late-life marriage of friendship—was very different from his four-decade love affair with Nell Stead.

Helena Zimmerman died in December 1971 at the age of ninety-three. She had outlived two husbands and three of her four children, and left a British estate worth £140,732 (from which £68,895 was taken out in death duties), not to mention the hefty American trust fund.

There was only one beneficiary—her last surviving child, Mandy.

Mandy's oldest sibling, Alice, had died in 1962 from complications during hip surgery in a Mexico hospital. She had moved there in 1948 after the shocking death of her sister, Louise, because she wanted to be near their brother, Edward. She then stayed after meeting and marrying an American architect named Fendall Gregory.

Even though Mandy's money worries were finally over, it seemed as if the dismantling of the Kimbolton estate was never-ending, such was its size and scope. Every once in a while an article would appear in a British newspaper mentioning the sale of an item from the castle: 'A letter written in verse by the poet John Donne in about 1612 was sold for £23,000 at Sotheby's today. The letter was the property of the Duke of Manchester.'

Some prized assets from the Kimbolton fire sale of 1949 had been salted away. Some were sold when markets improved and others, like the autographed Donne manuscript—'A Letter to Lady Carey'—were discovered as experts slowly combed their way through the castle records. In 1977, when the Museum of Tobago opened, with its oldest exhibit a deed signed in 1647 granting 20,000 acres (8090 hectares) to three London merchants, in a bid to encourage investment on the island. The document had been buried in the records of Kimbolton Castle for three hundred years.

Other auctions were of rare books from the vast library, among them a seventeenth-century copy of famed Amsterdam cartographer Carel Allard's book *Atlas Minor*, a 1639 tome called *One Hundred and Thirteen Diseases of the Eye* and a 1735 compendium of French inventions titled *Machines et inventions*. In 1973 there was a sale of furniture from the castle, including William and Mary armchairs and seventeenth-century Japanese black lacquer cabinets.

It seemed inevitable that the last vestiges of Kimbolton would also go. In July 1975, the *Evening Standard* announced the Duke 'and his heir, Viscount Mandeville' were severing their remaining links with Kimbolton. There were 3250 acres (1320 hectares) of farmland and woodland—containing six farms, and eighteen houses and cottages—with an asking price of £1 million. It was no surprise, but there was one note of concern: Mandy was described as 'the ailing Duke of Manchester'.

There was no mention of illness in 1976 when the sale was finalised for 'slightly less than asking price'. Instead, there was praise for the Duke and assurances that life for his now former tenants was unlikely to change.

'The present Duke, a war hero who carried ten men to safety after dashing into a bomb store, did his utmost to pull the estate together following its decline under the former Duke,' a report in the *Cambridge Evening News* noted, adding that he had transformed his Kenyan ranch 'from scrubland into one of the most productive mixed farming enterprises in Africa'.

It read like an obituary and was clearly a response to news that the Duke of Manchester had throat cancer, and had been forced to have a life-saving operation that reduced his voice to a whisper through an electronic box. At times he found it easier to communicate with a pencil and a notepad; his travel between Kenya and America lessened and, instead, he spent more time in London over the next year receiving treatment.

But the end was inevitable. On 23 November 1977, Mandy passed away in a London hospital. This time the obituaries were real, lauding his wartime bravery and noting his protest against hated death taxes as well as his determination not to be forced from Kapsirowa by the Mau Mau. 'When we bought our farm in 1946 we lived in a mud and wattle hut,' he had said. 'My son and I worked on the land from sun-up to sundown and although we did not get our own house built for six years, we meanwhile built a school for one hundred African children.'

Mandy was cremated in Cambridge and his remains placed beside Nell's in the family vault at Kimbolton five days later, the funeral service overflowing outside St Andrew's even though friends from America had not had time to fly over and attend. There was a wake back at the George Hotel, funded by £100—a tidy sum—that Mandy had left in his will for the tenants and estate workers, of whom he once told his son Angus: 'These are your real friends, this is your family, you look after these people.'

News quickly reached the Hawaii Big Game Fishing Club where Mandy, or 'Manny' as he had become known locally, had regularly competed in its annual billfish competition. 'He once philosophised that a marlin in Hawaii was much like a marlin in Africa,' a club newsletter noted, quoting the Duke. 'Either the fish is there and hungry when you come by with your bait and strikes or he does not even see the lure. All the same, you either go home with a fish—or you don't.'

The most touching obituary was written by the writer James Wentworth Day, a close friend with whom Mandy had often hunted at Kimbolton. 'Easily one of the twelve best shots in England,' Wentworth Day declared, recounting Mandy's abilities with a gun and his joy at hunting in the fens. 'We both loved the place and came to it stealthily before dawn when most men were asleep, and sat or waded about there all day, wet and happy, living on bread and cheese and bottled beer.'

Wentworth Day regarded his friend as a humble, bleeding hero who had carried 'half a score' of injured men from the bowels of the HMS *Eagle* and should have been given the Victoria Cross. He had seen, firsthand, his friend's love for Kimbolton and his frustration that he and Nell had not been able to save the family history. 'Today the fen is drained. The buck has fled. The estate is reduced to woodland. The castle is a school. And now the man who loved and treasured it all is dead. An era has ended.'

31

MORE DUPE THAN DUKE

Sidney Arthur Robin George Drogo Montagu, the 11th Duke of Manchester, was not particularly interested in farming. Despite his early efforts, helping his father to carve the Kapsirowa ranch from virgin bush, Lord Kim had long moved on from the satisfaction and challenge of growing coffee and rearing cattle.

Instead, he made his money as a mechanic and a driver for film companies doing location work. He had given up motor racing, which included a record nineteen successive years as a competitor in the East African Safari Rally, after he was involved in a serious accident that left him with a permanently injured tear duct. Instead, he learned to fly and would expand his business repertoire to include air-charter services.

Barely a year after his father's death, Kim arranged to sell Kapsirowa to the Kenyan government as part of its land acquisition program. The new seat of the Montagu family was a modest three-bedroom house on 2 hectares of land on the outskirts of Nairobi.

Kim's personal life had been messy. Just three months before his father died, he was divorced from his first wife Adrienne Christie, the daughter of a diplomat, to whom he had been married for twenty-two years. The couple had no children, and their marriage ended unceremoniously in what a London court called a 'quickie-postal', based on the fact that they had been estranged for two years. But the damage had been done long before.

Alcohol was blamed for the couple's lack of children as well as the disintegration of the relationship. Both were heavy drinkers. Adrienne, known by her middle name, Val, often stayed in a cottage called Chestnuts at Kimbolton.

And now Kim had found a new wife. Andrea Kent, thirteen years his junior, with three children from two previous marriages—the last to a well-known big game hunter—was the new Duchess of Manchester.

In 1977, when Kenya suddenly banned hunting, Kim saw a new opportunity as a safari guide, his clients armed with cameras rather than elephant guns. It was a decent sales pitch for tourists wanting the African experience led by an English duke, although he usually shied away from too much attention to his title. As Scottish vet Hugh Cran, who worked in Kenya for more than fifty years, noted in his memoir *Promises to Keep*: 'Kim Mandeville was a belted earl, a duke no less, a gentleman farmer with oceans of blue blood surging through his aristocratic veins. He was no ordinary mortal. But . . . he wore his ermine lightly and was as friendly and as easy going as you could wish.'

Unlike his parents and younger brother, whom he barely saw, Kim did not feel he had any strong ties to Kimbolton. The castle had played little part in his life, other than that he was born in one of its upstairs bedrooms. So it was no surprise that he continued to sell off the seemingly endless pieces of estate property left scattered around the village—several cottages and small parcels of land, as well as the golf course attached to Tandragee Castle, which yielded barely £40,000.

Coupled with his father's estate of £68,000 after tax, the continuing income from his grandmother's trust gave him a tidy annual income and for the first time in his life Kim had money in his pocket. He reduced his safari work and instead became involved in wildlife preservation groups.

He would visit London each year. On one occasion he attended the opening of parliament to take his seat in the House of Lords, while his wife sat in the gallery wearing the Manchester tiara, which had been borrowed from the Victoria and Albert Museum where it was now kept.

His trip to London in 1981 highlighted his disaffected relationship with Montagu history. His flight from Johannesburg had to be diverted because of storms over Heathrow; it landed instead in the city of Manchester. This meant that the Duke of Manchester was in the city of the family's dukedom, probably for the first time in its history. Oblivious to the significance of the moment, Kim chose to stay on the plane and wait for the storms to clear, rather than disembark and face a long bus ride back to London. He saw nothing of Manchester in the few hours he was there.

By the time he returned to Kenya, a month later, he'd had second thoughts about his decision and confessed in an interview to his mistake. 'I'm very humble and apologetic about it, but there it is. I've never consciously tried to avoid Manchester but somehow we have never got together,' he said, revealing he had accepted an invitation to be a patron of the city's art gallery. 'The truth is my family has no connection with Manchester. Technically, it should have been the dukedom of Godmanchester, an area centring on Huntingdonshire, taking in parts of Lincolnshire, Bedfordshire, Cambridgeshire and Northamptonshire, but it was such a cumbersome title that they decided to drop the *God*.'

His financial comfort was under threat in early 1983, when there was yet another legal challenge to Helena Zimmerman's trust fund. The Episcopal Diocese of Ohio—citing the original document drawn up by Eugene Zimmerman, which sought to honour his mother's wishes—laid claim to half the contents of the trust. But Helena had subsequently made two changes to document as part of her own will, the last of these to recognise her grandson just a year before she died.

Much to Kim's relief, the court confirmed his grandmother's right to change her own will, and her wishes stood. But it prompted his own concerns about legacy and, in particular, family heirlooms, including portraits by Hans Holbein and Van Dyck that his father had bequeathed to his second wife, Elizabeth.

It seemed incomprehensible to him that valuable portraits, which had hung for centuries in the Great Hall at Kimbolton Castle and then at Kapsirowa, would be given away to a rich American widow who lived in New York rather than being handed down through the generations to Montagu family members. The High Court agreed, sparking a search for the missing works and 'whatever else hasn't been sold'.

Kim was growing restless and he looked to America to find a future, drawn, as his father and mother had been, to its possibilities. In 1983 he bought a 200-hectare ranch in Tennessee, 30 kilometres north of Nashville. 'We're very, I think you call it, "into" conservation,' he told the local press. 'The thing that sold me was an aerial photograph of the farm with three deer standing in the picture.'

But the couple's plans to develop the land would come to nothing. On 3 June 1985, just after they arrived at the property from Nairobi, Kim suffered a severe asthma attack. As he was being driven to see a doctor in nearby Ashland City, the fifty-six-year-old had a major heart attack, slumped forward in his seat and died.

Angus Montagu was waiting to be tried for fraud in the Old Bailey when he was told of his brother's sudden death and that he had become the 12th Duke of Manchester. To make matters worse—if indeed they could be—his oldest son and heir, Alex, was in the dock of an Australian court weeping as he was told by the judge that he was likely to spend time in jail for his part in a bank scam.

The House of Montagu was being burned to the ground and the British newspapers couldn't help but report on its demise, particularly when a third legal stoush emerged, this time initiated by Angus in a bid to stop his first wife, Mary McClure, from referring to herself publicly as a 'duchess'.

Lady Mary laid claim to the title even though she had been divorced from Angus for fifteen years. 'It has taken me twenty years to educate taxi drivers that I'm really Lady Montagu . . . now they're going to think I'm a pub,' she told a newspaper less than forty-eight hours after her former brother-in-law's death.

It was true that Angus's three children with Mary—Alex, Kimble and Emma—had inherited formal titles, but not so his former wife who, at a stretch, could continue to call herself 'Lady'.

Angus had long since moved on to his second marriage, to a bank clerk named Diane Plimsaul, whom he married in a registry office in 1971 and celebrated in a room above a cafe in Ealing. But after fourteen years, that relationship too was also on the rocks and they would be divorced just months after he inherited the title.

In October 1985, he stepped back into court to face charges that he was a conspirator, with others, in a £38,000 swindle. The group had allegedly forged US bonds as security for a loan and blackmailed a bank manager after arranging for him to spend an illicit weekend with a strip-club dancer named Diana.

After two weeks of evidence, the jury acquitted the new duke on the basis that he was naive and had been duped by his business partners. Angus's name had been used to dazzle the compromised bank manager, but he did not escape the wrath of the judge, who was scathing: 'On a business scale of one to ten you are one or less and maybe even that flatters you. You are an absurdly negligent and stupid person.' Angus walked free from the court, but his business reputation was forever shattered, at least in Britain.

Angus was now almost forty-seven years old and alone—although, like his paternal grandfather, he always seemed to have an attractive young woman on his arm and the appearance of having money in his pocket. The truth was he was virtually broke, except for a moderate stipend from the family trusts; he lived in a flat in the market town of Bedford, 20 kilometres south of a castle that, if not for a mix of circumstance and incompetence, might have been his home.

He was socially inept, but he presented well and loved to flaunt his title, padded out with stories about his ties with royalty and movie stars. He made his job as a film extra in the 1960s sound like he had been rubbing shoulders on set with the likes of Esther Williams and Marlene Dietrich.

He was also protected by a coterie of sympathetic friends, who tried to help and bought him drinks to satisfy an unquenchable thirst. Although overweight, he remained very strong and would frequently step forward in East End pubs when challenged to do fingertip push-ups. Angus never lost a bet.

Despite the camaraderie, by the late 1980s his life on both a personal and financial level was empty. Contrary to media speculation about a Montagu fortune—some suggested there was £60 million waiting for him in America—there would be very little money attached to his inheritance of the title.

His older brother had left everything, heirlooms aside, to his second wife, Andrea, and her three children from previous marriages; their inheritance included the Tennessee ranch, which had cost close to US$1 million and had been largely funded from the sale of Kimbolton assets. It highlighted the toxicity of the fallout between the two brothers, created partly because of Angus's boorish behaviour, but also because Kim had felt aggrieved at the attention his younger brother had received as a child compared to his own struggles.

Marcus Scriven interviewed Joss Kent, one of Kim's step-children, who recalled a conversation just a few weeks before his death. Kim had become aware of the fraud case against Angus and was lamenting its impact on the family. When asked by Joss who Angus was, Kim had replied: 'He's my brother; I'd rather he wasn't.'

There were still several family trusts but two of them—the American trust started by Angus's great-grandmother Consuelo and the English trust of his grandmother Helena—had become discretionary after Mandy's death. Now the trustees could control how much was handed out to the new duke, whose debts had spiralled to more than £100,000. They bought him the Bedford flat. He would later add the adjacent flat and join it to the first to create a larger living space, but the trustees were reluctant to release more money for fear that he would simply spend it.

The trustees were right to be wary. As soon as he got his hands on the remaining family silverware and furniture, Angus flogged it as a job lot for £50,000, despite promises to the dowager duchess Andrea that he would 'keep it forever'.

'He had champagne tastes and lemonade pockets,' one female friend told Marcus Scriven. Angus was not only a physical copy of his grandfather, the 9th Duke, but he had a matching outlook on life and money, insisting on hiring limousines when going to the theatre as a 'ducal gesture'.

He quickly found solace in the House of Lords, where the food was free and the drinks and cigarettes heavily subsidised. All the while he pocketed a generous daily attendance allowance of £23 per day and £60 overnight, which was substantial given that he attended more than six hundred times during his tenure. In that time he made only one speech: to warn that England would lose its sovereignty if it signed the Maastricht Treaty, the foundation of the European Union. He rose to his feet at 3.55 p.m. and sat down three minutes later, at 3.58 p.m. 'I'm not a great speaker, so I kept it short,' he explained.

He accepted a role as figurehead of The Dukes Trust, a charity aimed at raising funds for deprived children, and took up an offer to appear as a guest speaker aboard the P&O liner *Royal Princess* on its cruise from Japan to Hawaii, then on to Texas and New York. It was all about creating the fantasy life of a duke, which slotted neatly into his personality as a fabulist.

In 1989 he married for a third time, to a divorcee named Louise Taylor, the daughter of a Yorkshire doctor, who was quite happy to play the costume role of duchess.

Angus's fortunes seemed to be changing. He received £500,000 when a relative died without an heir and then received news that he stood to inherit the jewels left by his great-grandmother, Consuelo, including those pawned by the 9th Duke all those years before. The stipulation of her complicated will meant that he had to wait until 1998, twenty-one years after the death of his father—the only other male Montagu alive when Consuelo died in 1909.

But his impatience would get the better of him and he began to raise loans with the jewels as collateral, even though he had not yet inherited them. To compound matters, he also ploughed the £500,000 inheritance windfall into a series of investments—housing developments, drag racing, casinos, even the purchase of a Caribbean island—all of which inevitably turned sour. The money was gone.

Worse was to follow. In 1991, having reconnected with one Keith Cheeseman, Angus was persuaded to accept a position on a company called Link International, which had been set up by Cheeseman and others. As well as a shopping mall in Florida and a scheme to sell water to Saudi Arabia, the company was also about to take a slice of the Tampa Bay Lightning, an ice hockey team.

The US$50 million Tampa Bay deal was announced with great fanfare in June, with Angus front and centre accepting a hockey shirt emblazoned with 'The Duke' and the No. 1 from club president Phil Esposito, who declared: 'Great isn't it? We don't yet have all the financing in place. We got us a Duke. Nothing shabby about the Tampa Bay Lightning.'

But it was indeed shabby. A simple check in Burke's Peerage by a reporter from *The Tampa Tribune* revealed the details of Angus's 1985 fraud trial and that he was among the poorest British aristocrats. Claims that he controlled trust funds worth

£200 million were spurious. Just two months later the plan was in tatters when Link couldn't raise the money. Investors began pulling out; the deal collapsed and so did Link International.

Fast-forward four years and Angus was fronting a Florida court on four charges of wire fraud and one of conspiracy. He was by himself. Keith Cheeseman was in jail on another matter and the other three partners were on the run from the FBI.

Louise stood by him and his lawyers offered the same excuse: that he was vain and gullible, led around by the others like a prize bull at a show, but not a criminal—'More dupe than duke'. The jury didn't buy it this time; he was convicted on four of the five charges and sentenced to almost three years in prison.

Angus was contrite, telling the judge: 'Since the beginning of this thing I had every intention of turning up . . . and serving my time. I'd also like to apologise, most profusely, for any trouble I have caused you and your court.' His lawyer was convinced that, if he had pleaded guilty, he would have paid a fine and walked away with a suspended sentence, but he had refused.

He served his time at the Federal Correctional Institution in Petersburg, Virginia, and emerged in November 1998 insisting that he had learned 'humility and tolerance'. But there would be consequences, not the least of which was his marriage. Although she had testified on his behalf and visited him in prison several times, Louise was gone, filing for divorce as a means of financial preservation against the mounting debts that Angus had run up.

No matter. On 22 April 2000, at the Swedish Church in Mayfair, he was married for a fourth time, to a fifty-eight-year-old former model named Biba Hiller, who had been married three times herself. Their union would last barely a year.

His income from the family trusts had dwindled as they paid off his legal debts, so he tried using his title to pursue a coach-tour business: 'heritage tours' to places like Stratford-upon-Avon, for which American tourists paid £250 a head to travel with a duke for the day. 'I really love doing the tours,' he said. 'The guests are honoured to see an English duke, and once you put them at ease they're wonderful people.' It failed.

He returned to the House of Lords, briefly, before the House of Lords Act 1999 banished most hereditary peers. In desperation he returned to Kimbolton and removed Catherine of Aragon's chest from the family vault, selling it for a paltry £350.

But alongside his money worries, Angus's health had suffered. Although he had lost weight in prison, by 2002 he was again grossly overweight and clearly had breathing difficulties. On 25 July he suffered chest pains and called an ambulance. By the time paramedics arrived at his upstairs flat, he had suffered a heart attack and died there. His body was removed by a crane from the building's third floor.

Angus's notoriety ensured that over the next few days he had more words written about him than any other Montagu male in two hundred years—even his spendthrift grandfather, the 9th Duke. Newspapers had a field day with their gleeful character assassinations. He was absurdly stupid and negligent, a hapless duke and an incompetent peer: 'he failed as a trouser salesman in Sydney, but survived wrestling with crocodiles', concluded *The Guardian*.

The funeral took place at the Bedford crematorium on 5 August. His two youngest children, Kimble and Emma, were there, as were two of his former wives, Louise and Diane, and his stepmother Elizabeth. Mourners packed the building and the wake, which was held at the Bedford Rowing Club.

Despite his clear character flaws, Angus had been a popular man and the last in the family to sit in the house of Lords and play a role in the affairs of Britain. Although the name and title has continued since, there was a feeling that his passing heralded a finality to the import of the House of Montagu.

EPILOGUE

The 13th Duke

There was one significant person who was not at either the funeral or the ceremony the following day when Angus's ashes were interred in the family crypt at Kimbolton: Alex, 13th Duke of Manchester.

Angus had publicly 'disowned' his oldest son in 1991 when, just as he was launching the Tampa Bay Lightning scam, news came that Alex was about to be deported for entering Canada illegally. Alex had not told officials that he suffered from bipolar disorder and had a police record in Australia that included twenty-nine convictions for fraud and assault.

Aged twenty-nine, he was interviewed by journalists while staying at the CA$25-a-night Skid Row Hostel in Toronto, alongside his new girlfriend, Katie, a former agent for strip-club workers. 'I've lived with the rich and famous, and I just wanted to be a bum and see how others live,' he said, adding that he was a cousin of Diana, Princess of Wales, and fifty-second in line to the British throne. Both untrue.

Alex had always been troubled, with some justification—as the judge in his 1985 trial for fraud observed. As a young man, he had been diagnosed as having a personality disorder; this was compounded by a lonely childhood, during which he was pushed from one private school to another, with little or no contact with his family.

It smacked of the problems faced by his father and uncle, although Alex's were born of neglect rather than circumstance, as he battled with depression and developed fantasies to deal with his loneliness. His grandfather, Mandy, attempted to intervene at one point and bring him to the UK for schooling, but it fell flat because Angus was not interested in his son.

Alex was just twenty-one when in 1984 he married a thirty-three-year-old model named Marion Stoner. The relationship lasted two months before she fled, accusing her angry husband of firing a speargun at her leg. He denied this and later told a newspaper: 'If I attacked my wife with a speargun, why am I not in jail? Why would I not just shoot her with my Walther P5? I never, ever miss.'

Despite his criminal record, Alex managed to migrate to the United States where, in 1993, he married a second time—to law-firm receptionist Wendy Buford, with whom he had a son, Alexander Jr, and then a daughter, Ashley. The marriage lasted thirteen years before the couple divorced. A year later he married a third time, to a California real-estate agent named Laura Ann Smith.

Then the already complicated story became twisted.

In 2009, the now Duke of Manchester suddenly stopped making child support payments to his second wife for their children, who were aged sixteen and ten. The reason for his non-payment was that the marriage to Wendy Buford had been bigamous and the children were therefore illegitimate. The Montagu family trusts would not pay up.

In the British High Court case that followed, it emerged that Alex had not bothered to divorce Marion Stoner until 1996, three years after 'marrying' Wendy, who would later recount how Alex's mother, Lady Mary, turned up at her door one day asking that she sign papers to finalise the divorce. She readily agreed.

But Mr Justice Floyd ruled that Alex's sloppiness was not relevant and neither did it matter where he or the children lived. Alexander Jr and Ashley were his children and therefore his legitimate heirs. 'It follows that I consider that the family trustees are entitled under the terms of the settlements to provide for Alexander and Ashley,' he concluded.

The case sparked a rash of publicity. Wendy Buford and Marion Stoner were both tracked down and interviewed about their relationships with 'the bigamist duke'. Stoner had not even been aware that Alex had remarried. Laura stood by her man, insisting that they were simply youthful indiscretions.

In the years since then, Alex has moved around the US, from Newport Beach to Las Vegas and finally to Laura's home in Michigan. There has been an array of business ventures, including renting executive jets and security, while Alex and Laura have used social media to rail about the unfair changes to the Manchester trusts, orchestrated by his uncle Kim, which meant that Alex had been stripped of his financial birth rights.

There have also been occasional brushes with the law. One case, in 2016, attracted prime-time news in Nevada, where he was interviewed behind bars. 'I've made mistakes and it's embarrassing to be here, but I'm proud of who I am,' he declared. Aged fifty-three, Alex had been arrested for a bizarre burglary in Las Vegas when a woman woke in the early hours of the morning to find a shirtless and shoeless man entering her bedroom. He ran away when she phoned emergency services and was found soon afterwards in a nearby house, where he said he lived.

In his defence, Alex Montagu-Manchester, as he called himself, claimed that Laura had attacked him with a box knife and cut his thumb: 'He's been saying a lot of things,' she responded, denying she had even been in the apartment. 'He needs help. Something's going on and people can see it.' Alex would spend fourteen months behind bars.

Perhaps the answer to his obvious distress lay in the fact that he and Laura had just returned from a trip to Britain, during which Alex had made a nostalgic return to Kimbolton Castle. There he had wandered through the stately rooms and halls opened to tourists while the school's students were on summer holidays.

Alex was accompanied by two volunteer guides, keen to take care of their esteemed aristocratic visitor. They patiently answered his questions about the castle and even showed him the family crypt below, where the coffins and cremation urns of his forebears—dukes and duchesses and family members, including his father, Angus, and his grandparents, Mandy and Nell—lay stacked floor to ceiling.

It was a bittersweet moment—family heritage that he could see, but not touch. He videoed inside what was once the great White Hall, with its grand eighteenth-century family portraits still on the walls and its Pellegrini frescoes on the ornate ceilings.

The Duke's commentary is clearly audible on the video, which he posted on his Facebook page. 'This is what my son wanted to see,' he told the guides. '*Our* castle.' Even though nothing physical remains of the Montagu estate, and the trusts of Consuelo and Helena are all but empty, he had not been able to let go of the sense of ownership of the most tangible evidence of the family's once-great position.

Although an empty vessel, without even a seat in the House of Lords, the title itself remains, and the heir presumptive—Alex's son, Alexander Jr—will one day become the 14th Duke of Manchester.

BIBLIOGRAPHY

Ashburner, R.W., *The Shorthorn Herds of England, 1885-6-7*, Warwick: H.T. Cooke, 1888.

Bankhead, T., *Tallulah: My autobiography*, New York: Harper, 1952.

Blixen, K., *Out of Africa*, Putnam: London, 1937.

Bly, John (son of Frank John Bly): interview with the author.

Boyce, G., *Cheers: Amusing tales of a life lived in Egypt, Kenya and the UK from the 1930s to the present day*, London: G. Boyce, 2010.

Butler, N., 'Kimbolton Castle in the 1930s: The Housemaid's Story', *Kimbolton Local History Society Journal*, no. 24, Autumn 2020, pp. 21–24.

Byron, G., diary, 28 March 1814: https://pastnow.wordpress.com/2014/03/27/march-28-1814-lord-byron-moves-into-new-apartments/

Catalogue of the pictures at Kimbolton Castle, circa 1900: held by Kimbolton School.

Cran, H., *Promises to Keep: A British vet in Africa*, Ludlow: Merlin Unwin Books, 2015.

Farson, N., *Last Chance in Africa*, London: Gollancz, 1949.

Guile, M. 'Foreword by Dame Elisabeth Murdoch' in *Clyde School 1910–1975: An uncommon history*, Geelong: Clyde Old Girls' Association, 2006.

Hansard, House of Lords: 12th Duke of Manchester's maiden speech.

'Herbert Gabler's reminiscences', *Kimbolton Local History Society Journal*, no. 12, Autumn 2017, pp. 2–4.

Huxley, E., *Nellie: Letters from Africa with a memoir*, London: Weidenfeld & Nicolson, 1980.

Kimbolton Castle auction catalogue, Hanover Square, London: Knight, Frank and Rutley, 1949.

'Kimbolton Castle', *The Kimboltian Magazine*, July 1950, p. 16.

Kimbolton School governors' letter to Mandy's solicitors, 1949: Kimbolton School Archives.

Kitale School newsletter, 2021.

Macquoid, P. and Edwards, R., *The Dictionary of English Furniture*, Volume I, 1924, p. 170.

Manchester, W.A.D.M., *My Candid Recollections*, London: Grayson & Grayson, 1932.

Mandy's and Nell's letters with Frank Cowlard: Hunting Archives (Ref: KHAC6/6074/7).

Nell Stead's letters to son Sidney: Hunting archives (Ref: KMAN1/A/18/1).

Rudderham, Janice: Unattributed interview notes kept by the Huntingdon Archives.

'School notes', *The Kimboltian Magazine*, July 1951, pp. 3–4.

Scriven, M., *Splendour & Squalor: The disgrace and disintegration of three aristocratic dynasties*, London: Atlantic Books, 2009.

Stead, Nell, Diaries: Montagu family archives.

Taylor, S., 'Lunch with . . . Paddy Hopkirk', *Motorsport*: March 2009, pp. 74–80.

Twain, M., *Following the Equator: A journey around the world*, Hartford: American Publishing Company, 1897.

Wanjala Khisa, A. and Ombaso Otwere, E., *Examination of the Mutual Impact of Colonization and Peasantization in Trans-Nzoia, Kenya, between 1920 and 1970*: Mount Kenya University, 2022.

Woodward, C., *Lanterns Alight: Journeys to far places*, Chicago: Normandie House, 1939.

THE HOUSE OF MONTAGU

Sir Edward Montagu, 1488–1557
m. Cicely Lane, Agnes Kirkham, Eleanor Roper (17 children)
Chief Justice of the King's Bench, one of 16 executors to Henry VIII's will

|

Sir Edward (son of Edward), 1530–1602
m. Elizabeth Harington (12 children)
Treasurer to Mary Queen of Scots, Sheriff of Northamptonshire

|

The Earls of Manchester (created 1626)

Henry, 1st Earl, 1563–1642
m. Catherine Spencer, Anne Holliday, Margaret Crouch (3 children)
Lord High Treasurer/Lord Privy Seal, confidant of Charles I, Star Chamber judge who sentenced Sir Walter Raleigh to death, bought Kimbolton Castle in 1615

|

Edward (son of Henry), 2nd Earl, 1602–1671
m. Susannah Hill, Anne Rich, Essex Bevil, Eleanor Countess of Warwick, Margaret Countess of Carlisle (4 children)
Major-General in First English Civil War, Oliver Cromwell his second in command, Knight of the Order of the Garter, opposed trial of Charles I, confidant of Charles II

|

Robert, 3rd Earl, 1634–1683
m. Anne Yelveton (9 children)
MP for Huntingdonshire, Gentleman of the Bedchamber to the King Charles II, High Steward of Cambridge University

|

The Dukes of Manchester (created 1719)

Charles Montagu (son of Robert), 1st Duke and 4th Earl, 1662–1772
m. Doddington Greville (4 children)
Envoy to Venice and Ambassador to France, confidant of William III and George I

|

William Montagu (son of Charles), 2nd Duke, 1700–1739
m. Isabella Montagu (no issue)
Knight Companion of the Order of the Bath, Governor of the Foundling Hospital for abandoned children

|

Robert Montagu (brother of William), 3rd Duke, 1710–1762
m. Harriet Dunch (4 children)
Lord Chamberlain to Queen Charlotte, Lord of the Bedchamber to George III

|

George Montagu (son of Robert), 4th Duke, 1737–1788
m. Elizabeth Dashwood (6 children)
Lord Chamberlain of the Household to George III, Ambassador to France, signed the Peace of Paris to end the American Revolutionary War

|

William Montagu (son of George), 5th Duke, 1771–1843
m. Susan Gordon (8 children)
Governor of Jamaica, oversaw abolition of slavery, Postmaster General of UK

|

George Montagu (son of William), 6th Duke, 1799–1855
m. Millicent Sparrow, Harriet Dobbs (6 children)
MP for Huntingdonshire, Deputy Lieutenant of County Armagh, Ireland

|

William (son of George), 7th Duke, 1823–1890
m. Louise von Alten (6 children)
MP for Bewdley and Huntingdonshire

George (son of William), 8th Duke, 1853–1892
m. Consuelo Yznaga (3 children)
MP for Huntingdonshire, declared bankrupt in 1890

William (son of George), 9th Duke, 1877–1947
m. Helena Zimmerman, Kathleen Dawes (4 children)
Captain of the Yeomen of the Guard, bankrupted on numerous occasions

Alexander (son of William), 10th Duke, 1902–1977
m. Nell Stead, Elizabeth Fullerton (2 children)

Sidney (son of Alexander), 11th Duke, 1929–1985
m. Adrienne Christie, Andrea Joss (no issue)

Angus (son of Alexander), 12th Duke (last to serve in the House of Lords), 1938–2002
m. Mary McClure, Diane Plimsaul, Anne-Louise Taylor, Biba Jennians (3 children)

Alexander (son of Angus), 13th Duke, 1962–present
m. Marion Stoner, Wendy Buford, Laura Smith (2 children)

NELL STEAD'S MATERNAL LINEAGE

Married, 1927

Great-great grandparents
Lieutenant-Colonel George Bain Johnston, 1764–1823
NSW Corps soldier, Rum Rebellion leader, pastoralist
m. Esther Juliana Abrahams, 1771–1846, convict and landowner (7 children)

Great grandfather
Captain Commander Robert Johnston, 1792–1882
Sixth child of George and Esther, first Australian-born naval commander and pastoralist
m. Frances Weller (15 children)

Grandmother
Penelope Brooks Johnston, 1842–1933
Eighth child of Robert and Frances
m. Samuel Dickinson, businessman (8 children)

Mother
Jessie Lilian Dickinson, 1873–1926
Fifth child of Samuel and Penelope
m. David 'Sidney' Vere Stead, 1861–1929, only child of Irish farmers David Stead, 1797–1886, and Mary Jane Belcher, 1824–1916 (4 children)

Nell Vere Stead, 1902–1966
First child of Sidney and Jessie

Nell's siblings

Marie Erin Vere Stead, 1904–1976
m. John Frederick Thornton Grimwade, 1905–1992 (1 child)

David Vere Stead, 1906–1959
Single (no issue)

Penelope Brooks Vere Stead, 1913–1970
m. Jon Bowie Somerset, 1908–1983 (2 children)

ACKNOWLEDGEMENTS

Reconstructing a life story like Nell Stead's is particularly challenging given that there are few, living firsthand sources and only scattered documentation. For that reason places such as the Huntingdon Archives are so important, and I would like to thank staff members Esther Bellamy, Carys Fyson and Sue Sampson for their help.

Likewise, Nora Butler at the Kimbolton Local Historical Society was very generous in answering my questions and finding items from the society's archives. Kimbolton resident Dawn Gooderham provided insight into the castle during the 1930s, and John Bly and his reminisces of the 1949 auction and his father Frank's purchase was a wonderful addition to the story. Huw and Mark Boyce, and Giles Remnant were able to shed valuable light on Nell and Mandy's later life at Kapsirowa in Kenya.

I want to acknowledge author Marcus Scriven and his book *Splendour & Squalor: The disgrace and disintegration of three aristocratic dynasties*, which was an important reference, particularly concerning the life of Angus, the 12th Duke, as well as the interviews he conducted with people like Grey Duberley and Patsy Bowles, who have both since passed away.

Regrettably, family members can sometimes be reticent to discuss their relatives. While I respect the decision, it means the portrait of a person they admire can be less than it might otherwise have been. It was therefore fantastic to have found Nicholas Hodgkinson-Montagu, great-grandson of Nell and Mandy, who not only was able to help me bring Nell to life through access to some of her diaries but also provided photographs from the family's albums.

The ageless Richard Walsh continues to be a wonderful supporter of my books, as does Annette Barlow and the ever-generous Patrick Gallagher, while I cannot thank Clare Drysdale enough for continuing to bring my books to life in the UK.

Finally, thanks to my wife Paola Totaro for her patience and encouragement over the past two decades and giving me the opportunity for a second career that would otherwise have been impossible.